JFK: The Unwrapped Enigma
Rites of Passage of a Master Spy

Dr. Julio Antonio del Marmol
The Cuban Lightning

© Copyright 2017 by Dr. Julio Antonio del Marmol
All rights reserved. No part of this publication may be reproduced, stored in a retrieval system, or transmitted, in any form or by any means, electronic, mechanical, photocopying, recording, or otherwise, without the written prior permission of the author.

ISBN: 978-68588-022-4 (sc)
ISBN: 978-68588-021-7 (hc)
ISBN: 978-68588-023-1 (e)

Because of the dynamic nature of the Internet, any web addresses or links contained in this book may have changed since publication and may no longer be valid.

Any people depicted in stock imagery provided by Thinkstock are models, and such images are being used for illustrative purposes only. Certain stock imagery © Thinkstock.

The Cuban LightningTM is a registered trademark of The Cuban Lightning Enterprises, LLC

Acknowledgements

I am a very lucky man because I have a great group of people by my side that I not only consider my friends but who also are the most capable, sacrificing professionals equal to the ones I've risked my life with over the past 50 years in their dedication and values. This group has made possible the publication of this book. To them, with all my heart today, I give the best of my love, gratitude, and sincerest thanks to every one of these fantastic warriors.

In order of seniority, I would especially like to thank O'Brien: a great friend and a great individual with extraordinary values. Thank you for the contributions you have made in many different ways to this project, as well as being loyally by my side and watching my back for almost all of my career. I know for a fact you have never done that before for anyone. To my right arm and great friend, Tad Atkinson: for your dedication to every detail in research and many hours of hard work with me, never hesitating to sacrifice even your personal and private family time in order to make this happen. To Steve Weese: thank you for the many pieces of computer and graphic work as well professional enhancement of photos to improve the quality of the book. To Carlos Mota: my thanks for your dedication and multiple contributions and sacrifices you have made in order to make this happen. To Gervasin Neto: for your constant loyalty and many hours standing on your feet or hiding between cars in order to maintain our security with your group of people you've coordinated to watch our backs, continually keeping us informed of any suspicious activity that occurs in our surroundings. To Chopin: for your great companionship, loyalty, and support for the last 50 years with me in our fight for freedom you've displayed by my side all these years. To our editor, Jen Poiry-Prough: who managed to make this book easy to read, using her magic touch to polish this piece of coal and bring to you, the readers, what I consider to be a very rare diamond. It makes all of us very proud to be involved in this project. Your professionalism, vast knowledge, and dedication, have made this book a great piece for future generations. To all of you, my friends who remain in the shadows, who contributed in one way or another in making this book and help me to bring the truth to the public, you have given the best of yourselves, putting forth your best effort to educate future generations. God bless you all. I embrace you as the Christian warriors that you all are.

Dr. Julio Antonio del Marmol

Introduction

At the age of twelve, the author, Julio Antonio del Marmol, found that his destiny had taken him through extraordinary circumstances that happen only a few times in history during widespread social chaos—like those seen in the deranged turmoil of the Cuban Revolution in 1959. The supreme leader, Fidel Castro, nominated this young boy to be the Commander-in-Chief of the new army for the future.

As Fidel Castro went through his own changes of heart at the start of this tumultuous time, the youth went through his own conflict as he watched his childhood friends abandon the island, discontented with the complete disruption of democratic establishment and the institution of Marxist ideology by the new leaders. Julio Antonio del Marmol, the Young Commander, sadly remained behind and daily observed the freedom of the Cuban people evaporate as promise after promise was broken. In spite of the commitment to equality for all without distinction based on political or religious belief, the Castro brothers and Che Guevara ruthlessly hunted down and exterminated all opposition. His admiration towards the leaders turned into disappointment and frustration, as he watched the Castros' forces execute their enemies and commit the most horrendous crimes humanity had ever seen in their ambition to maintain power.

He concluded that this is not what the Cuban people had fought their revolution for and decided, before sharing these horrible experiences with anyone, including his father, to abandon the country as his friends had done. When he did share these intentions with his uncle, he received the most shocking surprise: his relative was a veteran master spy. His uncle proposed that he be trained to be the next in line, and Julio Antonio del Marmol became the youngest spy in modern history at the age of thirteen.

In this story, the reader will find seemingly unbelievable and undoubtedly controversial details about the blueprints to create communist revolutions, spread corruption, and commit assassinations so outrageous that nobody ever could create this as a fiction.

The years are 1962 and 1963, as the young spy races against the ever-increasing momentum to prevent the most heinous act conceivable: the assassination of a sitting U.S. President!

The author tells the story not merely as a narrator; he was an active participant in these events as part of his first steps in his life as a thirteen-year-old spy, as he tried to retrieve what he felt to be important documents for his friends in his intelligence network. He perceived the relevance and import of what he had obtained. Readers will draw their own conclusions and put the facts together. Only when the author's friends reviewed the data did he realize the sheer magnitude of what he had accomplished in unwrapping the enigma surrounding JFK.

The Cuban Lightning

Volume VI of Rites of Passage of a Master Spy

JFK: the Unwrapped Enigma

Prologue: Treason and Forgiveness

When I was six years old, my Uncle Gollito had

professional fighting cocks in the backyard of his house. Every Sunday he went to a club and placed bets on the roosters. Having seen him do this all my life, I started to fall in love with cock fights. He taught me how you had to shave all of the legs and bottoms of the roosters and daily rub 90% alcohol to toughen the hide so that the spurs would be blocked as much as possible. He also taught me that there was a great deal of money involved in this industry, because the champion birds that built names for themselves could later on be used to stud. Eggs fertilized by these roosters could command phenomenal prices—as much as $100,000 USD.

He asked me, "Since you like the roosters so much, why don't you raise bantams[1]? Their spurs are actually longer and stronger than the ones grown by the professional roosters, and they're very hard to find. My friends will be willing to pay good money for the spurs from your birds. With that money, I could then sell you one of the chicks of one of my good professional roosters."

This motivated me to start my first business. I did extra work for my father in order to increase my allowance. As soon as I got a few dollars, I broke it for some coins. I went out into the country to some of the farm kids and held out a handful of coins to see if it was enough for me to buy one of their roosters. My strategy was simple—a handful of coins looked like more money at first glance than a couple of bills. Eventually, I found someone willing to sell to me, and I bought my first rooster.

Eventually, I had between forty and fifty of those small

---

[1] What we called in Cuba *kikiriki*

roosters in our backyard. Mima started to complain because of the noise they made in the morning. The black spurs were the most valuable, fetching as much as $100.

One of my best friends in Guane, Carlito, helped me. My uncle gave me the secret recipe of feeding them: soil, ground up beef, and other ingredients. This feed would make them very strong and feisty, as well as improving the strength of the spurs they grew. He taught me how to use electrical shears to shave the roosters. Carlito came to be my partner, and we recruited several of the neighborhood kids into this trade.

In another neighborhood, we had a rival group of kids. We lost several cock fights to them, because their birds were much more powerful than ours. My uncle's education in building a better breed, however, enabled me to save enough money to buy one of my uncle's wounded warriors. He only had one eye, but his record was 70 wins and 1 loss (when he lost his eye). My uncle had used him for several years as a stud, but he parted with him for $70—a large sum of money in 1953.

I bred him with my bantam hens, and before very long we had much better roosters. One of them had the same silver-grey plumage as his father, except smaller. We waited patiently until he grew up, training him with the others. True to his lineage, he was much feistier than the others. His fighting style was unusual, as well. We called him the Runner because of his tactic of running his opponent in circles to exhaustion before going in for the finishing kill.

We had fought him against the other groups of kids, but not against our rivals yet. The Runner was still too small, and the prize fighter they had was only a little smaller than the big professional birds. The owner of this bird was Mallito.

Carlito finally arranged for the fight between my Runner against Mallito's rooster. We improvised a ring using sugar cane and rice bags filled with sawdust to form the border of the circle. The bags we slung from sticks driven into the ground to form a barrier to keep the fighters in the ring. We asked my uncle for advice leading up to the fight to prepare my rooster for his match.

I noticed that Carlito was a little nervous and a little withdrawn the night before the match. I asked him what was wrong.

"I don't know. I don't think you should fight him. I think he'll kill your rooster, and the joke will be on us."

"Well, I don't know. We'll just have to find out, won't we?"

That night, Mallito managed to break into the patio of our home with some of his friends. They beat my rooster with the stick end of the broom while he roosted inside his cage. The rooster limped around on the ground. Not satisfied with that, they took the pressure hose used for cleaning and sprayed him with it. Then they left.

The first thing I did every morning, even before I brushed my teeth, was to check on my roosters. I was shocked to find my Runner lying on the floor, moving weakly, almost like he was dying. I picked him up and ran to my uncle's house, ignoring Mima's protests. I explained to him what had happened to the best of my knowledge.

My uncle said, "Don't worry. We'll give him some B-12. Go to school and let me handle it. Before you leave, let me ask you something."

I turned and sobbed, "What?"

"How did those kids know which rooster to beat up, when you have fifty of them on your patio in cages?"

I stopped and wondered about that. "Maybe nobody beat him up. Maybe it was some animals..."

"No," my uncle interrupted. "Look at these bruises. This was done by a stick or something on purpose. It had to be done by somebody you know who knew about the fight. Go to school, think about it, and come and let me know what you figure out."

I went home very sad. I listened patiently to Mima's reprimand for not being in school. I explained the situation to her, much to her disbelief.

She sent me to school, and the first thing I did there was tell Carlito about the incident. I was still emotional and a little teary-eyed. Carlito started to cry as well.

"What's wrong with you?" I thought at first that he was sympathizing with me. I patted him. "It's OK, my uncle is going to give the bird some B-12 injections and take him to the vet."

I noticed, however, that he wasn't responding to that. During a recess break, we both came out to the patio, and I said, "If I catch whoever did this, I swear I'm going to break his head." I noticed that he had quite literally urinated in his pants. "What's wrong with you?" I demanded again.

We were sitting on a bench outside, eating small guava pies. He threw his pie on the ground and said, "Forgive me, forgive me." He knelt down before me. "I was the one who told Mallito in what cage he could find the Runner. Your uncle is right. They told me they were only going to get a little rough with him, but I had no idea they were going to almost kill him."

The blood rushed to my head. I grabbed him by the shirt front and slapped him with both hands. "How could you betray me like that? You're my best friend!"

"I'm sorry, I'm sorry. They told me they were going to give me one of their roosters."

"Just for that, you betrayed me? I've got fifty I could let you choose from! Why didn't you ask me for one?"

"You never offered," was the weak reply.

"I never offered to have you do anything so despicable, either. If you had asked, I would have given you one of my roosters."

"No, you wouldn't. You love your roosters too much."

I grew furious. I went back inside the school and did not speak to him for the rest of the day. After school let out, I snatched up my books and ran to my uncle's house, where he surprised me no end. Runner was up and well.

"What did you do?"

"It was only stress. We gave him vitamins and he's OK. He's just a little bruised, just like when you get beat up. He's in perfect condition."

"I could fight him."

"Oh, that might be too much. If you fight him against a rooster that's been rested, it might be too much. You should wait a week before fighting him."

Happily, I took Runner home. Mima expressed her surprise at seeing him appear so healthy. I put him on the patio. To my surprise, when I came into the house, Mima said, "Mallito and his friends are on the porch, looking for you."

There he was outside, waiting with his rooster to fight as we had agreed. Mallito said, "Since you didn't show up at my house like we had agreed, I came here. You going to fight or not?"

"We have to wait until next week. Something happened last night, and my uncle said I should wait a week to rest him."

Mallito and his friends started making clucking noises to indicate they thought I was being cowardly. He stared at me and said, "I knew you would back out. I knew it! Your rooster is a piece of shit, anyway. I don't know why I bothered. Carlito even told me that your rooster is only so-so."

"Carlito told you that, huh? You know what? Go around to the patio. Let's fight them, and let's see what your bird has."

A couple of my friends had come with them and looked at me doubtfully. One said, "Are you sure you want to do that, man?"

"Sure," I said. "Let's see who the real chicken is."

I went out to the back and got Runner out of his cage. Everyone gathered around, and Mallito let go of his rooster. I held on a second longer, and we stepped out to let the fight start. The two birds came together with a crash. Runner tried his usual tactic, but his injuries slowed him down. His opponent kept catching up with him, so it wasn't working. When Runner was thrown onto the ground and Mallito's rooster was about to administer the *coup de grâce*, I raised my hand to stop the fight.

Right at that moment, Runner brought both spurs together and dug them into the neck of Mallito's cock. Mallito looked up at me in shock.

"What were you about say?" Mallito asked.

"Oh, nothing, I was just stretching." I scooped Runner up and put him in my cage.

Mima said to me, "Carlito's out front, looking for you."

I walked out onto the porch. Carlito said, "I'm sorry for everything."

"It's OK." I forgave him. I hugged him to me and said, "We won, after all!"

"I'll never betray you again, Julio Antonio," he promised fervently.

"I know," I replied, "and to prove you wrong, for all your help, go ahead and pick whatever rooster you like, and it's yours. And from now on, Runner is fifty percent yours."

Tears welled up in his eyes. "Really? Thank you! I don't deserve that."

"Anyone can make a mistake, but you're still my best friend."

JFK: The Unwrapped Enigma

Other People's Pain

The pain and suffering of others is merely salt in water in the minds of those who have not experienced the consequences of that anguish and misery.

Dr. Julio Antonio del Marmol

Dr. Julio Antonio del Marmol

Chapter 1: Justice for Kimbo

I went to the Volga, my heart pounding, as I expected at any moment to hear Raimundo the veterinarian calling me to come back before I could get in and start the car. I finally reached the car and started to drive away, and my nerves made me feel like a thief with the police hot on his tail. It was like I was worried that at any moment I was going to be caught in the possession of the illegal morphine.

I drove straight to the Cafe Labiada. I bought one of the best brands of Scotch whiskey that I could find imported to Cuba. I also go a nice plate of hors d'oeuvres—shrimp, cheeses, olives, sardines, pate, and anchovies. I made sure that everything was very salty—I even ordered them to put salt and garlic powder on it as well.

I drove to Captain Augustin's house and asked him to do me a favor. "Whatever you need, Commandantico," he said. "You know you're my buddy."

"I need you to go to the G-2 building and ask them for the report on the arrest of Leocadio. In a friendly way, not in any kind of imposition, tell them you have orders from the Superior Command to get all the information possible in that case and report it directly to Escalona. He wants to know for sure what happened in this case: the names of the agents involved and what triggered the arrest. Even if you have to say a few things that aren't nice about me, use every trick you can to see what they tell you. Flatter them a little bit, but get the information we need."

I explained to him that I was personally conducting an investigation for Fidel in Havana so that he could present to Ramiro Valdez a complaint against the actions of these agents. Of course, I didn't tell him my real purpose. I wanted him to act as naturally as possible so that I would have a cover in case something didn't go as planned. I would then have Captain Augustin on my side as a witness as to what my intentions were in getting a copy of that report. I gave him the telephone number of my house and left him with instructions to call me as soon as he had the report in his hands.

We said goodbye and I drove back home. I took the bottle of whiskey and tray of hors d'oeuvres to my room. Without breaking the seal, I used a syringe and a long needle from my mother's medical kit to remove some whiskey from the bottle. Leaving the needle in the cork of the bottle, I squirted the whiskey into a ceramic bowl and then dissolved several morphine pills in it. I sucked the liquid back into the syringe and reconnected it to the needle. I then injected the mixture into the full bottle and carefully removed the syringe, this time removing the needle. Once I was finished, I used a match to light a red Christmas candle to melt wax and cover the tiny hole left by the needle. I carefully scrutinized the seal to make certain the colors matched.

I nodded, satisfied. The bottle was ready.

I put the bottle to one side and took the plate. I picked up a bottle of sauce. I poured some into the bowl. It was an expensive sauce and so fragrant that I stuck a finger in to taste it. It tasted like tartar sauce and made me hungry, so I picked up a shrimp and dipped it into the sauce before doctoring it. The restaurant at the café was very expensive and all the food was delicately flavored. I put nearly all of the remaining pills in the bowl and added some olive oil to remove any sour or medicinal taste. I returned the dip to the tray and sealed the tray. As I did so, I heard a knock on my door.

"Who is it?"

Mima's voice answered, "My son, Captain Augustin is calling for you on the phone."

"Very well, Mima—tell him I'll be there in a moment." I ran down the stairs two at a time. I put the bottle of whiskey and the tray in one of the bottom drawers of the refrigerator. I went into the library and answered the phone. "Captain, is everything OK?"

"Commandantico, mission accomplished," he said happily. "Where did you want to see me? I got more than what you asked for."

"Great. Wherever is most convenient for you. If you want, I'll come back to your house."

"No, no, no. I have a ride from my sister. I'm not even at my house. I'm very close to the *Jupiña* factory on Cabada Avenue, close to the Kiosko de Felipe."

"Oh, my God—I live only a few blocks away! Very well, I'll be there in ten minutes." I left the house and got into the Volga. I drove to the small vendor's stand that was situated in the middle of nowhere. As I approached the kiosk, I saw Captain Augustin enjoying a popsicle that was the special creation of the owner of the stand.

He handed the folder to me. He said, "What a popsicle, man! Made from a pumpkin! I never heard of such a thing. When I saw the sign, I asked for one out of

JFK: The Unwrapped Enigma

curiosity. What an innovative creation!"

"Yes," I said, "Felipe is a great entrepreneur. He surprised everyone here in the neighborhood with his creativity. You know what makes it so good?"

"No—what is the secret?"

"It's no secret—he tells everyone. He uses condensed milk."

"Oooh, no wonder!" He didn't pause his licking as he spoke. "It's so sweet and delicious! This is great, Felipe," he said to the vendor.

"Thank you," Felipe replied with a pleased smile.

"You see, you have a new customer," I said to him.

"Keep bringing new clients, Commandantico," he said to me, "and I'll give you free popsicles every once in a while."

I smiled and waved my hand. "Thank you, but that's not necessary, Felipe."

I opened the folder. In addition to the report, I saw that he had pictures of each of the three men named in the report as the arresting officers: Ignacio Gutierres, Rogelio Rodriguez, and Serafin Sanches. With the pictures in my hand, I nodded in pleasure. "These are the individuals, eh?"

He smiled sarcastically. "Yes, the three *cabrones*[2] that beat up your friend and killed your dog Kimbo." He pointed to the fattest one of the three. "This one, by his own admission, is the one who shot all the dogs. I spoke with all three of them. He's big, six-foot-eight or nine, and to use his words, he killed those 'sacks of fleas' because they annoyed him with their barking and aggressive

---

2 Pricks

attitudes. Of course, there's no reason to kill a dog unless it's attacking you. This man must be a psycho." Augustin's face was disgusted as he spoke.

"How did you manage to get those pictures from the archives?"

He pointed at his captain's bars on his uniform. "This is very powerful, Commandantico. Of course, yours are even more powerful."

"Thank you very much. I really, really appreciate it," I said. "You don't know how happy this makes me."

"All I ask in return is that you take me home in your car. I got a ride over here from my sister, and she left to head to the capital. Is it going to be too much trouble to take me home?"

"Of course not! Jump in the Volga, and I'll take you all the way to Havana if you want." He smiled and got in.

On the way to his house, he said, "Those men from the G-2 are not only abusers, but they're all drunkards and corrupt. I know Serafin, the fat one, very well. All three of them are lazy bums. When they're not harassing people, they hang around in the bar section of the *El Chino Pepin*[3]. They're there all the time, eating Chinese food, drinking, and playing pool until the very late hours of the night. I don't know how they manage to go to work. I don't think they actually work, since all they do is harass people. By the way, they invited me tonight to celebrate Serafin's birthday, and they want to give him a little surprise. I politely declined, telling them I have another commitment tonight. Already knowing the kind of people they are and what they did to your friend Leocadio, I

---

3 The Chinese Restaurant/Bar

didn't want to hang around with that kind of scum. I wouldn't enjoy their company."

We arrived at his house, and we said goodbye. I drove home as fast as the traffic allowed me to do, because I needed to make an urgent phone call. When I got home, I called Chandee's house in Havana. To my surprise, Chandee answered. "Oh, my God, I knew it was you! That's why I ran to the phone when I heard it ring. Maybe I had a hunch."

"Really?" I asked.

"Really!" she said. "I know you cannot live without me."

"You're right, honey. I miss you so much that I need you here tonight if possible. Leave everything, whatever you're doing, because I have something extremely important that I need your help with. Don't ask me what, just tell me yes if you can do it. Tell your parents that I will return you to the capital this very same night. But I need your help with something extremely important."

"Don't worry," she said. "If my father doesn't need the car, I will be there in a couple of hours. If I cannot use his car for any reason, it will take me longer, you know. I'll have to, as you say, convert myself into a proletariat by taking the inter-provincial bus. One way or the other, I will be there with you in a while."

I smiled in satisfaction. "Thank you, sweetie. I will be here waiting for you with open arms. I want to ask you a favor: bring with you two dresses—very feminine— because my plan requires two young, attractive women tonight, and a couple of wigs for our disguises."

"Very well."

After we hung up, I walked up to my room and took a

long shower. All the time, I revolved around in my mind my plans for the evening, focusing on each step and detail to achieve my objectives. A few hours later, Chandee arrived. I gave her the full details and laid out the plan, and I took the tray and bottle out of the refrigerator. We left in her father's car, driving towards the Chinese restaurant.

El Chino Pepin

It was located in one of the most central streets in the city. The place was always crowded. It was one of the few places in the city open twenty-four hours a day, and it served the best Chinese food at a reasonable price. For this reason, prostitutes frequented this place in their attempts to obtain a bowl of the famous wonton soups to recuperate from the heavy exercise they put their bodies through every day. That special wonton soup was noted for making anyone sweat from all the protein in it. The special recipe included shrimp, octopus, beef and pork meatballs, as well as the more standard ingredients. As we drove, I asked Chandee, "Will your car be OK?"

"Yes," she replied in surprise, "why?"

"I don't know—something smells like it's burning in here."

"Must be that diesel truck that passed us. His exhaust smelled really bad."

Chandee parked in an alley behind the restaurant about half a block away. I selected a particularly darkened area, so that no one would be able to identify her car in case something went wrong or my plans didn't work as I had laid out.

We changed into the feminine clothing she brought. She applied some makeup to my face and put a wig of long, straight black Chinese hair on me. She kissed my lips, "You look so good."

I laughed. "If anyone watches us, they'll think we're lesbians."

She grabbed my crotch. "Uh, huh—you would give it away immediately. You cannot fool an audience for too long. Try not to kiss any women, OK?"

We left the car, walked along the main street, and entered a hallway that ran between the buildings. We had the plate of hors d'oeuvres and the bottle of whiskey inside a paper bag. When we reached the door to the place, a couple of bums tried to be fresh with us, perhaps because we looked too young. Or perhaps it was because we looked too attractive for that place. One of them tried to grab Chandee's leg as we walked in. My dress had some leather strings as adornment, and I used it to slap his bare hand soundly. He snatched his hand away. "Ouch! You are very violent. I only wanted to check the merchandise."

Before I could answer, Chandee said, "Don't get confused *compañero*. We're not prostitutes. We're members of the militia. One phone call from us, and you'll sleep in the G-2 for at least a week."

The man looked at Chandee fearfully but remained mute. We walked inside and looked for a table. It was hard to spot one for all the bodies in that place. Finally, one of the waitresses saw us and brought us to a small table in a corner. It looked like all the Pinar del Rio night life was gathered in this place.

After we were seated in that dark corner, it took us a while to get the waitress' attention. She finally returned, and we placed two orders for fried wontons, a shrimp cocktail, and two Coca-Colas. From where we were sitting, we could see the small dance floor packed with people. At the far end, by the corridor that led to the bathrooms, we could see through a set of glass bead curtains people playing pool in the room beyond. Even above the music we could hear the excitement surrounding the game as people cheered when a player sank a shot.

I said to Chandee, "I'm going to check to see if all the birds are in the nest. At the same time, I'm to take the opportunity to change the oil in my kidneys." I stood up and walked towards the bathrooms slowly so that I could locate the three individuals whose images I had memorized from the pictures. I could see only two of the men. The big man—the birthday boy—was not present.

I continued towards the bathroom, nearly entering the men's room by mistake. At the last moment, I corrected myself and entered the women's. To my surprise, I saw a group of women, one of whom was completely naked over one sink as splashed water from a glass to wash her genitals. Another was washing her armpits in another sink. I was a little shocked by this display and immediately headed to a vacant stall and locked myself inside. Just in case someone was watching, I sat down to urinate. It was awkward to do it this way, but I wanted to avoid discovery by the experienced women of the night.

On my way back out, they all looked at me enviously, but I rushed on out of the bathroom. I returned to the table and sat down. "Oh, my God. Without even realizing it, I nearly went to the men's room. By pure luck, I reacted naturally and continued on down to your bathroom."

She smiled. "Even if you dress the monkey in silk, you can always see his tail. In this case, it's really a tail! Are your birds in the nest?"

"I could only corroborate two. I don't think the third one is in yet, and he's the biggest and fattest one of them all."

At exactly that moment, a huge man walked through the door. It was Serafin. I watched him greet the bartender and one of the waitresses familiarly. Both people followed him silently as he walked through the beaded curtain. As they broke through, the waitress and the bartender started to sing "Happy Birthday," and we could hear the others in the pool room join in the song.

I looked at Chandee. "The third bird has arrived."

She said, "Wait for me here. I will find what we need."

She walked behind one of the waitresses who was walking towards the end of the hallway leading to the bathrooms. Chandee disappeared into a utility room.

Fifteen minutes later, she re-emerged dressed as a waitress and carrying a tray in her hands. She came over to me, and I handed her the hors d'oeuvres and the bottle of whiskey. Rapidly, she pulled them out of the bag and arranged them on the tray. Then she walked off towards the pool room.

    I followed her a short distance behind but remained outside the pool room watching through the glass curtain. Chandee approached the table where Serafin and his friends were playing and set the tray down on a corner of the pool table. She started to sing the birthday song. Serafin's partners and the rest of the men playing at the other tables stopped what they were doing and formed a men's chorus that followed Chandee's lead. After the singing was done, she curtseyed to Serafin and said to him, "This is a birthday gift from one of the tables out front."

    Ignacio opened the tray and exclaimed, "Oh, my God! This is from Labiada—this is high class, man!"

    Rogelio yelled as he raised the bottle, "This is one of the best bottles of Scotch—one of the best brands in the world! Who the hell loves you so much to make such an expensive gift to you?"

    Serafin turned to look for the waitress to inquire as to who sent the gift, but Chandee had already gone. She ducked into the bathroom where she had left her clothes.

    I returned to the table and sat down to wait for her. From my table I could see Serafin stick his head through the glass bead curtain as he tried to locate the waitress, but she was nowhere to be found. After that, Ignacio and Rogelio also appeared in the curtain as they tried to solve the mystery of who had sent the gift. They looked around for a few seconds, but finally disappeared back into the pool room to enjoy the food and drink, forgetting for the moment the issue of who had sent the gift. Lured by the desire for the expensive food and drink, they were anxious to have their share to sample.

Fifteen minutes later, Chandee returned, dressed as she had been when we had entered. This time, however, she wore a black beret to cover her face. She reported, "The birds are hungry and thirsty. When I looked into the room, they'd eaten almost half the tray and drunk about a third of that bottle of whiskey. They must have been drinking it like water."

"We'll stay here for a while to observe the results of our plan and the behavior of these criminals. When we're satisfied, we'll leave. I don't know what's going to happen to these guys. Not even the veterinarian could assure me what kind of reaction they'll have. I don't want to kill them. I only want them to suffer like they made Leocadio suffer and to make them pay in some way for killing Kimbo and Leocadio's dogs. Let's hope they get a lesson they'll never forget."

A few minutes passed. We hadn't even finished our fried wontons when we heard shots inside the pool room. We heard someone scream, "Please don't kill me! Please!"

Several men ran out of the room, dropping their cues on the floor in their panicked rush. The music stopped, and everyone in both the restaurant and the bar froze. Security headed in the direction of the pool room to see what was going on.

One of the men who had come out said, "One of those guys went crazy. He shot my friend, claiming it was his turn to use the table! He had his own table, for God's sake. Why did he need to do that?"

Ignacio, the skinniest, burst out of the pool room, breaking some of the glass marbles. He was stark naked, his pistol in his hand. With the butt end of a pool cue, he was tapping his naked rear end like he was riding a horse, making clucking noises with his mouth. He "rode" around the room, everyone frozen and wondering what was wrong with him. Finally, the security, helped by his two friends and some of the customers, managed to disarm him and tackle him to the floor. By this time, the local police arrived. They handcuffed him and used a tablecloth to wrap around his body. Virtually dragging him, they removed him from the restaurant.

An ambulance arrived to attend to the man who had been shot in the leg. He was taken away in a stretcher. I said to Chandee, "Well, this man will probably be expelled from the G-2 for his crazy and inexcusable conduct as well as damage to public property and the shooting of an innocent civilian."

The police and ambulance had not even been gone five minutes. Calm began to return, though some people began to leave. I said to Chandee, "The veterinarian said the drugs affect people with lesser body weight more quickly. That's why that guy was the first one to succumb."

A few more minutes passed, and more screaming erupted from the room. Chandee smiled and said, "Another bird fell into the trap."

This time it was Rogelio. He was a man of middle height and slightly overweight. He screamed in hysterical terror, "I'm burning! I'm burning! My body's on fire!

Please help, call the fire department!" He went from table to table, snatching glasses of liquid, whether water or beer, and dousing his body with the contents. Everyone froze and did nothing, as his pistol was in his hand. Serafin ran in behind him, attempting futilely to calm him down.

After several minutes, the security guards aided Serafin in wrestling Rogelio to the floor. He wasn't giving up, however, and continued to scream hysterically as he attempted to rip his own clothes off. The police arrived once more, this time even more rapidly. One of the policemen said, "We were expecting something like this to happen. Usually, when one case of hysteria strikes, another one isn't too far behind. Did the Chinese put something weird in the food tonight?"

It took several policemen to drag Rogelio out, handcuffed as he was. He still had extraordinary strength, and his seizures didn't help—nor did his maniacal strength like that of a schizophrenic.

After the police took him away, Serafin sat down at an empty table left behind by one of the recently departed customers. Exhausted and sweating, he looked around in confusion. The table at which he rested was not very far from us. He tried to mop the sweat off his face with his handkerchief. One of the waitresses came over and asked him if he wanted something cool to drink.

Serafin replied, "Yes. Please, bring a Bacardi *añejo* double, on the rocks. No, no—triple!"

"OK," the pretty Asian girl replied. When she turned to leave, but Serafin grabbed her by the arm.

"Do you remember who sent us that bottle of whiskey and the hors d'oeurves?" he asked.

She clearly had no idea what he was talking about, but seeing his condition she had no desire to contradict him. With a smile she shook her head. He let go of her arm and waved her away with his right hand. He pointed towards the bar to direct her to go fill his order.

I looked at Chandee as she moved in her seat slightly to obscure her face from his view. At the same time, she adjusted her beret to cover the side of her face so that he couldn't identify her. I smiled and said quietly to calm her down, "You don't have to worry about it. Every single waitress in this place is Chinese. With the uniform and hat, they all look similar enough that he won't remember details. I assure you, that to him, all of you look the same."

She smiled, unconvinced. "When do we leave here? It looks like this guy hasn't ingested too much of your medicine. He doesn't show any visible effect. It's possible those other two gluttons ate and drank the whole thing." She shifted again and adjusted her dress. She was clearly uncomfortable with Serafin's close proximity. "I want to remind you that at any moment, somebody will find the waitress I left behind in the utility room, and that will create a big commotion. That particular waitress can easily identify me."

I understood her concern. "Just give me five or ten more minutes." I held up my hand, my thumb and forefinger barely apart. "I want to see what effect that triple Bacardi has. He's the biggest and fattest of the three, so it might take longer for him than the other two. Even if he didn't drink much of my cocktail, when he mixes it with the Bacardi, it could be the fatal spark that blows his fuse. I doubt he drank little, given his size and weight."

Chandee sipped her Coke, but the glass was nearly empty. The waitress was passing by with Serafin's order. She put the glass down on his table and came back by ours. She asked Chandee, "Do you want another Coke?"

She tried to smile. She knew that giant nearby could go berserk at any moment or possibly even recognize her. "Yes, please."

The waitress turned to get Chandee's order. I watched Serafin squeeze a little lime juice into his drink and then add a little salt from a shaker on the table. He then downed his triple rum in a single gulp, leaving only ice in the glass. The waitress returned with Chandee's Coke. Serafin caught her attention with gestures as he held up his empty glass. He indicated that he wanted another. The waitress walked over to get his glass, but he snatched it away from her violently.

He said, "I asked you for another drink, not to take this one!" He took the glass once more and attempted to sip from it.

The waitress was unhappy with Serafin's improper behavior. As she turned, we could see her roll her eyes as she shook her head in exasperation. She walked past us. She hadn't gone very far before the chain reaction began to affect Serafin. This time, it was very violent.

I had been waiting for this. He started to slap at his face and body like he was swatting mosquitoes. He picked up the glass and banged it down all over the table as if he were trying to kill insects. He yelled, "Damn fleas! Those damn filthy dogs! They're jumping all over me!" He began to hit himself in the head and arms. He picked up the glass and began to hit his chest with it, spraying the scared customers with ice. The few people who were left from the previous two incidents began to leave the restaurant.

 The waitress was returning with Serafin's order. She watched in horror as he took the glass and slammed himself in the forehead with it, shattering the glass and badly cutting his forehead. She paused and turned to retreat. Serafin saw her and yelled, "Hey, where are you going? Come back with my drink, you bitch!"

 The waitress yelled for security. Between her leaving with his drink and her calling for security, Serafin grew angrier. He picked up the vase of flowers and threw it at her feet. It shattered and sprayed shards of glass all over the tile floor. Another waitress entered from the hallway leading to the utility room and bathrooms. She yelled, "There's a dead woman, naked and bound in one of the closets!"

 Everyone started to race from their tables, and security split into two directions. One contingent went to handle Serafin, while the rest went into the back to find out what was happening there. Before the security guards could reach him, Serafin stood up and grabbed a couple of chopsticks. He gouged both of them into his cheeks with enough force to pierce the flesh. People screamed, and I took Chandee's hand and said, "That's good enough. Let's get out of here."

 We didn't run, but walked at a normal pace through the room. I felt that the drugs had released the demons each of those evil men carried inside him, unbinding them to harm their own hosts. We saw as we walked away the chopsticks sticking out of Serafin's cheeks. One security guard was tossed through the air by the big man, landing flat on his back against the wall of liquor bottles behind the bar, shattering bottles and mirror.

Chandee looked about to panic again, so I murmured in her ear, "Don't run. Walk. Stay calm, and quietly walk out of here."

Finally, we managed to get out of that place and walked into the alley. Several police cars were arriving. We got into the car, and as Chandee started to drive away, we could see the police blocking off the alley and street behind us.

I said to Chandee, "Drive very slowly; don't be in a rush. We don't want to call attention to ourselves, and an accident right now would be catastrophic, since it would place both of us at the scene of the crime. Drive straight to the park. It's not too far from here, I'll direct you." I started to remove my dress and makeup as Chandee drove.

As she drove, she kept checking her outer rear-view mirror, as I was using the interior one to remove my disguise by the dim light. I was nearly finished cleaning my face when I heard her say, "Uh, oh."

"What's up?" I asked in concern. "What happened?"

Her eyes were glued to the mirror. "I think we have a police car behind us."

I twisted the mirror I had been using to look behind us to see for myself. It certainly was a police car. It was keeping its distance from us, but it was definitely pacing us. I turned the interior light off at once and leaned back in my seat. Using a calm voice to keep Chandee from panicking, I said, "Turn left at the next corner. As you approach the park, look for any empty space and pull in." I placed an index finger to my temple. "Remember, you're here in the city to visit me. You just arrived from the capital, only minutes ago. We left my house to go for a ride. That's it—can you remember that?"

"Yes," she replied unhappily as she nervously gulped. She nodded her head to show her understanding. "If we get stopped by these policemen, I have never in my life set foot in that restaurant. I don't even live in this town—just a visitor."

"Very well," I said, smiling in approval. I patted her shoulder reassuringly. When she had gotten into the car, she had taken off her beret. I now stowed it in her travel bag. Methodically, I folded up the clothes and wigs and concealed the evidence also in her travel bag. I zipped it up and put the bag behind my seat as she turned the corner towards the park. I saved that until the turn to conceal from the police behind us the activity. I tried not to look behind us. I said to Chandee, "Do not go past the speed limit, whether it's twenty-five or thirty kilometers per hour."

She smiled and replied, "I've been keeping my eyes on my speed."

"It could be nothing. So far, they haven't hit their lights or indicated they want us to stop. Don't get nervous. As soon as you find a space, pull in."

We finally reached the park. Chandee spotted a vacant parking space a short distance away. She opened her mouth to say something about it, but at that moment smoke started to bellow from under the hood and filled our compartment. It was white smoke, like water vapor, much like the car was overheating. She pulled into the space and we both got out.

The police didn't even notice what had been going on

with our car and continued cruising past us. I breathed a deep sigh of relief. I told Chandee to open the hood. She popped the catch, and I raised the hood up. As soon as I did, I could feel the heat of the vapors. The car had been overheating for quite some time.

"What happened?" she asked.

"Remember when we parked at the restaurant and I asked you if something was burning? Apparently this has been going on for a while, and you've got a hole in a hose or the radiator, because you're completely overheated and out of water."

We could see the water dripping and running off into the gutter. I tried to open the radiator cap to get a better look by the light of the street lamp. The main hose leading to the radiator had a slight crack in the seal. When I opened the cap, steam shot into our faces.

Chandee asked, "Do you know any mechanics in this area who can help us?"

"Yes, a few blocks from here is the house of the mechanic who fixes my father's cars. If we go over there, he will probably be home by this time. He might be able to help us. It's not far from here. The only problem is that everything by now will be closed if we need to buy parts for him to repair your car. But you never know—these mechanics sometimes have spare parts in their shops, and he might have what is needed to fix it. This is really unexpected; I hadn't counted on this. It's not good for this to break down so close to where we just were."

"Don't worry—we'll fix the car, and I'll be on my way back to the capital in no time. Let's go to your friend's house." She closed the hood and walked towards the side of the car. She opened the door and started to get in.

"What are you doing?" I asked
"We're going to the mechanic's house."
"Yes, but we have to walk."
"Why?"

I shook a finger at her. "You cannot drive this car without any water in the radiator, not even for one block. You'll completely ruin the engine, doing more damage than has already been done. I don't think your father will like that very much."

"Are you sure?"

"Absolutely! My brother ruined my father's 1951 Buick driving less than a block without any water in it, and he blew the engine up."

"That bad?"

"Yes—that bad."

"But you said he lives very close."

"Yes, but as I said, you shouldn't even start the car after such intense overheating. As soon as your car overheats, you should pull over and stop the engine, or you could cause major damage to it. Why do you think they put the gauge for the oil pressure, temperature, and so on right in front of your face on the dashboard?"

She shook her head. "I'm sorry. I don't know very much about cars. OK, how do we get there?"

I tapped my legs. "The oldest form of transportation. Roman will tell us what the problem is and how quickly he can resolve it. He may even have to tow it to his shop, but don't worry about that. The only thing that cannot be fixed is death. Let's hope that's not the same case with this car."

"Are you trying to cheer me up?" she asked half-accusingly.

I smiled and shook my head. "No, honey. I've learned with cars, you have to be like a dog. Whenever you smell something unusual, stop at once, or you'll be very sorry."

She made a face. "OK, I've got it now. Next time I smell anything, I'll pull over immediately and ask someone to help me with my car."

Guane

Tobacco Fields

Tobacco Storage

Chapter 2: Sandra's Wedding

I smiled and we started to walk towards the mechanic's house. In the distance, we saw an old Catholic church with flood lights, cameras, and a large crowd gathered. The sidewalk leading from the street up the steps of the church was long and white. Parked on the street was a beautiful white horse-drawn carriage with a black roof. Hitched to the carriage was one white and one black horse. The man in the driver's box wore a black frock coat with long tails, a top hat, and white gloves. He waited patiently, the leather whip in his hand.

Chandee looked at me, smiling radiantly. "Look at that beautiful wedding! Let's get closer. Maybe we can be lucky enough to get a view of the newly wedded couple as they come out of the church. That is so beautiful! Oh, my God!" she exclaimed as she tried to drag me faster. "Hurry up, hurry up! There they are! Did you know it's good luck to happen upon a wedding spontaneously? That's the proverb."

I smiled and shook my head incredulously. "Do you really think that superstition Is true? Really?"

Chandee shook her head a little embarrassed at the guilty admission. "A little. In reality, though, weddings are so beautiful, and there's nothing wrong to believe a little bit in those old wives' tales. Maybe there's some truth to it, since happiness breeds happiness. Don't you think so?"

I nodded, though still unconvinced. With a resigned

expression, I decided not to spoil her happiness. "Well, maybe you're right. Those old sayings usually have some kind of truth behind them."

She turned and looked at me with a broad smile. She knew I was trying to please her. She took my arm and said as she tried to rush me over to the crowd, "Let's go! We're going to miss it if we don't get there quickly! Thank you, you are very patient and complaisant. These qualities are very special in a man, especially one of your age."

I smiled and shook my head. "For my age? Thank you, thank you, thank you."

She smiled and continued to drag me along.

We were a short distance from the wedding party. The newlyweds had already descended the stairs to the sidewalk. The powerful lights illuminated their faces for the cameras. Chandee looked around at all the happy faces and squeezed my arm in her attempts to hurry me even more so that we could get close to this event. The bride was dressed all in white with a long, beautiful train held by a little boy and a little girl, similarly attired. She had delicate lace gloves on her hands. Her veil covered her face, but she looked absolutely radiant.

Next to her stood a young officer in his dress uniform. His shoulders bore the stars of a commander, and he wore a vast, bushy black beard. She held his arm as they walked down the steps. The photographer snapped pictures from different angles, and two crews manned large video cameras. The crowd started to toss rice as the newlywed couple politely ducked the bombardment of grains to avoid getting hit in the face or having it caught in their hair. They continued courteously as people yelled the usual wishes for a newly married couple. They proceeded along the sidewalk, adorned with flower-draped poles. The coach was utterly resplendent with flowers, the blossoms continuing up to the necks of the horses.

    A smile on his face, the coachman held the door open for the couple. In front of the coach, a red and white carpet had been laid down over the sidewalk, lending a distinguished and very elegant aspect to the entire event. I realized that in Chandee's happiness and excitement about the wedding she had completely forgotten about the broken-down car. She continued to push and drag me between the people in her attempt to get close to the newlyweds. The bombardment of rice continued unabated, and the festive mood continued. One of the young girls yelled, "Don't hurry back!"

    The bride turned as she let go of the groom's arm. She faced the crowd of people, mostly women. She tossed the bouquet to the side where we were. Chandee dropped my hand and dashed in to attempt to catch it. She ran and jumped through the air like she had been shocked by a high voltage current, and she snatched the bouquet before any of the other girls could get it. The other girls looked at her in irritation. She waved the bouquet over her head and yelled, "Julio Antonio, I got it!" She pumped both of her arms in the air in her joy. The bride heard her and looked in my direction.

    When the bride had thrown the bouquet, I had noticed an object fly off her hand, sparkling under the lights. It landed on the carpet and rolled towards me. I was waving to Chandee and so was very conspicuous. I looked down at the carpet and noticed that object had rolled between my feet and stopped by the instep of one of my boots. It was the bride's wedding ring. I bent over and picked up the precious object. The bride, realizing what had happened, was already moving towards me, dragging her train and the two attendant children behind her.

I handed the ring to her with my right hand and she held out her left hand to receive it. With her right hand, she lifted her veil. I was frozen in astonishment when I recognized her.

A woman's voice yelled, "Sandra! Fix that ring or you'll lose it! It's too big for your finger."

Sandra, my ex-girlfriend, was mute and paralyzed in disbelief at seeing me there. With the two of us in stasis at that moment, my hand remained extended towards her outstretch hand in a tableau. Time seemed to stop for me, though perhaps only a few seconds actually passed. The groom realized something was wrong. Chandee was trying to push her way through the crowd to get back to me. Finally, she reached me. Holding the flowers up, she looked back and forth between Sandra and me, the three of us remaining completely mute.

Chandee took my arm affectionately yet determinedly, as if sending a message to Sandra. The groom came over to us and took the ring from my hand. "Thank you," he said abruptly. He grabbed Sandra by the arm and virtually dragged her a little away. He leaned in and whispered in her ear in apparent displeasure.

Whatever he said must not have been very nice. Her face snapped towards him and she leaned away from him, her face registering shocked displeasure. She yanked her arm away from him. She walked rapidly away from him towards the coach. When she reached it, the coachman politely helped her into the carriage.

We followed them, our eyes glued to the couple. From inside the coach, Sandra turned towards the crowd, but her eyes met mine. There was sorrow and perhaps a shade of repentance in her face as she looked at me. I had never seen such a sad expression in anyone's eyes until that day. She wiped away a couple of tears with her finger. With a smile that was clearly forced, she waved to everyone, but her eyes remained fixed on mine, her left hand keeping the veil up so that she could maintain eye contact.

I turned my face away to avoid that guilty look and said to Chandee, "Let's go. It looks like that party you wanted so much is over."

As we walked away from the crowd, I said to Chandee, "My God! Sandra getting married. She never even mentioned this the last time we saw each other about seven months ago. Life is just pregnant with surprises. A new baby can be born when you least expect it."

Chandee held my arm and felt my sadness. She certainly perceived my change of mood and demeanor. In an attempt to sympathize with my depressed state, she looked at the bouquet and smelled it, and then dropped it in a trash can we passed by as we walked along the street. "If I'd only known, I would never have told you to come with me to see that wedding."

I said, "You shouldn't have thrown away that beautiful bouquet of flowers. You put so much work into obtaining it."

"If I only knew for one second that it was Sandra's wedding, I guarantee you that this baby would have been born an orphan, and I would have saved you from the unpleasantness you just went through."

I smiled with gratitude for her compassion. "If only we'd known or could have imagined how criminal and unscrupulous the liberators from the previous dictator would become, no one would have supported them, much less shed a tear over their promises. The unpleasant surprises are identical to the pleasant ones; they are both unpredictable. Besides, they give you valor and prepare you for the next battle. If you have true values and love, they will never change for anything." I took her hand and squeezed it. "You possess all those true values and love capable of fulfilling the most demanding man on this earth, and you can give him all the happiness he deserves."

Chandee stopped in the middle of the sidewalk and looked deeply into my eyes, hers filled with tears and worry. She hugged me fiercely. She pulled away and kissed me tenderly on the lips. "Thank you," she said. "I know that really came from the bottom of your heart."

I returned her kiss, and it became passionate. We continued kissing until the blast of the horn of a passing car broke us out of our idyllic reverie and snapped us back to reality—standing on a public sidewalk where people could interrupt us without a care for what we were feeling in the moment.

As we walked, we both felt very close to each other, bound by the words we had chosen to support each other during that not very pleasant surprise and the even more unpleasant embarrassment it represented for Chandee. We walked silently to Roman's house, glancing periodically at each other with small smiles. We couldn't feel completely at ease—not after that incident.

When we arrived at Roman's house, he received us with his usual courtesy and offered us refreshments. We declined and explained to him the problem with the car. At once he put a shirt on over his overalls and the three of us got into his tow truck.

We were only a few blocks from his house when we felt two objects hit the truck—one on the roof and one to the rear of his truck. It was like something had dropped from the sky. At the same time, we heard the rotors of a propeller airplane, perhaps a Cessna, flying so low that it might have caught the power lines running along the street. The impacts started in the back and moved forward. A bundle slid down the windshield of the truck: magazines bound together by a wire. We then saw the plane, and it continued flying at that dangerously low altitude, dropping bundles on the cars parked along the side of the street.

The magazines were *Bohemias*. The headline read, *Dirty Communist Hands of Cuba*. As we drove, Roman tried to avoid hitting the large bundles, each about 18 inches thick. He abruptly twisted the wheel as he slammed on the brakes. Chandee and I grabbed the dashboard desperately to avoid hitting the windshield with our heads.

The bundle on the windshield rolled off and fell to the sidewalk. The wire binding sprang open, spilling the magazines all over the sidewalk. The truck stopped, the front wheels on the sidewalk, narrowly avoiding colliding with a light pole.

Roman turned to us in concern. "You guys OK? Are you hurt? I'm sorry, but I didn't want to run over all these things, these magazines. Heaven knows what they might have inside—maybe even bombs."

We reassured him we were fine, and we got out of the truck. Several large bundles of magazines lay in the bed of the truck as well as all over the street and on the cars parked there. People were coming out of their houses to see what was happening. Apparently this was a common occurrence, because the people ran to get the magazines. *Bohemia* was considered the only source of truthful news in Cuba at the time.

As people collected the bundles and gathered up the bundles of magazines, they looked around furtively, always on the watch for the police or G-2, knowing full well that this was illegal. It would not be very long before the authorities showed up to collect the contraband periodicals the government so desperately didn't want people reading.

Though it caught me by surprise, I later discovered that this *gratis* form of communication was sent by the owners of the magazine from Florida. Decades before, it had been an important form of communication, even going back before the Revolution. Initially, they had operated inside Cuba; but once appropriated through the arbitrary Socialist laws of the Castros, they relocated to Miami and sent it for free to their loyal readers to spread the truth of what was going on in the world. That truth was feared by the Cuban government. They tried very hard to conceal it from its citizens and change it through their propaganda machinery to something favorable to the government, covering the people's eyes with a black bandage. The lies they fabricated used people's dream of freedom and democracy following the collapse of the military dictatorship that had previously held sway on the island.

People continued to scurry about, snatching up the packages wherever they could grab them. Roman took a handful of magazines and put them under the driver's seat in his truck. In a very short time most of the magazines were gone. As Roman tried to clear the truck off, people would even snatch them out of his hands before he could put them on the sidewalk. Men, women, even children came to him like the magazines were hot bread that they were anxious to eat. In the distance, red lights started to flash. We knew the police were approaching, and with the police would come the G-2.

"Get into the truck!" Roman said. "Quickly!"

We ran and got back into his truck. We passed by several more streets that had already received their deliveries. We saw several arrests as the police confiscated magazines. Several of the bundles had broken when they dropped, and individual issues were more difficult to confiscate. Several G-2 civilian agents pursued people, running after anyone who appeared to have something in their hands. They were frustrated in that they only caught a few people. Because we were at the first drop point, we had lucked out. By the time the plane had reached the end of the street along which we traveled, the police had already been alerted, and so it was more difficult for people to obtain the precious cargo.

Roman tried to excuse himself to us. "I'm not a political individual; I don't even care who is in power. To me, they're all the same—liars. I know of no politician who has not broken his promise. They tell you only what they think you want to hear to get your vote. Once they're in power, they kick the people who put them there in the rear end. Unfortunately, people never learn, and they think the next politician is going to be the best, hoping he will be the one who will change everything. Instead, it's just another fraud. Like an adulterous wife who promises that the last man she got caught sleeping with is the last one for her and then goes right out and sleeps with another man, and the stupid, betrayed husband believes her." He smiled and shook his head, his face showing his disappointment. "That magazine I put under my seat? I'm going to use it to clean the grease off my hands and nothing else. I don't care what they've printed there. To me, it's all filthy politics."

I looked at him and smiled. I turned and looked at Chandee, who sat next to the window. She rolled her eyes and shook her head incredulously.

We were nearly in the park where we had left her car. I put one of my hands on his shoulder and said, "Remember, if you use that magazine to clean the grease from your hands or wipe your rear end, that's your business and not anyone else's—including this government, which intends to put its nose even in your underwear if you allow it. I will give you a little advice. Before you throw those magazines away and wipe your greasy hands on those pages, I don't think it would be a bad idea to discover its contents. Nothing they print in that magazine, if you're a man of conviction, can change your ways of thinking and your ideology. Maybe, though, it could be of essential importance for your education, principles, and morals. It's very good to be well-informed and educated. That is the only way to prevent anyone from ever pulling a fast one on you and tell you one thing when it's another."

Roman was parking next to Chandee's car. He looked at me with surprise in his eyes, taking in my uniform and pistol. He limited himself to simply nodding his head.

In an attempt to change the conversation, he said as he opened his door, "Well, let's see what kind of surgeon this patient needs."

We got out of the truck. He put some red cones before and after his truck to signal his workspace. He turned on the red and yellow lights on the roof of his truck and asked Chandee for the keys to the car. He opened the hood and checked the oil. He wiped the dipstick and thrust it back in. He touched the oil with his fingers and then smelled it. He shook his head and made a sound of disapproval.

He walked to the back of his truck and pulled out a five-gallon container of water and filled the radiator. He got into the car and started it and then walked to the back of the car. He put his hand near the muffler to feel the vapors. He turned the engine off and wiped his hands on a rag. With a sad face, he said, "You told me it's a hose, but I believe it's something a lot worse than that. I think the head gasket is burned, so the water has started to mix in with the oil pan. Did you guys run this car with the temperature gauge marked hot?"

Chandee and I exchanged glances. I didn't want to say anything since I hadn't been driving it, and she remained silent. Without an answer, he persisted, "Who was driving this car when it started to smoke?"

Chandee replied quickly, "I was the driver. Why?"

Roman shook his head and asked again, "Where did

you drive this car from?"

She didn't understand his question, but answered, "From the capital—in Havana."

He scratched his head and made a sour face. "Did you check the water before you left?"

"No, I filled the tank up with gas. I had assumed my father had done it and everything was OK."

Roman tried to make her feel better as he saw her face. "Don't feel guilty. It's very possible that one of the hoses developed a small leak. Because it had been leaking for a while, your father didn't notice that the car was low on water. When you drove it that long distance here, the water evaporated, and you didn't notice the temperature gauge indicating the engine was getting hot. That engine heat burned the head gasket, and so now the oil is mixed with the water. You can't drive it now. If you do, you could blow the engine and utterly ruin it." He scratched his head again. "My personal suggestion is to open it up and see what's really going on. This is just a superficial diagnostic. You're in luck—when I started the motor, it sounded like nothing was damaged. But to fix this problem, I'll have to tear apart half the engine and replace the heads and gaskets. This will take a long time."

"How long?" Chandee asked anxiously.

"Could be four or five days—and that's if we don't find any major complications. It could be a damaged valve, which it doesn't sound like, but I won't know that for sure until I open it up. What I've given you now is a visual preliminary best-guess diagnostic."

I said, "Take it to your shop and do what you have to do. Don't worry about it. I'll take care of everything. You don't even have to worry about my father, I'll handle that for you. I know you're very busy, but if you work fast, do a good job, and give it a priority, I will compensate you greatly for your consideration. Chandee is a close friend of mine, and this is her father's car. She needs to get back to the capital as soon as possible."

Roman scratched his head once more. "I'll do whatever is possible to have it ready in the shortest time I can."

"Thank you very much. Now we need you to please give us a ride to my home, if it's not too much of an inconvenience."

"Oh, please, Marmolito! Let me get the car hitched to my truck, and I'll drop you guys wherever you want to go. I have nothing else to do, and I'm at your service."

We thanked him, and he got the car hoisted on his tow truck. With Chandee's car trailing behind us, we drove to my house. When we said goodbye to Roman as we removed Chandee's travel bags from the car, I drew close to him and asked, "Can I ask you a personal favor?"

He smiled. "Whatever. Not only are you a good kid, but you're a great guy as well as the son of one of my best friends. What do you need?"

"If it's not inconvenient, could you give me one of those magazines?"

He looked at me and raised his eyebrow. Wordlessly, he leaned in and pulled a magazine out. A grave look on his face, he handed it to me, still obviously wondering what I might do with it, Revolutionary as I appeared to be in my uniform. I rolled the magazine into a tube and rapped him soundly on the shoulder with it. I smiled and said, "I will save it, not read it. Maybe it can serve me on some occasion as you say to clean the grease off of my hands when I have a flat tire."

He looked at me closely for a moment and then smiled. Slowly he nodded and winked at me. "You are too smart for your age."

He got inside and started the engine. He rolled down the window and tapped his temple. "Remember—you never got that magazine from me. You picked it up in the street, OK?"

I nodded and smiled.

He saluted me in a military style. "Stay out of trouble," he said and drove off.

Chandee's face was still long and full of worry. I put my arm around her shoulder. In an attempt to cheer her up, I said, "You should not worry at all. Thank God you stopped the engine in time, or by now your father's car would be ruined. After all, though your car changed my plan by breaking down, we actually have the best outcome. In a few days Roman will have it ready, good as new. Call your father from my house and tell him that we will need you and his car to complete my work for several more days. If he needs a car urgently, I will drive over there in the Volga to let him use it, and I'll come back on the bus if necessary. But it's very important we finish what we're doing. Don't tell him the car is broken or anything like that—this way, you will avoid upsetting him with bad news. I know Roman is a great mechanic and will make it better than it was before."

Chandee asked, "How much will all of this cost? You didn't even ask him that, and he said he needs to take almost half the engine apart to discern it."

I touched her face and looked into her eyes. "Don't worry. Che will pay for all the repairs. The best part is that he won't even know he's paying for it!" I smiled mischievously.

She shook her head. "You're something!"

I nodded and winked at her. I helped her bring her bags into my house, and we walked to the phone in the library. I left her there to speak in privacy with her father. I walked into the dining room. Most of the family was asleep by now, but Mima was still up, preparing some things for the following day. I had the magazine concealed behind my back and said to her in a singsong voice, "I have a surprise for you."

"What do you have—pastries?"

"No," I said, "something even better."

"What do you have?" she asked eagerly. "Tell me!"

I pulled the magazine out and opened it. She clapped a hand to her mouth. "My God, where did you get that? Everyone in town's been talking about it, but most people can't get their hands on one. Every time the plane drops them, the police and the G-2 are right behind, picking them up. Then they burn them."

"I have connections," I said nonchalantly.

She sat down at the table. "Oh, my God!" she exclaimed softly as she began to flip through it, looking through its contents in fascination. "Are you going to leave it here?"

"Yes, but put it in a very secure place, or they'll create a big fuss and accuse you of being a Counterrevolutionary. Keep it safe, because when I have a chance, I want to read it, too."

"Oh, my God, my brother Goyito has been asking about this magazine, because they're talking about the whole state of Pinar del Rio."

After I told her how I had happened upon this copy—with it almost literally coming to me from out of the heavens—Mima thanked me for bringing it to her. She had been really anxious to see the information they printed in the magazine from the outside world. She offered to squeeze some orange juice for me.

"OK," I said.

Chandee, her conversation with her father completed, returned as I started to drink my orange juice. Mima offered her one as well, and she accepted.

As Mima squeezed some more oranges in the juicer, Chandee sat down next to me. She said in a much more relaxed manner, "My father told me not to worry about it. He'll be leaving tomorrow to Guantanamo with the Professor and will be staying there for at least two weeks. He told me to take whatever time is necessary to complete whatever we're doing."

I nodded and said, "I told you. Whoever worries about tomorrow today worries twice. And in the end, the problem tomorrow might resolve itself, and all that worry and preoccupation prove unnecessary."

Mima listened to me with a smile and nodded. "Who taught you that, my son?"

I smiled and nodded as well. I bowed and saluted her with my nearly empty glass. "Who else but my beautiful Mima, who has always been my best teacher."

Mima set a small plate and a glass of orange juice in front of Chandee. She gave me a kiss on the cheek and said to her, "You have to be careful with this guy. When he wants something, he puts so much honey at your feet you won't be able to move."

Chandee smiled at that.

I said, "By the way, Mima, if anyone asks for me, I need you to tell them that I left with my friend Chandee who came from Havana to visit me early in the afternoon to the town of Guane. After so many months of absence in the literary campaign, I wanted to see your parents, Lorenza and Jose, for a few days."

"Oh, that is a very good idea," Mima said with a big smile. "Give them a kiss for me and send them my regards. You should have told me that ahead of time so that I could prepare some sandwiches and food for your trip."

Chandee looked at me in perplexity. I nudged her with my foot under the table and nodded slightly. "Don't worry, Mima—we'll stop someplace and buy some food. Don't stress yourself."

Mima said as she looked at her watch, "It's kind of late. Why don't you guys wait until early tomorrow morning? It's not safe to drive at this hour."

I looked at her warningly. "Mima, the reason I need to leave now, and should have left already, is because of something you'll probably read about tomorrow morning. Something that happened here in town—you know the sort of things. I don't want those bad kids at the G-2 to assume I had anything to do with it."

She understood my meaning at once. She stood up abruptly from where she had been sitting. When she spoke, there was a little worry in her voice, "In that case, what are you waiting for? You guys should be out of here already."

I smiled. "I will. I'm glad you understand. For those who understand, a few words is enough."

I took Chandee by the arm, who had also stood with

my mother. We said goodbye and left. We stowed my travel bag along with hers in the trunk of the Volga, and left in the direction of Cafe Labiada.

"I still have the munchies after those hors d'oeuvres we gave our enemies. If they had that pleasure, we should have it, too. It's part of my plan, anyway. Whenever we have the opportunity for some enjoyment, we will also share it with my grandpa and the rest of the family. Even though we had an unexpected breakdown with your car, the experiences of the past couple of years have turned me into a master of improvisation—although I don't like it. Originally, I thought to have you return at once to Havana. However, they say everything in life happens for a reason, and that sometimes works out better than you had planned, when you look at it positively."

Chandee smiled. "I have no doubt that you are an incorrigible optimist without any remedy."

I raised my arms and said as I opened the door to get in, "I'm very grateful to God and Mother Nature that I wasn't born a pessimist. Only the thought of being that depresses me."

Chandee started to get out of the car, but I stopped her. "No, wait here. I want them to see me—only me. That is a part of my plan, just in case we have any problems for what happened tonight."

I went into the restaurant. As I walked in, I saw a large tray with a sign marked "free samples" filled with fish-shaped crackers. I took a fistful and ate some. I asked the waiter, "What is in these crackers that is so good?"

"It's something new we're doing. We're going to put them in boxes. The flavor will be different: beef, pork, chicken, and fish."

I took another handful and put them in my breast pocket. I really liked those crackers. I placed my order with the waiter—the exact same plate of appetizers I had served to the three miserable men, along with the same brand of imported whiskey. I meticulously folded the receipt and put it in my other breast pocket. I took my order and put it in the back seat of the car. I handed Chandee another handful of crackers I picked up on my way out.

"What is that?" she asked curiously.

"Eat it," I said. "You'll see."

She popped a few in her mouth. "Mmmm! Where did you get these?"

"In there—and they're free. You want more?" I started to get back out.

"No, no," she said, stopping me. "But these are delicious."

I drove off through the city towards the exit for the Pan-American del Caribe Highway to head towards the southern side of the island. When we reached the outskirts, I saw a long line of cars that looked like a checkpoint. This was new, especially on this highway. Reacting very quickly, I turned the wheel to my left to pull into what appeared to be an abandoned gas station.

Chandee, her mouth full of crackers, asked worriedly, "What happened?"

"Don't worry. I think they're conducting a search. It may have nothing to do what we did a little while ago, but when in doubt, stop." I opened the door and removed my belt and beret, dropping both in the seat. "Wait for me here. This won't take me long. I just want to make sure that we're not the ones they're looking for."

Chandee nodded. "Very well. Be careful, OK?"

"Don't worry, I will. If by any chance you have a problem, blow the horn as often as you can. That line looks like it's half a kilometer from the bridge where they have the check station. For me to hear you at that distance, you'll need to blow the horn repeatedly."

"Don't worry, take it easy. Now go."

I closed the door and crept into the bushes bordering the highway. I walked for a while until I could see the guards conducting the search. I passed several drainage pipes on my way, and soon I was under the bridge near the guards at the roadblock. They had erected wooden barricades to form the checkpoint. As I walked through the dark, I stepped into soft mud at the border of the bridge. I sank into the muck up to my right knee, nearly falling onto my face in the black, smelly goo. Fortunately, there was a large tree growing there, and I was able to catch myself on one of the branches. I pulled my leg out of the disgusting mess, and saw the filthy water running from my pants to my boot. It smelled of rotten fish and human bowel.

I waded through the water. Though it was not completely clean, it was better than the filth I had stepped in, and I used it to clean myself. I had to use my fingers to scoop out the accumulation of that mess that had formed in the border between the elastic hem of my uniform pants and the top of my boot.

From my position under the small bridge, I could hear the voices of the soldiers and the drivers of the vehicles they had stopped. Some of the voices sounded very angry, protesting the long wait and unnecessary search when nothing bad was going on in the area. One of the truck drivers told the soldiers that he drove that trip to make a living, and he had been waiting for half an hour burning diesel in his truck. He demanded of the soldier whether the government was going to pay for it.

The soldiers limited themselves to expressions of helplessness and said that all complaints should be made of the Minister of the Interior. When I heard that, an alarm bell rang in my mind. I knew this was not a regular search, which was ordinarily performed sporadically by the highway patrol to make sure that people were paid up on their license plate fees and other taxes and licenses. This search had been initiated by the Interior of the Ministry—which could, in this case, mean the G-2 or possibly the DTI. They were after somebody or something in particular.

This highway ran through the mountains, and the bridge spanned an arroyo which would channel water during flash floods. As such, the road was built up as it approached the bridge to around 40 feet above the ground, with an easy 30-to-40-degree grade for the slope. I had to maneuver my way up this in order to identify who was in charge of the search. After I crawled to the top of the highway, I hid behind the bushes growing along the side.

I lay flat in the wet grass and saw two cars from the G-2 a short distance away. They were parked facing opposite directions, poised to immediately pursue anyone who attempted to escape the search. The guards were dressed in civilian clothes but were armed to the teeth and were wearing bullet-proof vests.

I shook my head in disgust. That indicated they were

looking for us. The fact that the G-2 was present meant there was something to worry about, especially after what we had done to three of them a few hours before. I didn't want anyone in authority, much less the G-2, to know the exact hour Chandee and I had left the city.

Two soldiers approached in my direction with two large black Rottweilers that started to bark. The starch in my uniform helped me to slide admirably, and without much effort I was able to allow myself to slip down the grade over the wet grass. The dogs continued barking as I descended. One of the soldiers asked, "What do you hear? What's going on? Is it something for real this time, or is it a jack rabbit coming out to eat that wet grass?"

I finally felt my feet touch firm ground. I didn't move, but stayed there glued to the side of the slope. I was well concealed inside the bushes. The dogs started to growl as the barking became frenetic. I remained immobile for several seconds. I knew it was very possible for the guards to be watching the area towards which the dogs were barking. I heard a different guard say, "I don't see anything down there."

At the same time, I could see the beams of powerful flashlights flickering through the bushes. A third voice asked, "What's happened? What's going on?" This voice was more authoritarian, like that of someone in command.

"I don't know," replied the second voice. "The dogs are going crazy. They never bark like this."

This time three lights began to search the bottom of the slope. I froze, not even daring to breathe. The lights started to move towards my right. I used the opportunity to slide to my left, towards where I planning to break away. I was beginning to worry about getting caught there.

Slowly crawling, I moved all the way towards my left until I found some rocks and the first buttress for the bridge. I crouched and began to creep down along the border of the wall. I needed to get out of there as soon as I could. I looked at both sides of the bridge, and saw that the flashlights continued searching the area where I had been before and further away from my current location.

I decided to break from my cover and run to the left, towards where I had left the Volga. As soon as I did that, I heard the dogs going crazy. Even though I ran silently by human standards, the sharp hearing of the Rottweilers picked me up. Possibly they also caught my scent in the wind. An authoritative voice yelled, "Let the goddamned dogs loose! I saw some movement over there at the bottom of the bridge."

As I ran, my heart sank. This was not in my plans at all, and I prayed to God to help me get out of this situation. *Forgive me, Jesus*, I prayed silently, *for bothering you at this late hour of the night, but please shield me from my enemies and those dogs.*

I had half a kilometer to cover before I could get to the Volga, and I had to move fast. This was why I had left my heavy weapons belt in the car. However, the reality was much different, in spite of my forethought. I ran, my heart pounding in time with my feet pounding along the ground, sweat pouring down my face. I hadn't run like this since that incident in the mountains so many months before.

I went through the drainage pipes once more, though these were smaller than those by the bridge. While the larger pipes were simply to drain the excess water during flash floods, these smaller pipes served to channel the water away from the road, preserving the asphalt from erosion. I practically flew past the first one as I jumped over the water.

It sounded to me like the dogs were gaining on me. I had nearly reached the second pipe. I realized they were getting too close and there was no way I would be able to make it to the Volga. Thinking quickly, I decided as I caught a glimpse of my ring that there was a possibility of getting clear of all of this if I made certain that the dog approached me from the front rather than attacking my back.

I turned abruptly to my left and entered the pipe. It was large enough for me to stand up in it. I walked to the center and crossed my arms to protect my chest in a combat position as I made sure my back was against the wall. At the same time, I made sure my ring hand was free. One of the dogs entered after me. I saw the light glint off his eyes as he searched for me. He no longer barked but continued to emit a low growl as he slowly approached me. He stalked me and came so close that he was able to smell the boot that had sunk into the rotten mud. I started to bring the ring down but stopped. As he smelled me, he had lost most of his aggression. I couldn't be certain what he was doing, but I remained immobile, every muscle taut, ready to strike with the ring at the slightest aggression.

It was miserable in that pipe. The water increased the humidity in there, combining with the heat from the day to make conditions inside like a foul sauna. The dog continued to smell me, and I suddenly realized that we were alone. I wondered where the other dog had gone. I had seen for certain two dogs, and I worriedly looked around even as I kept my attention on the one at my feet. I prayed again to Jesus Christ to help me, because I did not want to use the poison on that beautiful animal. I had nothing against it personally, even though it belonged to my enemies.

Suddenly, the dog looked up at me, raising his head, and his growling stopped. Abruptly, he sprang up to place his paws on my shoulders. I raised my left hand in preparation to sink the needle into his neck, when I noticed he was smelling one of my breast pockets—the one that had some of those wonderful crackers. I halted my attack. I kept my left hand raised and ready to strike, and slowly moved my right hand over to undo the button on the pocket. I reached in and took some crackers out. I held them before his muzzle, and he practically inhaled them. As he chewed the crackers, he went back down onto all fours, sitting as he chewed. He looked at me as he ate, licking his chops. I realized he wanted more. I reached in and pulled out almost all of the crackers I had left, carefully dropping them in front of him, still keeping my left hand ready. I thanked God then, because he completely changed from an aggressive attack dog to more like a family pet enjoying a treat.

As I straightened up, I used my right hand to pet him on the head in a gesture of affection and gratitude. I said, "Good dog."

I slowly turned and backed away. Keeping my back to the wall and my eyes on him, I slid along the pipe to the other side. I was perhaps ten feet away when the other dog arrived carrying a dead rabbit in its bloody mouth. It dropped the rabbit on the floor and started to growl and bark aggressively at me as it approached me menacingly. I stepped back inside the pipe, resuming my combat ready pose, slowly backing away. I was prepared for the worst as I said, "Good dog. Calm down. I don't want to hurt you. I'm your friend."

This dog looked more aggressive than the other. He bore a massive scar from his left eye down his face, as if he had been in a big fight or someone had cut him badly. As I backed away, he continued his advance, growing more aggressive. I knew he would jump for me soon. I tensed every muscle in my body in preparation for that moment. I moved from one side of the pipe to the other to catch him by surprise. At that moment, he jumped. As he did, the other dog leaped for him, and a dogfight ensued. I slid slowly away from the battle as the two animals fought each other, spraying water and mud all over the place. I finally got outside the pipe, and looked around. Perhaps thirty feet away, I could see the flashlights of the soldiers. I didn't take time to think about it—I took off at a run.

I heard one of the voices call the dogs by name. "Protector! Satan!" I thought, *Oh, my God. I'm right in the hallway between Heaven and Hell.* I smiled to myself, thinking that at least I was past the worst. As I ran, the sound of the demonic dogfight faded as I put distance between myself and the scene.

One of the voices screamed, "Goddamned dogs, shut up! What the hell are you doing? You should be following the scent, not fighting each other!"

I heard pained yelping as if they were being beaten. I shook my head as I ran, sympathizing with those poor dogs. I ran faster to increase the distance as rapidly as I could.

Eventually, I no longer heard either the voices of the soldiers or the dogs. I crossed the last of the drainage ditches and then reached my destination. Chandee was still there, and I felt joy in my heart as I realized I had gotten out of that dangerous situation. I had not expected the kind of trouble I had nearly veered into; it was like the Devil had specifically set some of his dirty traps to ensnare me. My body was drenched in sweat, and my heart was pounding. I stopped for a few seconds to catch my breath. I could see the lights of the highway and was close to where I had left the car.

My breathing grew more regular, and I walked on at a normal pace. I crossed over the ditch and climbed the wall on the other side towards the highway. As I started, I saw a silhouette come out from behind the concrete support pillar. It looked like a soldier. His pistol in his right hand, he yelled, "Put your hands up, and don't try anything stupid if you don't want to die here tonight."

I froze a few steps away from the shadowy form of that person. I could see the pistol in his hand but I could not see his face. I raised my arms in surrender. I asked, "What is the problem, *compañero*? I only came down here to the ditch to go to the bathroom. I ate something at dinner that didn't settle well in my stomach." I lowered my left hand and touched my stomach. "I had terrible stomach cramps."

This time, as I rubbed my stomach, the man commanded nervously, "Don't move! Put your hand up where I can see it if you don't want to get shot."

He took a couple of steps toward me aggressively. He

was obviously prepared to shoot me on the spot, pointing the weapon right at my head as he walked up to me. The muzzle touched my forehead. His other hand reached out to pat me down as he checked me for weapons. "Where did you leave your pistol and big knife?"

I said, "Be very careful, *compañero*. That weapon could discharge by accident, and then you'll be in a lot of trouble. I am the Commandantico, one of the most favored in the first ring of Fidel. You could wind up in front of a firing squad for this."

He stepped back. He interrupted me with a yell, "Shut up! I know who you are, and I know what you and your Chinese friend did this evening at the Chinese restaurant! You guys are going to pay a high price for that to my colleagues in the G-2. I'm on a special mission, assigned by my boss Piñeiro, to find some evidence. Now I have that evidence, and you've been caught with your hands in the cookie jar. This is your last adventure, Commandantico—or should I say, Lightning? Isn't that what the Commander-in-Chief calls you?"

He pulled a flashlight out of his belt shone it into my face. "Really—I'm sorry, because I didn't want to believe that you are that famous spy in service to our enemies. But tonight I confirmed for myself that Piñeiro has been right all along. It will be an even greater disappointment for Fidel. I want to tell you to not even bother defending yourself. I don't care what you say. What you did with your friend tonight in the restaurant is your ticket to the firing squad, my little Commander. Like I said before, I'm really sorry, because of your age. But *que sera*." He held the beam of the light up to his own face. "Don't you recognize me?"

By the light I could see him clearly. He was familiar, but the exaggerated shadows obscured enough of his features that I couldn't place him. I ran that image through my memory to figure out where I had seen him before, using the natural gift I possess to remember facial features. I attributed this momentary block in my memory to the adrenaline rush I was suffering at that moment. The fact that he had mentioned Piñeiro's name didn't help matters, either. He had taken me completely by surprise and produced an extremely negative impact on me. For the first time in my life, I felt trapped like a wild rabbit in the forest between a wolf and a vast cliff face.

He smiled and pulled the flashlight a little lower and shone it once more into my face. Observing my silence and insecurity at that moment, he said, "My name is Jose Manuel Castellano." I kept my silence, confusion and discontent at war in my face. "I am the one who asked you before to put the handcuffs on when we took you to Villa Marista, the night of the painting auction when we took you out of the Belles Artes palace for questioning. Remember now?"

I nodded, memory flashing back to me. "Of course I remember you, Jose Manuel Castellano. It's an extraordinarily great pity that you didn't follow my recommendations." As I spoke, I could see shadowy movement behind him. "If you have a good memory, you'll recall that I told you to look for another job with anyone else, and to stay away from Piñeiro. He would only wind up bringing major problems to you. I see now that you're in very deep trouble." He looked at me in perplexity. "If you ask me, you're in a dark alley without any exit at all."

He smiled in surprise, touching his chest with the handcuffs he had just pulled out from his belt. "I, in an alley with no exit?" He laughed. "Don't make me laugh. I think you have the whole thing inverted." He held the handcuffs out towards me. "You go ahead and put these on yourself, but this time it's not a regulation procedure. It's an order, and do it quickly! I don't have any time to waste on you." I smiled and looked at him ironically. He stared at me oddly. "Laugh all you want, but your arrest will guarantee the promotion I've been waiting for all this time. After all these years, I'm the one who put the handcuffs on the famous spy that everyone, even Piñeiro, has failed to catch."

I still could not fathom what assurance he had that the spy was me. What we did in the restaurant was not proof that I was a spy; it just meant that I was angry or upset with someone.

My look became very serious. I took the handcuffs from him and raised them up. "Are you sure you want to do this? This is your last chance."

He glared at me and shoved the pistol in my face. "Put on the goddamn handcuffs and don't fuck around with me any—"

He never finished the word. Instead, he uttered a gurgling breath and opened his mouth as he gulped for air. He froze there, his eyes bulging out, and the huge sword blade of my Commando knife erupted from his mouth. Chandee stood behind him, having used the massive blade to stab him through his neck, into the base of his skull. The beam from his flashlight bobbed and rolled around as he danced in his death throes. Losing stability, he fell to his knees before me.

Before he reached the ground, Chandee snatched the pistol out of his hand before a reflexive convulsion could squeeze the trigger. She put her knee against his back and pulled the knife out of his body. He remained there in the kneeling position, as if he were begging for pardon.

I had recognized her form in the darkness from her long hair as she had made her stealthy approach from behind him. I had continued speaking to him to not just hold his attention but also to muffle with our voices any chance sound her feet might make. My worries, however, were unfounded. Chandee was as silent as a mountain lion and had eliminated him very efficiently. Clearly, she knew that he had to be silenced as soon as she heard his intention of bringing both of us in front of Piñeiro for no other reason than to secure his promotion. I could only assume that he had more evidence that convinced him of my identity as the spy they had been trying to catch for so long.

I knew taking his life was no easy decision for Chandee. I looked at the kneeling body in pity. He was a victim of his own ambition, an unscrupulous desire to create whatever fiction he had to in order to please his master and thought that I would be easy prey when he accepted the mission.

After we removed his clothes and personal effects, we dragged the corpse clad only in its underclothes towards the sewer access. We opened the manhole and dropped it down there. We both crossed ourselves, and I said, "Rest in peace, wherever you are going. Now you have to render an accounting to the Supreme Judge of the Universe."

Dr. Julio Antonio del Marmol

Chandee uttered a prayer, and we replaced the cover. We walked along the ribbon of water under the bridge. We washed our hands and the blade of the knife in it. I put my right hand on her shoulder and said, "Thank you." She nodded silently, and we started to climb the gentle slope until we reached the border of the highway. We walked over to the abandoned gas station where we had left the Volga.

Before we got into the car, I hugged Chandee. I knew she needed my support at that moment. She looked at me with luminous eyes filled with tears. I could see a little guilt there. "Are you OK?" I asked.

She bit her lip and nodded. "I had no other choice. It was either him or us. He would not only have brought us down but also Heaven knows how many others with us." Her voice was very sad as she spoke.

I squeezed her neck by the collar bone. I said to her in a sympathetic tone, "I would have done just as you did. You are a very good person to feel as you do in this moment. Thank you again for intervening so opportunely when you did."

She looked unconvinced. "Thank you. I know for a fact you would have done the same for me. Let's get out of here as soon as possible before we encounter another similar situation."

I shook my head. "I think this was a lone wolf. Piñeiro knows that's the only way he can trap me. I would be suspicious of a group of people, and so he hoped that one person would escape my notice and be able to get close enough to me to catch me in the snare."

I opened the door of the Volga for her and gave her a tender kiss before closing the door. I walked around and opened the driver's door. I got in and drove to the only other exit from the city, in the opposite direction.

Cafe Labiada

Dr. Julio Antonio del Marmol

Horror and Indifference: Accomplices in Our Time

The ocean is burning. I feel the heat on my face and in my heart, the tremendous scorching of his fire. The sun is angry, and the sky weeps as the world breaks into a thousand pieces. I can hear her pain and feel her cry. As the human race grows more deranged like never before in our tremendous killing sprees, hunting each other like rabbits in the desert night, I watch you and the rest of humanity cry out for love and peace as our political leaders ignore us, doing nothing about it. Our sisters, brothers, and friends lose their heads, though our leaders have the power to stop this madness; instead they frivolously play sports and games when they should be working to stop these crimes. While our world shatters into smithereens, they who are supposed to be our brothers and sisters despite their prominent political positions, sit in silence drinking beer and watch my friends die as if nothing was happening, looking at all that happens with incompetence and ignorance. As I watch this leader's indifference, my blood boils in my heart and my stomach grows nauseous with disgust. To our leader I say: in the eyes of the Father, my friend, this beyond any doubt makes you an accomplice to all these despicable crimes.

Dr. Julio Antonio del Marmol

Chapter 3: Sexual Slavery in the New Socialist Society

The Luis Lazo Highway was an old, forgotten highway. It was extremely narrow—only two lanes near the top of the hills that passed along some copper mines on the way to Guane. It was uneven, with steep grades to slough water off the roadway and cement channels along the cliff side to direct the water downhill. The locals had nicknamed the highway the Devil's Serpent to reflect the dangerous, continual hairpin turns that slowed the trip. There was no doubt in anyone's mind, however, that the view of the tropical forest was breathtakingly beautiful, augmented by the cascading waterfalls and dense jungle which provided coconut and papaya fruit right along the border of the highway. It was a kind of Amazon rain forest with an abundance of wild flowers.

One could travel for hours without seeing a sign of civilization. Large mining trucks filled with copper from the Matahambre[4] mines created a new danger to drivers, as they had a tendency to hog the road. Once the new highway was built, all these factors, combined with the frequency of fatal accidents, generally discouraged people from using it. Virtually the only traffic now on that road were those trucks. It had certainly earned its

---
[4] Killer of Hunger

nickname with honors.

"I don't like this route at all," I remarked as we entered the highway.

Like everyone else who started along this path, I crossed myself. "When I was a little kid on my first trip with my father when we lived in Guane, we traveled this road in his first brand-new car. He had just bought a 1951 white and bottle green Buick. I remember clearly the accident we had that could easily have cost us our lives.

"He tried to pass an interprovincial bus, right at one of the short pieces of straight road. It was the only opportunity he'd had in the last half hour. Apparently the driver hadn't slept well the night before and kept nodding off at the wheel. At the exact moment we passed him, he started to fall asleep. The bus drifted towards us, and the wheels of my father's car nearly ran on empty air. Dad blew the horn to wake the guy up. I was sitting in the front passenger seat and saw the sparks erupt as the side of the bus touched the side of our car.

"Thank God that small Buick had a powerful horn! My father leaned on it, and the driver woke up and jerked himself back to his side of the road so abruptly that the other side scraped against the rock face. When I saw our left wheels virtually in the air, I thought we were going to die. Dad was able to get back onto the highway and regain control of our car.

"Once he'd passed the bus, he pulled over, as the bus also did, so that the damage could be assessed. All the passengers on the bus left in panic and conglomerated in the highway, gawking at the damage to the bus. Our little Buick's right side was completely smashed from front to back. It was so bad I couldn't even open the passenger door. I had to get out by the driver's side. My door was actually welded shut. Naturally, the driver apologized to my father and tendered his excuses. Dad waved it off understandingly and calmly—even the driver's offer to pay for the repairs."

When I finished my story, Chandee looked at me fearfully. She turned to face her window, which looked out over the cliff. She said, "Please, drive carefully. We're not in a rush. Thank God it's dark so I can't see how far down that cliff goes!"

I smiled. "Why do you think I've been driving so slowly? From the moment I entered this highway, the memory of that accident's been playing in my head like a movie. I was perhaps only seven or eight years old at that time. To tell you the truth, that day was the first time in my short life I saw fear and desperation in my old man's face. He is always so sure of himself and in control in every situation. I'll admit it to you—that was probably the first time I ever felt my hands sweat so much, like running faucets. I left the marks of my fingers on both knees I gripped them so tightly and swayed back and forth with my father in an attempt to keep the car's equilibrium. All that panic is something I remember, and I can't explain to myself why I'm holding my knees now and swaying so we don't fall down that cliff."

She smiled and caressed my cheek with her left hand. "Maybe, in your innocence, you tried to help your father in his attempts to get out of that horrible situation."

I smiled and shook my head. "I never in my life saw my old man with so much fright and uncertainty in his face. That is probably what scared the hell out of me." I shifted my position a little and turned the radio on. "Let's not think of bad memories and play some music instead. Maybe that will bring us some good vibes."

By luck, the radio was playing a beautiful song by Benny More, "Santa Isabel de las Lajas." We looked at each other and smiled. We were fans of the popular singer and enjoyed the music as we drove through the mountains. Our enjoyment was short lived, however, because the mountains started to block the signal. I leaned forward to adjust the reception. The signal grew weaker as we went deeper into the mountains. I continued to fiddle with the dial to pick the station up again.

Suddenly, a military truck appeared behind us like it was erupting out of hell. It was a transport vehicle with benches in the back filled with women. It passed us at a speed unusual for that road and was escorted by two police motorcycles. The women were dressed in civilian clothes. Between my surprise and my preoccupation with the radio, I almost lost control of the car.

The driver cut violently in front of me, and the motorcycles followed his example. I struggled to maintain control, and Chandee and I exclaimed in surprise at the sudden encounter. The women were extremely young and bounced all around the back of the truck. One of them lost her grip on the rail, fell, and began to roll around on the floor of the truck. She very nearly was thrown out of the vehicle, which would have been fatal, one way or another. By luck, she grabbed one of the cargo nets along the side of the truck, and was helped back to her place by some of the other women.

Not long after this encounter, a red and white Pontiac Catalina, perhaps a 1955 or 1956 model, passed us in the same way as the truck, as if it were in pursuit of the military vehicle. This car was moving even faster than the truck.

To my surprise and consternation, the Pontiac rammed the police motorcycles from the rear. One of the motorcycles flew out over the cliff and into the darkness. The other lost control but managed to maneuver onto the runoff ditch. After struggling with his bike for a few seconds, he was able to regain control and returned to the highway. The Pontiac, however, didn't let him rest. As soon as he got back onto the highway, he got back in front of the car, and the Pontiac floored the accelerator to hit the bike once more. This time, the bike flew against the side of the mountain, seeming to ride along the cliff face like a circus rider for a moment before gravity reasserted itself. Unlike a circus rider, he had no net. This was one of the sharper grades, and when he hit the asphalt again, he slid back into the concrete ditch, the motorcycle breaking into the several pieces. One wheel bounced back onto the road, and the Pontiac ran over it. The Pontiac tried to pass the truck, blowing its horn insistently.

The women in the back of the truck apparently knew who the driver of the Pontiac was. They were gesticulating as if trying to signal. I thought at first they were agricultural volunteers for the government, being moved from one part of the island to another. I realized now that they were dressed too nicely for that and were too young. They looked like they were returning from a party or a dance.

Chandee and I exchanged surprised glances. The lights of the Volga became spotlights for the drama that was unfolding before our eyes. Two men leaned out of the passenger windows of the Pontiac, waving at the driver of the truck to stop. Their voices could be heard as they yelled at the truck. Instead of obeying the shouted commands of the men, the driver increased his speed, and began to swerve against the Pontiac, attempting to crush it against the mountainside. The car slowed down, however, and avoided that.

I slowed even more to allow the Pontiac in front of me. Instead of slowing down to avoid the truck, the Pontiac's driver swerved to hit the right rear wheel of the truck. It careened dangerously towards the abyss next to the road, the women screaming and flailing at the air in panic. Seeing this, the truck driver slammed on his brakes to counter the Pontiac's attack and to throw it off the highway and into the runoff ditch.

I had slowed to less than 25 kilometers per hour to avoid colliding with the Pontiac. The driver realized that he had no hope in a fight like this against a truck and that there was no way he could force it to stop. The men in the car leaned out again, this time with pistols in their hands. Again they yelled at the driver, reinforcing their demands for him to pull over by offering to shoot him with the pistols pointed at him. The truck driver ignored them, hitting them once more. It happened so suddenly that one of the men didn't have a chance to get back inside. The man in front was crushed between the two vehicles, while the man in the rear seat managed to duck back inside just in time.

The driver of the Pontiac managed to avoid the ditch. When he got away from the truck, we could see the body of the unfortunate man dangling limply from the side of the car, his gun bouncing along the highway. The truck driver, seeing his success, decided to hit the Pontiac without waiting. The car driver was taken by surprise, and the two left wheels went off the edge of the road. The side of the mountain prevented a full flip, and the Pontiac ran on its side for about fifty feet before being pushed back onto all four wheels by the same mountain, sparks and stones flying everywhere all the while. The Pontiac fishtailed for another fifty feet as the driver struggled to bring the car fully back onto the roadbed. Not wanting to get hit again, the truck driver accelerated in an attempt to get away. We had by this time slowed almost to a stop.

The Pontiac regained control and got back onto the road. The driver of the car changed his tactics, now employing a more radical approach. He accelerated to get directly behind the truck. He rammed into the back of the truck, which could not match the Pontiac's speed, and floored the accelerator. He steered toward the left to force the truck into the runoff ditch and away from the open side of the road. The greater mass of the truck would make getting back out much more difficult.

The truck driver started to zig zag in an attempt to get rid of the mosquito on his tail, when suddenly one of the large semi-trucks from the copper mine appeared, blowing its air horn. Both vehicles swerved to avoid the impact. The Pontlac slowed down, and unfortunately for the military vehicle, the truck driver did the same. Before our eyes, he lost control. In his attempt to get out of the way of the semi, he swerved too close to the open cliff. He slammed on his brakes, the entire truck skidding around until the rear wheels hung off the edge of the cliff. Some of the women were flung out of the bed and smashed against the side of the mountain, others flung along the road or into that terrible chasm, but some managed to retain their grip on the rails. The only survivors were the ones who were still in the truck, and they were now screaming in terror.

This happened so fast that the Pontiac was unable to stop before running over one of the women who had landed immediately in front of the car. We could see from the Volga two men get out the Pontiac, their hands clasped to their heads in grief as they looked at the woman they had just hit. They ran over to the truck and looked into the window to make certain the soldiers were dead or unconscious. They then went over the top of the truck to help the surviving girls out. I stopped my car, understanding that any survivors had to leave immediately. At any moment the balance could be upset enough, and that truck would soon plummet the approximately two thousand feet to the bottom of the cliff. I aimed my lights towards the truck and left the engine running.

I took Chandee by the arm. "Wait for me here, please, until I find out what's going on, and who the good guys and bad guys in all this are." I pulled my pistol and cocked it. I handed it to her. "Keep this so you can watch my back."

"You keep it to take care of yourself." She pulled a small .25 pistol out of her purse. "You crazy, going over there without a weapon? We don't know what's going on here, and I don't think it's a good idea to even stop."

I rolled my eyes. "Just pure humanitarianism. Some people could die if we don't assist. Don't get out of the car, though, until I give you a signal that everything's OK."

I clasped my hands together in front of her. "You know. And if I see anything wrong or dangerous, I'll take my beret off. If that happens, carefully get out of the car. Watch your surroundings at all times."

"Very well," she replied.

I kept my pistol in my right hand. I got out of the Volga and shielded it with my leg. I yelled, "Do you need any help?"

One of the men from the Pontiac was on top of the truck. "Yes, yes—we need a long rope to get to these poor girls hanging on to the rails of the truck."

I continued to carefully walk towards them, keeping an eye on my immediate surroundings at all times, my pistol glued to my leg so that no one would notice it. As I drew close, by the lights from the Volga I saw what was going on in that truck. I intentionally kept myself in the lights so that Chandee could see me. I saw one of the utility compartments in the truck's side was open. Through the door I could see what appeared to be a roll of chain. I approached the truck and began to pull the chains out, thinking that this might help in lieu of rope. As I pulled the chain out, something strange caught my attention. Every three or four feet there were handcuffs attached to the chain. I looked at them in surprise. Were they transporting prisoners?

I wrapped the chain around my forearm until I had what I judged to be sufficient length. I walked around the truck and went to the man who was bracing the truck with his weight. I handed the chains to him. "Maybe this can help you guys in some way."

It was a very young man. He handed them to the other man and said, "Morito, maybe these can help you." He looked at me gratefully. "Thank you very much for stopping and trying to help us."

When he slid the chains to the other man, the truck swayed dangerously and slid towards the edge some more. Morito slid the chains back. "That is too much weight!" he said in a panicked voice. The chains rolled along the bed of the truck and landed at my feet.

When I saw the truck move and heard his words, an idea rapidly formed in my mind. There were still six girls hanging on for dear life, and something needed to be done soon, as that truck was going to fall at any moment. I heard Morito trying to convince the girls to take his hand. The girls sobbed in panic, but no one wanted to let go long enough to grab his hand. Morito was a very skinny guy, and they didn't trust him to have sufficient strength to pull any of them up. They pleaded with him to get more help.

I picked the chains up off the ground and walked without a word back towards the Volga. The young man watched me leave. He must have thought I was offended, because he yelled to me, "Hey! My friend didn't mean to insult you. Where are you going? We need you here, man—come back, please."

I waved at him over my head and continued walking. I touched the metal bumper and realized it was far too flimsy for what I had in mind. I scrambled under the Volga and looked for the chassis. I tied the chain off as best I could to the metal structure. I then pulled the chain as far as it would reach, but it wasn't long enough. I left the chain on the ground and went back to the Volga. I told Chandee, "Everything is still the same—nothing's changed. I don't know who these guys are or what their agenda is. The only thing I can tell you is that they're trying to save a bunch of young girls from certain death. They're literally hanging by their hands in the air over that cliff."

Chandee asked, "Do you need my help?"

I glanced at her as I put the Volga into driving gear. "Maybe—but don't leave the car until we're sure who we're dealing with here. I need to be convinced for myself that everything is OK. Until then, you have to remain, for both our safety, out of the eyes of these people."

"OK," she said. "I understand perfectly."

I slowly drove the Volga as close as I could to the truck and put the emergency brake on. I got out and dragged the chain to the side of the truck. I climbed under and looked for its chassis. Once more, I tied the chain as best I could. I then ran and located the four largest rocks I could find and used them as wheel chocks to further brace the Volga against being dragged by the greater weight of the truck. Before leaving it again, I told Chandee, "If this car starts to drag forward towards the cliff, jump out of it at once. Keep your hands on the door handle."

I left the Volga and rejoined the two young men by the truck. The friendlier man saw me returning and received me with a relieved grin on his face. By now I felt a little more relaxed with the situation. I could see these young kids represented no immediate threat. I still didn't holster my pistol; instead, I pocketed it in my campaign pants.

"Thank you very much for what you're doing for us," the young man said. "God bless you for what you're doing. My name is Jose Aristedes Valdivia." He held his hand out to me.

I took his hand and shook it. "I am Julio Antonio del

Marmol. It's a pleasure."

"The pleasure is all mine. But do you think that little Volga is capable of pulling this big truck?"

"That is not my intention, but it's not a bad idea, at least to try. My original idea was only to anchor you guys firmly until you can get those girls out of danger. But your idea isn't that bad at all." I gave him a small smile. "Maybe we can try. You never know—maybe the little David can get Goliath out of trouble."

He nodded, clearly unconvinced. "If you are willing to risk your car ending up possibly dragged by the weight of this heavy truck at the bottom of that cliff, we can try it."

"That is the risk I was willing to take anyway when I tied the chain to both my car and that truck." I raised my right arm high. The drama between the girls and the other guy had continued unabated. "Tell everyone to hold on tightly, and tell your friend to come back over to this side. His weight will help out and the two of you can push against this wheel."

"Very well, I will try," Jose said. He turned away. "Morito! Come back here, quickly!"

I got back to the Volga, and I could tell Morito liked the idea. Frustrated from his futile efforts to persuade any of the women to take his hand and come to safety, I saw him do exactly as I had instructed.

Chandee looked at me incredulously. "What do you think you're doing?"

I replied with a little smile. "Let's see what this little *volgita* can do."

I put the Volga in reverse, since I knew that the reverse gear in any transmission was the strongest one. I had read that in both *Reader's Digest* and *Popular Mechanic*.

JFK: The Unwrapped Enigma

I pressed on the accelerator, and the wheels spun against the asphalt. To our collective surprise, inch by inch the tiny car began to pull the truck, which began to incline slightly to the left. This brought first the front of the cabin onto firm soil, and then the rear wheels, and finally the danger was past. The girls joyfully jumped onto the firm ground, hugging each other and crying. The two young men were hugged as well. As soon as I saw the truck was stable, I stopped the Volga. I repeated to Chandee, "You stay here. I'm still not sure what's going on, so let's keep you out of sight for now. Just in case."

I walked over to the group. Everyone was very happy to see me, and the men shook my hands as the girls embraced me. Jose made all the introductions. One of the girls was Morito's sister, Margarita. She began to tell me what had happened.

The men in the truck had kidnapped them, taking almost thirty women out of their *quinceañeras*. They handcuffed them, beat them up, and kept them for several days in a large tobacco curing house in the middle of nowhere in Guane. That afternoon they had been taken out of that place and put in different trucks to be taken to the port of La Coloma in Pinar del Rio. There was to be a large yacht waiting to take them out of the country to be sold into sexual slavery.

Morito said, "I found out last night that they would be transporting them today under police protection. It cost me every single penny I've been saving all my life, but I bribed one of the officials in the police in Guane, and he told me the exact time and day they would be transporting the girls. I vowed to get Margarita out of there if it cost me my life. Thanks to my friend Jose there and my unfortunate friend who died trying, Gollo, may God have him in Heaven. He was Margarita's boyfriend."

Margarita was weeping and gripping Morito's arm, shaking in complete shock and grief.

She looked around at the bodies of the girls scattered around the place in panic. Out of the fifteen girls being transported, only six had survived. They were all only fourteen or fifteen years old. I asked Margarita, "How many of you guys were there in the beginning of the kidnap?"

"Thirty at least. Maybe more," she answered. "I cannot tell you. They separated the youngest ones, those who were twelve or thirteen, and took them early this morning in another truck. They are probably already in La Coloma. The young women they had attending us where they kept us prisoners were left behind because they weren't too pretty. They will attend to the rest of the groups, feeding us and doing all the menial work."

She paused and dried the tears rolling down her cheeks. "One of the girls attending us told me that she had been a prisoner in that horrible place for two years. She confessed to me that it had crossed her mind many times to kill herself, because she couldn't continue to live that way. They worked her twenty-four hours a day without rest and forced her to have kinky sex with all these ugly and filthy men in the most perverse ways not even seen in Sodom and Gomorrah. Sometimes they make one girl sleep with three or four men at the same time. When I got to be friendly with this girl, she told me they would make her do such immoral and disgusting acts that she no longer wished to live. All these girls are religious Christians, and when they resist they get beaten almost to death. This girl lost three teeth because they hit her with a baseball bat. One of the men told her that it would make her better for oral sex."

I shook my head in a profound feeling of sympathy for the girls and disgust for the reprobate men. I was completely outraged at how the police—members of the Revolution—would have anything to do with something like this, something which had such horrible consequences for the community. I nearly wept as I listened to what those young girls endured during their captivity of the past few days. My feelings were of sorrow mixed with disgust. I looked at the two young men and asked, "What do you guys plan to do next?"

Morito replied, "Well, the first thing we want to do is return these young girls to their families. Then we'll have to inform the families of the girls who didn't survive the sad news so that they can come here to identify the bodies and see to it they receive proper burials."

As I spoke to them, their backs were to the truck. I looked at the cabin of the truck and saw movement. One of the kidnappers was regaining consciousness. I pointed to the truck. "Before you do that, I think you guys should make sure those bandits are secured. I can see one of them looks like he's waking up. I don't think it would be a good idea to let these two move around freely. Heaven knows what they might try to pull off."

Both of the young men whirled to look behind them. They pulled their weapons out and walked towards the truck. "OK, thank you," they said as they waved back at me.

Morito opened the door to the truck and pointed his gun at the semiconscious man. He ordered him to get out of the truck, and the dazed man obeyed. Dried blood caked his forehead, and his nose was broken. They tied him up as best they could with their belts and sat him on the ground with his back resting against the wheel of the truck. They went back and pulled the still-unconscious second man out of the truck. His face was a mask of blood, and they likewise bound him and lay him against the side of the vehicle. They returned to me after they were finished and thanked me for warning them.

Once I saw that everything was under control and that these were trustworthy people, I signaled to Chandee, who still waited anxiously in the Volga. She got out and joined us. I introduced her to the rest of the group and brought her up to speed with all that had happened. The two young men thanked me once more and said they would be able to take care of everything else. We got back into the Volga and left to continue our trip to the extremely small town of Portales de Guane where my grandfather had his tobacco plantation.

I drove silently, deep in thought. Even though a criminal underworld existed in Cuba as they did everywhere in the world, it seemed that such evil had flourished since the Revolution. The negative elements in our society had become integrated into the Revolution, turning the highest levels into accomplices to those parasites who preyed on society. Now these malcontents were able to demonstrate their frustration as they attained positions of authority within the government. These elements used those positions to enact the most horrific deeds and acts of corruption, like the Mafia taking control by suborning law enforcement agencies.

It was a paradox how the naïve and honest useful fools

like my father who had fought to eliminate the casinos and crime families that were so prominent under Batista never conceived the change that Castro promised with his high-flown rhetoric would be for so much worse, destroying utterly what ordered society previously existed.

I was so distracted by my thoughts that it seemed like no time before we arrived at my grandfather's. Before I turned left onto the property, Chandee asked, "What happened to you? You haven't spoken a single word since we left the scene of the accident. That was a long time ago. You've been so silent. Not that I blame you," she added. "I was shocked into muteness at the sight of the bodies of those girls spread all over the highway. I couldn't help but think that one of those innocent victims could easily have been me. How quickly life can vanish so violently. Anyone could be taken by surprise—anyone."

I shook my head and smiled slightly. "Yeah, you're right. In your case, though, if those kidnappers had run into you, they would have received an unpleasant surprise. Besides being very well-trained by the best people in our business, you always carry a small weapon with you. That is the great difference between those poor defenseless girls and you. Remember, those men have no souls. They are hunters. Hunters, like lions and other predators, always look for the weakest, easiest, and most vulnerable victims. They're lazy, and don't like to work hard. As hunters, they also have a great nose for smelling weakness in their prey."

Chandee nodded resignedly. "Yeah, you're right. I know for a fact that, even if they surprised me, I would be a big headache for anyone who tried to seduce me or take me down. Before they tied me up in those chains as a humbled slave, I would bring at least a couple of them down. I could never be that submissive."

I nodded and smiled once more. I drove up the dirt road to the farm house slowly. The car jerked slightly as we drove off the edge of the asphalt road onto the packed soil. By the time we drew near the house, we could see the large tobacco plants on both sides of the car by the headlights. From their size, it appeared very close to the time for them to be harvested.

Chandee looked to both sides, admiring the vast plants with the large, verdant leaves, the green displaying the health and beauty of the plantation. She had never in her life seen a tobacco farm, city girl that she was. I smiled and said, "Tobacco. This is one of the worst kinds of manual labor and one of the most costly and difficult crops to farm in agriculture, although some consider sugar cane to be worse. I can assure you, though, I've seen both very close and observed the process. In my opinion, there's no comparison to the level of labor and processing between tobacco and any other crop a farm can raise. The tobacco has to be planted year after year—it's only one annual crop. It's not like a fruit orchard. After you cut the leaves, you have to cure them, tie them to long sticks in curing houses that are very expensive to maintain. They have to be kept in the shade for the curing process to complete. It takes a long time for the leaves to dry out and brown, and then they have to judge the quality of each individual leaf and separate them for different purposes."

I shook my head. "Believe me, I've watched my grandfather and uncles go through this work for years without any rest, only to receive as payment whatever quality of leaves nature provided them. Some years it's great. They grow a majority of the highest quality leaves and make a lot of money. Other years, however, they get a bad crop. They can barely cover their costs and go into debt until the next year. It's criminal to me, to have to deal with this after an entire year's work. And after all this—what is tobacco good for, aside from giving pleasure to some addict?

"Sugar cane, on the other hand, regrows, and you don't harvest the entire plant. If you cut it properly, you don't have to do any replanting for many years. In the meantime, the only work consists of cutting the cane, loading it into the trucks, taking it to the mills, and processing the sugar we all need in our lives."

Chandee smiled. "Apparently, you don't like what your uncles and grandfather do here very much."

I shook my head. "Sincerely and personally, to me tobacco is the worst crop anyone could plant in this soil." As we drove along, I reached out the window and pointed at the ground. "But who is going tell my grandfather that, when everyone in my family is addicted to it? Even my grandmother chews tobacco."

Chandee smiled again and shook her head. She pointed to herself. "I will most certainly not be the one to tell them they shouldn't do it."

I smiled a little sarcastically. "Believe me, I've already tried. All you do is waste your time. To them, tobacco growing is a simple routine of daily life, year after year, that demands of them to remember God and pray to Him for the rain they depend on for their crops."

We had reached the house, and I noticed that even at

that early hour, the entire house was lit by kerosene lamps. It appeared the entire family was up and about as if it were the middle of the day. Some of them had looked out, seen the lights of the Volga, and walked out onto the porch to see who was coming to their hacienda at that time. By the time we parked, nearly the entire family had left the house, seemingly out of curiosity. At least, that is what I thought until I realized that they had come out for another reason.

After we parked, we got out and walked towards the gathering on the porch. To my surprise my big brother, Leonar, was present. I was doubly surprised by the pistol in his hand. He recognized me and called out, "It's OK, it's Julio Antonio."

I wondered what he was doing there, and more to the point what he was doing with that weapon. He repeated his call, this time turning towards the house to call to those still inside. "He's brought a Chinese girl with him."

My cousin Alberto came out of the front door holding a double-barreled shotgun. He yelled, "Oh, my cousin, the Commandantico!" He grinned broadly as his little sister, my youngest cousin, twelve-year-old Aisolin, and my uncle Pablo came out to greet us.

I said hello to everyone. Aisolin was the most beautiful and regal of my cousins. She had wavy, golden blonde hair and honey eyes framed by thick arched eyebrows and eyelashes the same color. She looked very exotic, much like a Viking princess. I had always been fascinated by her looks.

After I introduced Chandee to my family, we entered the house and sat down around the long, oaken dining table decorated with lions and engravings. They set a line of kerosene lamps down the center of the table. My brother and my cousin brought us up to date, explaining why he and his wife Blanca were there and why everyone was up at such an odd hour, including the beautiful and innocent Aisolin.

She had been kidnapped a few days before from the same party the girls we had encountered on the highway.

The youngest girl at the party was one of her friends, who had been hidden in the outhouse. Through a knothole in the wall, she had seen everything that went on and had stayed there until the men left. Afterward she ran to everyone's families and raised the alarm as to what had happened.

My grandfather and uncles had no idea at that moment what to do. All the families had gone to the local authorities without any result, and there appeared to be very little official interest in the matter. All the neighbors came to the conclusion that the police were either involved or had been bribed by the kidnappers to keep everything quiet. It wasn't the first time this had happened in that area. In the last two years, several hundred young girls had disappeared, and their families never heard nor saw anything of them again.

Knowing of my brother's military training, my grandfather had sent Alberto to Las Martinas. When Alberto told Leonar what was going on, my brother wasted no time in mobilizing several of his friends who had retired from the army and now lived in the surrounding area. Very rapidly, they got information about the kidnappers' routes so that an interception could be planned.

Based on the information they got from the police, the

second truck with the very young girls, like Morito's sister had told us, had also held Aisolin. They had gone in a different direction along the Panamericana del Caribe Highway. Luckily for them, our family caught them in a small town named San Juan y Martinez.

As before, two police motorcycles provided escort to the truck. When they stopped at a restaurant that appeared to be a regular stop for them, Leonar, Alberto, and the other military men took the kidnappers by surprise, killing every one of them, including the two police officers who tried to defend the reprobates. They took possession of the truck and the girls, liberating Aisolin. They returned the young girls to their respective families, but it looked like the local authorities had changed their story.

The new version, of course, was that the liberators were actually terrorists and assassins. An alert went out over the radio to all the local police stations to stop my brother and my cousin, dead or alive. They were identified by name as the criminals who had killed two police officers as well as several other people. Apparently San Juan y Martinez held an informant for the kidnappers who acted as their contact in that town, probably within the restaurant. He likely survived by not getting involved in the conflict and therefore was able to positively identify them. Now the authorities were searching for them everywhere. They even sent a patrol car that day to check the farm. However, they had hidden in the basement of one of the curing houses and so were not found.

The police had spent the entire day at the farm. Fearing that some harm might befall them after dark, they left as night fell. When my family saw the Volga, they thought perhaps the police or soldiers were coming back. My family was in a complete state of panic, not knowing what they were going to do. It was evident that if my brother and cousin did not leave Cuba immediately, they would probably wind up being killed in retaliation by the police, not just out of vengeance but because of their disruption of this filthy human trafficking business. This could certainly not become public knowledge, and so they had been marked for death.

I shook my head when I heard the full story. I said, "My God. You could say it was coincidence or by God's design, but on our way here we ran into the truck that was taking the older girls along the Luis Lazo highway. Unfortunately, those girls didn't have the same luck you did. Most of them are dead. One of the girls' brother tried to rescue them with her boyfriend."

Everyone at the table crossed themselves at my grim news.

My grandmother said, "There's no such thing in life as coincidence, my grandson. It's Providence. That is why you are here today." She reached out and touched my shoulder.

After I finished the story of our encounter on the highway, my grandfather said in an extremely worried voice, "If we don't get them out of here immediately, they will not be alive when the sun comes up. That is probably what the authorities are waiting for. They'll get reinforcements and then tear down everything here in their search. They're being protected by this government because it's been corrupted at the highest levels. What are we going to do? They have no hope."

I stood up and said, "I'm sorry, Grandpa, but they have a real hope. That is probably why God sent me to you guys today."

As we had been talking, I had been caressing the golf ball Lee Oswald had given me. I held it up in front of one of the lamps. "You see this? This was sent, as Grandma said, by Providence." I handed it to my brother. "Take care of this little ball with your life, because it and the rest of you depend on it."

Everyone looked at me in surprised incomprehension.

"There's no time to explain now, unfortunately." I turned to my grandmother. "I'm sorry—I have some delicious treats to give you, but I think we'll have to eat them on the road. We don't have time to wait for food to be prepared for the trip; we need to get out of here *now*. We'll have breakfast on the road. Grab whatever essentials you absolutely need, and quickly."

I expected that my brother would bring his wife and that my cousin would not want to leave his sister behind.

"If my grandfather is right—and we have to listen to his experience—and the local authorities are waiting for dawn to return here, we haven't a minute to waste." I pointed to Leonar and Alberto. "You guys are putting the entire family's lives at risk. You have maybe five minutes to say your goodbyes, put everything in the car, and get the hell out of here."

My grandfather stood up. "My son, you've told me several times you wanted to be an attorney. I believe, though, that destiny will make you a doctor. You always manage to make your visits so short, even more so than any doctor who comes to visit us!"

We laughed and hugged. My brother and cousin

grabbed their things and we got into the car. Amid tears we drove away from the plantation as fast as we could.

We had not even been at the house for twenty minutes. Leonar, Blanca, Alberto, and Aisolin sat in the back seat, Chandee in the front seat. We returned to the twisting route of the Luis Lazo highway. I left with a little sadness, because I had promised to show Chandee the colonial house in which I had been born in Guane. But Guane was half an hour further along, and it wasn't prudent now to take the added risk of either Leonar or Alberto being identified by the local authorities. I held Chandee's hand and said, "I promise you, next time, I'll take you to the house."

She smiled. "Don't worry. Let's get your family to safety. That's more important than anything."

After driving for a while, we came by the scene of the accident. A long line of cars waited to traverse the area, since one of the lanes had been closed. Ambulances, police cars, and other emergency vehicles were there. We could see medical personnel at work, picking up pieces of the bodies strewn around the road.

Aisolin started to sob, clasping both hands to her mouth as she shook. She could not control herself with the recent memories she had and then watching the bodies of young girls who had been friends of hers being picked up off the road. She had been born in that small community and spent most of her life there.

Chandee noticed she was getting more agitated. She turned around in the seat and took Aisolin hands in both of hers. In a maternal voice, Chandee said softly, "I know, this is horrible for all of us, but it's worse for you. Look at me. Look at me! You have to control yourself. The authorities are looking for your brother." She let go one of her hands and pointed at Alberto. Then she pointed at Leonar. "And your uncle. They will be looking inside each of the cars to see who is responding emotionally as you are. They'll want to ask you if you know these girls and what you know about the whole thing. We do not have the luxury of explaining to them anything. Do you understand? First of all, there's nothing any explanation we could give that will bring them back to life. Second, nothing we can say will change what happened here. The reality is that it would create a huge problem for all of us. If they detain us for questioning, we could all end up dead."

She thrust her face close to Aisolin's. "I know you're very young, but you're a smart girl. Please try to control yourself." Chandee's last statement was said in the tone of a mother disciplining a child.

After she finished, she let go of Aisolin's hands and sat forward once more as if nothing had happened. At that moment, the policeman controlling the traffic in our direction signaled our side to move forward while his partner stopped the opposing traffic to allow us through.

I slowly drove by the officer, who nodded to us with a smile, motioning us to move along. I was able to breathe more freely after we had passed the second policeman. Once past, I reached over and squeezed Chandee's shoulder in gratitude. "Thank you for your words."

I looked up at Aisolin through the rear view mirror. She had completely regained control of herself. Her eyes were still filled with tears, but she appeared calm, trying to be strong. I smiled, nodded, and winked at her. "Thank you." She smiled tightly and nodded.

We drove in silence for a long time, cautiously navigating our way between those cliffs and the sheer drop. The sun had risen, and in the light one could appreciate the dangers we had run. Occasionally, one could see scars along the side of the road with the ruins of cars dashed along the bottom that marked where people had lost their lives. The cliffs were so steep here that the authorities never bothered to go through the labor to remove the wrecked cars from the cliff bottom.

By the light of the sun, we could see the beauty of the scenery. We could also see small crosses with recently cut flowers that marked those who had died along that route.

Chandee was in a state of panic, one hand gripping the door, the other clutching the dashboard. She did not for one second take her eyes off that horrible cliff, even though I was driving with extreme care and well under the posted speed limit.

There was a patch so filled with hairpin turns and switchbacks that one easily grew motion sick. Because of this, in the middle of our trip I decided to take a break on a small plateau near the foot of the mountains by a large mango tree. I asked them if anyone was hungry and received several nods.

We had a nice picnic of finger sandwiches and quenched our thirst with the crystal-clear waters of the creek that flowed out of the mountains. My brother foraged and brought us papayas and wild fruit to enhance our brunch.

Using a large rock as a table, we sat down. I used this as an opportunity to give Alberto and Leonar the details about using the golf ball. I opened it for them and wrote an introductory note, telling them to only give it to the ambassador of the embassy they went into. I also gave them the telephone number and code signal between Chopin and me so that he could bring them presentable clothing, transportation, and housing should the situation in the capital make them take longer than expected to get extracted by the embassy security.

I told Leonar that, as soon as he got to the embassy, he should tell the ambassador what had been happening and to request political asylum. As we sat around that large rock at the foot of the mountain, we set in motion our future plans to remove them to safety with minimal risk so that they could disappear from the country. At the time, my idea had been to return to Oriente to cover both my back as well as Chandee's and to finish my responsibility and fulfill my promise to Maria de Los Angeles with the literacy campaign. After we finished our debriefing along with our brunch, we continued the trip until we arrived in Pinar del Rio, thankfully without complications.

We arrived at Roman's shop and were in luck. We did not have to wait long at all, as he was just finishing up Chandee's car. True to his word, he had left all other projects to one side and given all his priority to Chandee. I was very generous to Roman, not just for the prompt work but for his many considerations. Roman was embarrassed and protested that I was giving him too much.

"You deserve it," I replied. "This money is from the Revolution to help you. Take it." He didn't know what else to say, and so I was able to force him to take it. "Don't clean the grease off your hands with it," I teased.

We left the Volga at the Regiment. We said our

goodbyes at the train terminal. I said my farewell to Mima very briefly. I explained what had happened and why I couldn't let anyone into the house. She crossed herself and wished me well.

Late in the afternoon, as the sun was setting, Chandee gave me a big hug and a kiss on each cheek. I wished her luck on her trip back, and she drove away from Pinar del Rio towards the capital with those members of my family who were fleeing.

I felt at peace.

My train finally departed. I looked through the window at the trees moving past the window. As the locomotive slowly picked up speed, I looked at the city with tranquility flooding my heart, and a great satisfaction imbued my spirit. Once more, I had managed to bring justice and was able to make fools out of my enemies. That satisfaction took me all the way on my train trip to Oriente.

Swiss Embassy Havana

Dr. Julio Antonio del Marmol

Chapter 4: From Commander to Recruit—October Crisis and the Enigma Unwrapped

A few weeks later, I returned to Havana from the literacy campaign, through which Fidel sold to the ignorant world the false image of Cuba as the first country in the world to have stamped out illiteracy. The master of deceit received awards from philanthropic organizations and recognition in the press for being a great leader and benefactor to the poor. This genius of evil was able to once more, though these gigantic lies and machinations, pull the wool over the eyes of not just the Cuban people but the international community as well. This was neither the first nor the last time that Castro was able to get away with such things.

Soon afterward, I received a telegram from the Office of the Prime Minister. It was sent by the lady with the iron hand in Cuba, the woman feared even by the sinister G-2—Celia Sanchez Manduley, the lover and confidante of Fidel Castro. She possessed no official titles, but she had more power than anyone else as his personal secretary and counselor (among other things). She possessed the art of persuading the criminal leader to do even those things he didn't want to do. Ideas or plans the other leaders and ministers would not even dare to broach with Fidel, she made happen. It was certain within official circles, several high-ranking people assured me, that Huber Matos lived thanks to Celia. It was she who had intervened on his behalf for the sake of their long friendship. It was she who had introduced Matos to Castro. If it had been up to Fidel, Matos would have been executed the moment he received the famous resignation letter in which Castro was addressed not as a political leader but as a friend.

After a few days, I presented myself at the Prime Minister's Office, where Celia tried to persuade me in every way she could. According to her, to please Fidel I should go to the Soviet Union, where they would give me the education and skills to become a high intelligence officer in the Cuban international counter-intelligence.

I managed in a very pleasant, polite way to turn her around and gain her blessing to let me study music in Cuba at the prestigious National Arts School in Cubanacan. I studied there for nearly two years, navigating the many problems and demands this supposedly free Socialist scholarship imposed on me. It was mostly Communist indoctrination twenty-four hours a day, with volunteer work that bordered on slavery. I finally could not take it anymore, and I returned to my normal life in Pinar del Rio.

Just when I thought I had gotten out of my commitment to the government, they surprised me with yet another telegram. This time, it wasn't from the Prime Minister's office, much less from Celia Sanchez, but instead from the Interior Ministry's Obligatory Military Service. The irony was that, in spite of all my military training and being the youngest Commander in the

Dr. Julio Antonio del Marmol

Revolution as well as the Commander-in-Chief of the Juvenile Commandos of the Rebel Army, I was now going to be a simple recruit for the regular Army, just as my brother-in-law Canen had predicted.

This Revolution was like the Mafia: if you tried to abandon your post, they either smashed you or killed you. The tyrant was like a godfather, and you could not say no to him or displease him. In such a society, it was easy to go from being a Commander to a recruit.

Such was the case of Canen's good friend Homar Fernandez. He was the National Minister of Transportation who had also said no to Castro. He went from that high position to being a lowly doctor in a local hospital in Havana. He considered himself lucky, because many others wound up with twenty or thirty years in prison for the crime of contradicting the egotism of our dictator—if not ending in front of the firing squad.

After a few months in the military service, fortunately in the group of several good friends, I received some of the most inhumane and despotic treatment I had ever endured in my life. This particular camp was run by officers who had inferiority complexes and agreed with everything Castro mandated. Those who, like Canen, believed that it was their responsibility to change the black course the ambitious Marxists in power were pursuing in their Utopian dream of controlling the world by force had already left. The remaining sycophants proclaimed that they were protecting the poor as well as the climate through the erroneous theory that the capitalist world tried to destroy unscrupulously. I felt this was the greatest fraud any man could see.

After several rebellious fights and confrontations,

which once landed me in a punishment detail known as the doghouse in which I suffered the worst humiliations, I was accused of insubordination. I certainly was insubordinate to every abuse I saw. I was very sad the day one of my friends died. They said that he took his own life, but we all knew the leaders of the camp had killed him.

This place was called Military Unit 3234. The recruits received seven pesos per month and were obligated to work to the point of exhaustion on little food on not only military construction but also in agricultural fields. It reminded me of the construction of the Great Pyramids of Giza. Images of the movies I had seen continually played in my mind, and I asked myself how my civilized country, full of the prosperity and vibrant economy that earned it the nickname of the Paris of the Caribbean, could in such a short time regress to the point of transforming its youth to the level of slaves millennia before the time of Christ.

I realized that before things could get better, they would have to get worse. This was the natural course of things, and it came true once more very early one morning. I heard several trucks arriving in the compound while we were still asleep. We discovered when we awoke that something extraordinary had occurred that would later become historical: the October Crisis of 1962. The world had come to the brink of annihilation. Up until now, people have not known how close that truly came.

In the midst of all these terrible events, I received some excellent personal news.

The trucks that had just arrived brought with them hundreds of doctors, who were to be debriefed and quickly trained at our base before being sent to other units. There had been no age exemption in this draft, with physicians seventy years old being taken out of their houses in the middle of the night. The nation had declared war.

That morning, a doctor's courier came to me. After locating me in one of the smoking areas, I was told by several of my colleagues that an older man had been looking for me all over the compound. He introduced himself to me and then gave me the codes he had received from my uncle and the General. They and the others had sent him with the solution to my troubles.

This exit took me out of the inferno of physical and psychological abuse I had been enduring. I profoundly thanked the courier and immediately started on that magnificent plan that would gain me my freedom.

A few days later, things turned around as a result of some dangerous and very serious events. The Russian captain in charge of the Soviet garrison decided on his own recognizance with his new military toys to shoot down the American U-2, or what they called Target 33, when it entered his airspace. His unauthorized action put his superiors in Moscow in an absolute panic, since they had no idea on what else he might decide to fire.

On October 27, at 10:21 a.m., my unit was put on alert. They took several of us to pick up the pieces of what was left of that example of advanced technology which now lay in ruins. At that moment I realized fully the horrible intensity of what was going on and where it could lead at any moment.

As I picked up small pieces of that plane from the ground, a vision of the future unfolded for me. In only a few minutes everything could be reduced to ashes and dust. It might not even take minutes—perhaps only seconds. Over the past several years, I had personally seen the nuclear artifacts unloaded from ships onto the island, sent by that irresponsible leader who was himself being used and manipulated by the most powerful hand of the Soviet Union. They played a dangerous game, attempting to intimidate the free world and provoking friction such that even they didn't know if a spark might ignite a flame that would start the inferno of destruction that would spread from our small island and across the globe.

As the Professor told me several times, ignorance is daring.

I made up my mind to get out of that camp as soon as possible, so that I could continue my fight to impede our ignorant leaders in Cuba before they blew up themselves along with the rest of the world.

After two weeks of tension, the October Crisis finally ended in an undisputed victory for Castro and his associates. Fidel was angered at the international agreement the Soviets made to remove the missiles from Cuba, but after they explained to him the plan, Castro was much happier. Khrushchev, a very clever man, had come up with a way to pin the tail on the American donkey by breaking the promises he had made to Kennedy.

I personally took part in this particular operation. When the Soviet ships arrived in the Mariel port, my military unit continually loaded trucks filled with junk—broken agricultural equipment and old rusted-out Russian trucks, engines, and transmissions—and covered them with long tarps to disguise them as the missiles being removed from the island under the distant eyes of the U.S. Naval blockade.

    Unit 3234, located at Artemisa in Pinar del Rio, was activated in the middle of the Crisis. Under cover of darkness, we were transported in troop carrier trucks. Everything was done at night; when daylight came, our work stopped. We worked by flashlight and dim lights to prevent spy aircraft from being able to photograph what we were doing. We spent nearly a week filling those cargo ships with junk. At first, it didn't make any sense to anyone. We had no idea why the Soviets wanted all of this rubbish. Then, after the Crisis, we heard some officers laughing and making fun of the North Americans' acceptance that Khrushchev would keep his word and therefore upheld their word to not inspect the ships that were supposedly removing the missiles from Cuba; another slap in the face for John F. Kennedy.

    A few months later, my plans went as expected. I was honorably dismissed from the Army under a medical incapacity for a disorder to my nervous system and a liver deficiency. This required long treatment and rest under intensive care. I was therefore returned to Mima's side in our home.

    I have to say today, now that Canen has passed away, that I would never have been able to accomplish this without his help. As part of the plan, he met with my uncle, and they both spoke personally with the commander of psychiatric, Dr. Juari. He assured them that he would sign the final diagnostic for my condition, and under his responsibility and prognosis prepared my dismissal for Diagnostic Neurotic Reaction. He rendered the judgment that I was incapable of continuing in active service. It was thanks to Dr. Juari's coaching that I was able to exhibit the appropriate symptoms without jeopardizing either his professional reputation or his military career.

Our plan succeeded. With this dismissal under the hand of the Commander of Military Doctors, none of them—not Ramiro, not Piñeiro, not even Fidel himself—had the authority to reverse it. Once more the Lightning made fools of his enemies and walked out the back door of the same building they had forced him to enter in the front.

I would also be ungrateful for not thanking my guardian angel, Jesus Christ, for finally helping me depart that purgatory.

To maintain the façade, I had a few months of resting and visiting the private doctor Dr. Juari had referred me to at the Colonia Española. I continued my activities in accumulating data and espionage, but now I had to be extremely careful and watch every microscopic step I made.

Canen had been promoted to the Chief for Combat Preparation for all the troops in Pinar del Rio, Havana, and Matanzas. He was transferred to the main headquarters in Managua, where I sporadically visited him until some time had passed. Once we considered it safe, he and my sister Disa invited me to move in with them temporarily on a small family farm where they had relocated their family. It was in Santiago de las Vegas, near the military headquarters.

The farm was very suitable to our plans. It maintained the appearance of my recuperation in the countryside, only a short drive to Havana. I was by this time not involved in any way with the government, much less the military. However, I still had complete access to all the high commands of the Army anywhere in the nation, since I accompanied Canen everywhere he went.

We both enjoyed each other's company, and we were in complete agreement when it came to ideology and religion, although we left those conversations for the strictest privacy within the house. We could not trust even the soldiers in his escort, even though they had been handpicked by Canen and so did not agree with the political course charted by the Castros and Che for Cuba's destiny. Each year that passed deepened the economic disaster to become the worst in the nation's history. It was mostly owing to the millions of dollars spent daily in exporting revolutions by training terrorists who were then sent anywhere in the world they were needed.

Everywhere we went, everyone continued to address me as the Commandantico. Even though I no longer had any rank or the stars on my shoulder, I started once more to dress in military olive green. I had started to do this to prevent creating problems for Canen whenever we visited a military installation or an official ministry building, but I later realized that my status as the Commandantico followed me wherever we went. People recognized me at once in all the official circles. Like someone had snapped their fingers, I came back in by Canen's side with his escort. Ministers, high security clearance military bases, and the guards at the posts never even dared ask me for the identification I no longer had. Everyone still knew me as the favorite of Fidel and Che and knew nothing about my recent past. I felt cleaner, since I no longer had any association within the government, while at the same time I was able to maintain a status that not only followed me but would continue to follow me in the future for several more years. That reputation enabled me to cover my back on many occasions.

One day, at one of the missile bases, I did get a little nervous, even though I was with Canen and dressed in a military style, even wearing my sidearm. I realized that I had nothing to worry about. My record was exemplary. I'd completed my position with the Rebel Army from the age of twelve and went on the literary campaign. Unlike many young kids who couldn't take the abuse of the peasants, I hung in there and finished the campaign to the very end. My commitment fulfilled, I received my award. Then I had been recruited by the regular Army, and though my discharge had been for a nervous system and liver disorder, it was an honorable one. My record as a military man as well as a Revolutionary went beyond untouchable; it was exemplary. This was the perfect cover for my covert operations aimed at defeating that band of murderers and stopping the destructive Marxists' plans to enslave the globe.

What my enemies never even imagined was who I really was. Even though Ramiro, Piñeiro, and some of their confidants had suspicions about me, they could never produce any of the proof they would have given an eye to obtain. No one surviving could support their theories that I was the famous spy they pursued called the Lightning. Now, thanks to God as well as Canen, I came back into the game where I could give Ramiro and Piñeiro gigantic headaches for years to come.

Dr. Julio Antonio del Marmol

November 22, 1963

In the very early morning hours, I left our home in Santiago de las Vegas in the company of our escort. We headed towards the Santa Clara province as part of a military caravan. Some of the trucks held mortars, anti-aircraft machine guns, and other weapons, while others carried high-ranking officers from the headquarters in Managua. A military parade was to take place in that city, where major ministers were supposed to be present, along with Raul Castro and Che. Canen was going to direct these exercises and was to demonstrate before the Committee the superior training the troops had been receiving. It was his time to shine and show the results he had obtained in such a short time in the aftermath of the October Crisis.

We arrived at the Tribunal and took our seats among the high officials. Below us the troops began their parade and drills. I was sitting with Canen's escort, watching my brother-in-law direct the exercises. Hand-to-hand combat, anti-aircraft targeting, and marksmanship exercises all demonstrated military discipline and skill to the admiring applause of the onlookers.

I was utterly distracted by the show and did not see Che arrive after everyone else, nor did I realize that he had sat with his entourage a row behind us. Raul sat on the extreme left by Ramiro.

It was around 11:00 a.m., and the sun had started to grow hot. I felt a hand squeeze my left shoulder, and I turned around. I saw the not-too-friendly face of Che, who had leaned forward to get my attention. I saw how serious he appeared, and I thought at first we had mistakenly taken the seats assigned to him. I immediately stood up and offered my seat to him, but he waved the invitation off. He gestured to his ear to indicate that he could not hear me over the sound of the guns firing and indicated that I should come with him.

When he stood, his men started up, but he waved them back down. I walked down to meet him, a little unhappy at what he might now be cooking up in his mind. I hadn't seen him since our argument after he had accused me of being suspicious in Fausto's death. We had certainly not ended on good terms, and I was concerned with what he might want to say to me now.

We walked down the wooden steps of the improvised platform, and I followed him out to the parking lot behind the parade ground. I walked behind him, expecting the worst. A strong odor of sweat assailed my nose. His lack of hygiene had, if anything, grown worse. To get upwind of him, I tried to walk by his side.

We walked clear across the parking lot, and he opened the door of one of the Soviet jeeps. He said loudly, "Let's get in here. I want to talk to you."

I got in the passenger side, he in the driver's side. He offered me one of his Habanos cigars, but I declined it politely. He lit it, and both of us got comfortable in the jeep. He took a deep drag. "Do you remember Yuri?"

I nodded silently.

"They killed him last night in New Orleans."

I widened my eyes in surprise. I had no idea what was going on or what he was trying to say. I concentrated on containing my nerves. My hands were about to betray me as I felt a cold sweat breaking out on them. I was expecting at any moment he was going to confront me about my attire and being armed. In an attempt to disguise my feelings, I nonchalantly shifted in my seat and casually wiped the sweat off my palms on my pants. Che bit his lower lip and said, "They also killed our great comrade Arzate, the fifth wheel, our standby in case one of the others was killed before the operation in Texas was finished."

Che took another drag on his cigar, waiting to see if I would ask him who had killed Yuri. My silence, however, continued. He understood I wasn't interested in that conversation, and so he said, "I never trusted anyone until today. The reason is that I've learned through my career in politics and espionage that we cannot trust anyone. But this makes it very sad for anyone, especially when one is surrounded by carnivorous predators who want to eat you in order to take your place. This makes it very difficult for me or anyone in my position to make new friends, because no one likes to be distrusted. I know you've been a reliable friend by my side all this time. That's why I've decided to break all the rules and make you my real friend. We have to start at some point, if we want to have trustworthy people around us who will defend us from the other predators. Who better than you, who has already saved my life once? I want you to be one of those confidants. So I want to give you, from my heart, my deepest apology. I care for you as if you were my own son."

I looked at him askance in unconvinced surprise. I raised my hand and waved it dismissively. "Forget about it. Forget what happened. But I have to tell you something. It hurt me very much, the distrust you treated me with, because I never gave you any motive for that."

"I know, I know," he practically jumped to say. "That's why I ask you for forgiveness and have to apologize to you yet again. We know for sure now who killed Fausto. We already cut her head off, the same way she cut the penis of my good friend."

He took his beret off and scratched his head. "The saddest part of it all," he said with some resentment in his voice, "the perpetrator, Maggie, had my blood. But she was like an appendicitis, suppurating in my body. I had to cut it out before it did more damage."

In spite of feeling better at that moment for my exoneration, I could not help but feel a knot in my stomach at his last words. Che raised his hand and said cynically, almost boastfully, "Really, you have to have big *cajones* to decapitate your own daughter. But she was the same image of her *boluda*[5] mother—hysterical and stupid." He shook his head. He added with resignation, "I couldn't expect anything good could come out of that whore Maruca, so our daughter could never amount to any good. She had to be a lesbian and a murderess."

I shook my head silently.

He looked at me and took another drag. "The little shit tried to negotiate for her life with me in exchange for information. According to Maggie, she knew the identity of the Lightning. But I didn't take her seriously, nor could I believe such bullshit from a liar like her. I already know his identity," he added with a sarcastic smile as he pointed at me with the butt of his cigar.

I swallowed my nervousness.

"Even though Ramiro and Piñeiro both think that you

---

5   Argentinian word for stupid

are, and they've been trying to convince me and Fidel for a long time. But I know for a fact that you cannot be that spy."

I could breathe again.

"You see, I know, because I've been a master spy myself for many years, and I know better. I proved it to Fidel on several occasions with my vast experience in espionage when they almost had him convinced. Last night, I corroborated it. After several weeks, we've been holding and squeezing the ass of the true double of Lee Harvey Oswald, and he confessed to us under torture before dying that the CIA and other intelligence groups around the world don't call our spy the Lightning as we do. He is known to the rest of the world by the cryptonym JUBATERE.

"This son of a bitch, according to the confession of Oswald's double, intercepted one of my best men last night in New Orleans and killed him with a shot to the head, expecting to derail our plans. He didn't even let him finish his mission that will be accomplished today. We believe he killed Arzate this morning in his hotel room shower in Dallas. At least, Arzate has disappeared, and our people found blood on the shower curtain and one of the towels. Either because they're sloppy or were in a rush, the North American intelligence didn't clean up all of the traces. Our other agents didn't even know Arzate existed, since he was the cleaner. If they failed, he was capable of finishing the job by himself. He had also been ordered to clean up the entire mess without leaving any witnesses—including Oswald, Ruby, and everyone else involved. What JUBATERE doesn't realize is that taking one or two fish out of the water doesn't take all the fish out of the tank."

He rolled the sleeve of his shirt up to look at his watch. He smiled in reassurance. "This plan will complete at a high velocity. No one can stop it. In less than an hour, that son of a bitch Kennedy will be dead." His smile turned to one of satisfaction.

I thought that he was either an idiot or had taken too much Bacardi with his breakfast today. I certainly thought him capable of doing anything, and I had knowledge that this plan had been in the works for a while, I could not in my mind comprehend how they could have the capacity and muscle as well as the connections to really take this scheme to the next step. It was such a complicated plot and one of such magnitude.

He looked as though he were reading my mind. "What—you have any doubts?" He pointed the cigar at me again and said seriously, "Remember, what we say in here is completely confidential."

I spread my hands in disbelief in order to play with his mind, giving him an indignant look.

He looked ashamed and said, "I know, I know. I'm sorry. But I have to remind you, anyway. Even at this point, this is not the thing of major importance. It will happen very shortly, and no one can stop it now. To us, even if the entire world accuses us of being part of it, at least for a hundred years, if any one of us lives that long, we will deny it." He chuckled. "I don't think we'll be able to live long enough to tell it. But you are a lot younger and are a witness to history. You have the privilege and unique opportunity to meet some of the people who partook in this altruistic act of historical justice, and that will take me to my immortality. It will also take our

Revolution to immortality, for you are a part of it. It will take you and everyone who partakes in this process into posterity. Your names will be recorded in the history of humanity, especially you, since you were physically present while this was being created, and you played an important role at my side."

His tone betrayed his pride in himself to the point I didn't think one could stick a pin in his anus, as tight as it was.

I turned all of this over in my mind in an attempt to digest it fast enough for rapid analysis. I asked myself if it were possible. He seemed so sure of himself that everything appeared to be going exactly as he said with his plans, and were on the verge of realization. His demeanor and words indicated that he was sure that his clandestine intelligence agents had kept him very well informed of the progress that had gone on. He seemed to have been completely briefed on it. I remained serious as I thought, even though I hadn't had any idea about the name of JUBATERE that was my supposed codename within the global intelligence community.

It occurred to me that there might be another spy within our military circles. Maybe it was the General adopting my name, not only to give me cover but also to conceal their own trail. It was also possible that it was to completely throw Castro's counter-intelligence off the scent. It would not only enable him to work more freely by having the excuse of blaming the other spies, but also ensure that information which circulated in global intelligence was completely valid in the eyes of everyone else. This could be how the knowledge of the whereabouts of Oswald's actual double came out. It was beneficial for me, since he had convinced my worst enemy, who was also a KGB master spy, and so had restored his complete confidence in my person. He was so convinced that he had even apologized twice, something he never did to anyone.

Wiping away his smallest doubts was invaluable, and I realized this was a great opportunity. I had to use this benefit to maximum effect until another doubt was planted in his mind. I knew for a fact it wouldn't take very long until he started to wonder in this nasty business of espionage. It surprised me a little when he leaned back in his seat.

"I will tell you something very, very secret, classified, and special before it happens, so that when it occurs you will remember that it was I who told you first, and that I'm the one who started that investigation." He leaned back and looked me straight in the eyes. "I believe in reality that there's not just one JUBATERE or Lightning, or whatever *carajo* the gringos want to call this spy. I strongly believe that it's a myth. I think Piñeiro created all of this after they stole my portfolio in Pinar del Rio a few years ago. He is just trying to justify his negligence, and I believe our enemies are using the same weapon against us now in an attempt to confuse us. This is my first theory.

"My second theory is that Piñeiro started this dangerous game of disinformation to try and cover his ass, very cleverly. He not only fooled us but our enemies as well. He's gone to the extreme of leaking truthful information, no longer disinformation, but real, good quality information to our enemies in his effort and psychological sickness to convince all of us that this spy really exists.

"If Piñeiro is true under either one of these theories, and I'm convinced he is—he's certainly capable of doing so—there is no other name for him but a traitor of the Revolution. Without hesitation, he should be executed without any consideration at all."

He paused for a second. With his left hand he slapped the wheel of the jeep. With his right hand he brought the cigar up to his mouth and took a long draft as he thought about what he was going to say next. With a scheming smile, he said sarcastically, "Would it not be ironic if, after all these years of accusing you of being this famous spy, after all it is Piñeiro and his personal envy for Rolando Cubela[6]? All because he was always jealous of him and wanted to be in his place as a double spy and have his own nickname like Cubela's AMLASH! Maybe in his fantasy he created the Lightning or JUBATERE." He shook his head. "Nothing anymore will surprise me in the world of espionage, and the personal ambitions of some imbeciles. That is exactly what I told Fidel this morning when I debriefed him about all this."

I reclined in my seat, much more relaxed. I breathed more freely as I listened to Che's conspiracy theories. I stroked my chin. "Speaking of Fidel, what does he think of all this?"

Che stroked his beard. "Fidel told me that he is absolutely sure that if I'm not on the right track, then I'm

---

[6] Still alive in Spain, Cubela was one of the most brilliant Commanders whose ethical beliefs made him become a double agent for the United States, an action which nearly cost him his life.

very close to the truth. He doesn't think it's possible for anyone to be so good and meticulous enough to be able to get away untouched—not with the mechanism we have in place for counter-intelligence. At the very least, he should have made a single mistake. This goddamned spy cannot be so perfect or exceptional. He can't be a ghost, since we know they don't exist. So he's given me the green light to meticulously and very discretely check every single move 'Red Beard' Piñeiro makes from now on. If we follow the hen, we'll know where she lays her eggs. If we catch her in the nest, then we'll put her eggs in the fryer."

He flashed a sinister smiled as he enjoyed the thought. I certainly knew he hated Piñeiro's sycophant tendencies where Fidel was concerned.

At that moment, one of the men of the escort approached the jeep. Very respectfully from a distance, he said, "Commander, I hate to interrupt your conversation, but I have to give you an urgent message."

Che turned rudely and snapped impolitely, "Urgent or not, I don't give a damn. How many times do I have to tell you guys, even if the message is from Fidel himself, I don't want to be interrupted?"

The guard gulped and apologized once more. "Yes, yes, Commandante, I know. But you told me that if Marcelino called or left you a message to call you immediately."

"What? What? Marcelino, you say? Come here." He beckoned the guard over.

The guard started to whisper something I could not hear. As the guard spoke, Che rolled his cuff up to look at his watch once more. A diabolical grin split his face. He said to the guard as he pushed him away, "Go immediately and tell Raul that I have something extremely special to communicate to him. Tell him to get on the CB and call Fidel immediately. Tell the rest of the escort to get ready immediately. We're returning to Havana at once."

He dropped the cigar at the side of the jeep, full of energy and happiness. He checked his watch once more and said, "My God, this is efficiency and precision." He turned to me. "Commandantico, memorize this moment, this minute, this second, and remember it for the rest of your life. This is history. The serpent is decapitated. John F. Kennedy is killed. Out of combat!" He shook both fists in the air victoriously. "Bravo! Bravo for my guys!" He leaned over and hugged me, and then got out of the jeep to walk briskly towards the podium.

I got out of the jeep and started to follow him at a more normal pace. He stopped abruptly and turned. Che said euphorically, "In three days, at eight p.m. on Wednesday, in the house in Boca Siega, I invite you to the celebration party for this accomplishment. Then we will learn some of the details of the last-minute improvisation, straight from the mouths of our brave internationalist soldiers, Marko and Marcelino. If you want, bring your brother-in-law and your Chinese *miliciana* girlfriend with you. I like her. It will be a very unique, select group there."

"Thank you," I said.

He walked back towards me, pumping his fists in celebration. He hugged me exuberantly once more. He said in my ear, "I have the greatest plans for you. Don't disappear on me again."

I smiled and replied, "Don't distrust me again, and I

promise you I will not disappear."

He beamed and shook his finger at me as he rushed away. It was evident that he wanted to spread the news quickly to Fidel and the others before they heard it through conventional channels. He wanted to be sure they gave him if not all the credit, the greatest part of it, as he proved once more the efficiency of the communication within the select team he had under his command. It looked like they had managed to accomplish the unimaginable right under the eyes of the North Americans intelligence as well as the whole world.

I was still unconvinced about everything Che had been telling me. In spite of that, I was still very disturbed and deeply absorbed in my thoughts as I followed him at a walk. It wasn't just the death of Kennedy, which represented a massive setback to global democracy; I was deeply worried about the consequences this could bring in the way of escalation for us. If what Che had been telling me was true, I did not want to consider what consequences might come the way of Cuba.

I walked towards the polygonal stands before the parade ground. The exercises had concluded, and I could see in the distance Raul, Ramiro, and the others surrounding Canen as they congratulated him. As I drew closer, I could see Che by gestures separating the entourage of the leaders. After they said their goodbyes to Canen, they left in a hurry towards their vehicles with their guards.

By the time I got to Canen, they had all left. When he saw me, he greeted me at once and excused himself with the other officers. He walked towards me. As soon as we were together, he asked in a low voice, "What did you think of the exercises?"

"Excellent. You've managed to leave all these bigwigs with their mouths open in astonishment. There's no doubt that your military skills are far superior to any of the others I've seen before. I don't think anyone else can touch your level of expertise. I believe you will be promoted soon to be the director of the Superior War College—and in my opinion, you deserve it more than anyone else I saw there." I reached out and tapped his epaulette. "It's about time they took those three Captain's bars and replaced them with the Commander's stars. The only problem you have is that you're not a Communist. But for the rest, you are intelligent, disciplined, dedicated—a fine military officer. I tell you this from my heart. It's not easy to find someone with your level of dedication and integrity."

Canen grinned broadly. He put his arm around my shoulder. "You may not believe what I'm going to say to you, but your words are more appreciated by me than all those sons of bitches who patted my shoulder a few minutes ago. At least I know for sure that your compliments are sincere. About all those guys, I don't know if all they're doing is try to stroke my ego so that they can continue to use me."

I nodded. "You're probably right. All they are concerned with is using people."

He said goodbye to the other officers, and we started to walk to the parking lot followed by his escort. I remained silent during the walk. When we reached the car, he asked, "Why have you been so quiet? Today is a day in which to be happy."

I said, "Well, I'm a little worried about something Che

just entrusted me with a few minutes ago."

Canen looked at me worriedly. "What? What did he say to you? Is that crazy SOB screwing around with you again?"

I drew in close to him so that the soldiers behind us couldn't hear me. I said in a low voice. "No, no—it's not that. I believe these imbeciles have killed the President of the United States."

He froze and whirled on me in shock. "What? Are you kidding me?"

"Don't stop. Keep walking, and don't behave as though I told you anything unusual. One of the things Che told me is that until this moment this thing is completely and utterly confidential. I know your men are entirely trustworthy, but remember when we talked before? We can speak only at home in private to reveal our personal feelings. We could find a rock in the rice, and it could be very costly if it breaks one of our teeth. In this case, it could force us to wear complete dentures, and I'm too young for that."

He smiled. "OK, OK. Always with your sense of humor. But this is very serious."

"I *am* being very serious."

He stayed close to me until we reached the area of the lot where we had parked the car.

Before we got into the car with his guard, he asked, "Are you sure that's what he said?"

I nodded. "Of course, that is what he said. I don't believe anything anyone says. When we get in the car, let's put on the *Radio Reloj*[7]. It's the best station for news,

---

7   Radio Clock

and we'll be able to corroborate what he said."

Canen nodded his agreement. "You're right." We got into the car and he immediately tuned the dial to the network. We drove for half an hour on our way back without any major incident. When we least expected it, the signal like Morse code broke into the broadcast. We were told all the stations on the island were being linked together to bring the events of the last few hours.

I will never forget how Canen ordered the driver to pull over to make sure we received a clear signal. We stopped on top of a small hill the highway went over. The announcer broke in and said, "The President of the United States has been shot and is in critical condition." For the next hour we followed the news, until finally the grave news was delivered: "The shot removed a portion of the cranium and part of his brain."

Canen had pulled the transportable radio out of his Buick. We sat under the shade of a tree when we received that shocking news. None of the men in the escort made any comment, so numbed were they by the broadcast. To all of us, this sounded unbelievable. To this day, if I see that tree, that moment is forever frozen in time. Everyone repressed their feelings.

Finally, Canen said, "Let's go. Any man who has half his head blown off is done for. There's nothing they can do for him."

With sad faces, we got back into the car and continued our journey. We eventually lost the reception, but the signal returned approximately two hours later. The next breaking news we heard was that the supposed murderer of the President had been arrested sitting comfortably in a Dallas movie theater, after killing police officer J.D.

Tippit not too far from his residence, and the name of the killer was Lee Harvey Oswald. That raised the hair on my neck and gave me goose bumps. I understood then the whole course of the plan that Che and his KGB friends had crafted so perfectly.

If the President was assassinated at 12:30 p.m., and Lee were a professional spy (as I knew he was), why would he waste time to stop and kill a police officer so close to his house when he should be getting as far away as possible, searching for a refuge in a secure location? He should at least put distance between the scene of the crime and himself. According to the radio, the police officer had been killed at 1:15 p.m.—only forty-five minutes afterward. At 1:45 local police had located and arrested him: not the FBI, the Secret Service, or any other federal agency that had greater resources and training for tracking down such a high-profile criminal. The only answer was that the local police were supermen on steroids. We knew that they didn't possess the technical capacity to apprehend the killer in exactly one hour and fifteen minutes following such a public, historic crime, in front of hundreds of witnesses with multiple accounts. How could they possibly, in such a short time, get the arrest warrant and track him down?

Barring a miracle, this wasn't likely. The only reason that could explain it to my satisfaction was that this had been all carefully planned and calculated, and I had no doubt that this was indeed what had happened. I felt extremely sorry for Oswald. Canen put a hand on my right shoulder. With a very sad, resigned expression he told me, "Well, evidently Che has the ball completely in his glove."

I replied at that expression, "Yes, you're right. Now it's our turn to wait and see what kind of consequence that game will bring to us. Let's hope this doesn't precipitate an abrupt retaliation. Instead of bringing anything good to anyone, including Che and his friends, it could be the physical destruction of all of us." I shook my head. I looked at one of the soldiers. I added, "Time will tell."

Canen nodded. "Yes, we'll see what kind of crisis will come our way now. No sooner are we out of the October Crisis; now we might have the November Crisis, which could continue into the December Crisis so that we don't have any holidays."

The beeping on the radio announced a news update. The announcer said, "According to the Chief of Police for the city of Dallas, Texas, the assassin, Lee Harvey Oswald, after resisting arrest inside the theater, once restrained said, 'Well, this is it. It's all over now.'"

I thought with pain in my chest that of course for Lee at that moment, he would have to realize that he had been utterly framed. The announcer continued: "They have found in the possession of this murderer documents for another identity with the name Alec James Hidell." I remembered that Oswald had used that name under his cover as a double agent during the Brigade training for the Bay of Pigs in Guatemala.

I said to Canen, "Do you want to meet the doubles for the 'murderer' Lee Harvey Oswald—who has been arrested, tried, convicted, and sentenced before they've even booked him?" I pointed at the radio. "We are invited to Che's house in Boca Siega on Wednesday at eight in the evening. I think it will be very interesting. We'll get a history lesson, and it will be more interesting for you, since you haven't met these men yet. You will see in person the executors of all that happened today in Dallas, Texas."

Canen said me in surprise, "Che invited you for sure—but he never mentioned anything to me."

"Maybe in his euphoria he forgot. But he told me if I want, to go ahead and bring you. He also told me to bring my *chinita miliciana* girlfriend. Apparently he has a difficult time remembering a simple name like Chandee."

My brother-in-law removed his hat and scratched his head. "I wouldn't miss that for anything in the world. This will be extremely interesting. But I have to wonder, after almost a year of not seeing you, Che must be very impressed by you and your personality to invite you to such a highly-classified event. Or maybe, after all, he might possess a good quality—that of gratitude. For him, then, it would be very difficult to forget that you saved his life on this very highway to Santa Clara."

I nodded as that moment flooded my memory. A knot formed in my throat as I remembered all those deaths and the sense of guilt I had over those people who had sacrificed themselves and that maniacal fanatic who brought death everywhere he went. Now we could add President Kennedy to the list of people who had died around Che. It mattered not that I had saved his life only out of the pure instinct that stemmed from my good nature. If God had given me a few seconds to think about it, I felt that I would have let Che get shot. I regretted it now that I saw all the damage and death this man had created not just in Cuba, but all around the world, and I'd had the opportunity to stop much of it before it happened.

Dr. Julio Antonio del Marmol

The radio continued. "The assassin Oswald, after being asked by a reporter in the police station whether he had killed the President, has replied, 'No, I have not been charged with that. In fact, no one has said that to me yet. The first thing I've heard about it was from the newspaper reporter in the hallway who asked me the same question. I didn't do it. I did not do it. I haven't shot anyone. I am a patsy."

I shook my head in disgust, sadness, and pity for Oswald. I turned to look at the panorama passing by outside the window. I felt Oswald's pain of betrayal. We were entering Havana now. The last bulletin we heard said: "Lee Harvey Oswald has been arraigned for the assassination of President John Fitzgerald Kennedy. Oswald's words when he heard that were, 'Everybody will know who I am now.'"

I shook my head once more. *Poor Oswald*, I thought. *He thinks that his cover has been completely blown out of the water and that his career is forever ruined.*

I put myself in his shoes, and I could not avoid feeling the sweat running down the palms of my hands in spite of the air conditioning in the car running full blast. Moisture formed in my armpits, and I began to feel warm. I could not breathe comfortably.

Chapter 5: My Unknown Decoy

Fortunately, we arrived at the farm. As soon as the driver stopped and I entered the house, I told my family I had to run to the bathroom. I held the bottom of my stomach as if to indicate urgency.

I ran into my room and removed my watch, pistol, and other things I needed to worry about. I ran into the shower fully clothed and booted, and I let my emotions out. I had put myself entirely in Oswald's shoes and thought in that moment how the same thing could happen to me. I decided never to trust anyone completely. Even my own shadow could be a question mark and be turned from a part of me into my most implacable enemy.

Then I removed my clothes and after a long shower, during which I put my thoughts in order and brought both my nerves and emotions back under control, I went down to the dining room. My sister had called up several times for dinner, and when I got down there I saw that they had already started eating.

I apologized and sat down with Canen's driver, my sister, and little Sophie. Disa held in one arm her baby boy, Frank. Canen had given him this name to commemorate one of the bravest, most daring martyrs in the fight against Batista, Frank Pais.

It had created a small headache for the family, because the rhetoric from the new dictator was that we should hate the Yankee imperialists, and everything associated with North America. They insisted that Canen's son should be registered as the Spanish version of the name, Francisco, instead of as Frank. In spite of all the negative rhetoric from the Cuban Communists, the rebellious Canen, a true Revolutionary, stuck to his guns and insisted that his son be called by the Anglo version of the name. It was his right, as the father, to call him what he wished, and this was his firstborn son. He didn't care what anyone said, not even the government. The situation escalated to the point that my sister had to go back to the Civil Register Office several times, because the employees there did not want to register a child with a North American name.

Finally, Canen went to them and raised hell. When he made the argument that the child was named for one of the Revolution's martyrs, they had to capitulate.

It didn't matter that these were the same names; it was a question of principle to Canen. He'd won a small battle, and for the first time the Cuban Communists lost a direct confrontation over their extremely arbitrary regulations through which they imposed their points of view—the same way they had stolen from the Cuban people their democratic Revolution.

After dinner, I gave Disa a kiss on the cheek for the wonderful dinner and rubbed her belly, swollen with the next baby that was on the way. I smiled and said, "From the size of your belly, I think it will be twins."

Majito, in her usual animation, spontaneously yelled, "No, no, no! For God's sake, Julio Antonio, don't even say that, not even jokingly. I have my hands full enough with Sophie and Frank. Leave well enough alone with only one more baby."

Canen smiled and said, "Well, we already know it's another boy and that it's only one baby. Don't excite yourself, Majito, and I will call this one Noah, after the messenger of God who saved his family and the animals in the ark for the future of the world."

Both Majito and Disa clapped their hands to their heads. Disa exclaimed, "What excuse will you give the people at the Civil Register for that name? *Dios mio*, save us from this crazy man! You will go there this time. I'm not doing it. I'm not fighting that battle with these ignorant Communists in that office. I don't want to know what's going to happen!" She crossed herself, as did Majito—and the driver.

They said together, "God help us confess."

Everyone laughed.

I said goodbye to everyone, telling them that I was going to my uncle's house. As I left, Canen told me to take the Soviet jeep, which bore the military insignia of the Supreme Headquarters.

It took me a little while to arrive at the Hilton at L and 23rd. Even though it had been renamed during the nationalization in 1960, in my own mind I continued to think of it as the Hilton. I went to one of the public phones in the lobby and called Chandee, arranging to meet her there in half an hour.

I called my uncle. My aunt picked up, and after greeting her I asked to speak with my uncle, giving her the emergency code. He told me that he would meet me there in one hour.

Dr. Julio Antonio del Marmol

I went to the coffee shop and found a table from which I could see the exit and entrance by the only front door. I ordered a sugared napoleon and an orange juice. I was only halfway through my snack when I saw the beautiful figure of my *chinita* Chandee walk into the shop. At that time of the evening, it was very busy.

When I stood up to receive Chandee with her customary smile, she said, "Oh, my God! I like you a lot more with your hair in a short military cut. You look so attractive and masculine. I know what you're going to tell me—the dress doesn't make the monk, and I know you probably hate that recruit haircut, but mm-mm-mm." She nodded. "I like it."

I rolled my eyes and shook my head as I hugged her.

We had not seen each other for several months, and I noticed her body was more voluptuous. She truly had filled out, including her breasts, which she had always felt were too small. She noticed my admiration of her and reached inside her purse. She pulled out a recent photograph and handed it to me. "This picture is for you. When you left for the military service, I kicked myself in the butt, because I never gave you a photograph to remember me by."

I smiled. "I don't need a picture of you." I tapped my forehead. "I have you right here."

Chandee

We kissed each other, and as we sat down I asked, "Have you already had dinner?"

She smiled wryly. "Dinner has come to be a luxury in our Socialist society for many of the proletariat. According to the options we have, we can either have lunch or dinner. You cannot do both with the small amount of rations for groceries we get each month from this government. If you eat both, there will be a week at the end of the month during which there will be no food at all in the house."

I shook my head. "What are we coming to, eh?" I clucked my tongue. I smiled then and said, "Well, that ration book crap doesn't apply to me. You know me—I was a rebel even before I was born. I almost killed my mother at birth. Majito said I resisted coming out of her womb and weighed almost 18 pounds." I raised my eyebrows and asked, "Can you imagine it? I didn't want to get out of the warm womb, and I nearly killed my beautiful Mima."

Chandee shook her head. "My God! Eighteen pounds through that little hole! Ooh-la-la! The worst part is that you haven't changed a bit. What are you eating?"

"Just a little dessert, because I already had dinner at my sister and brother-in-law's house. Ask whatever you want. Here there is no rationing. Whoever can afford these enormous prices that only the tourists can pay are people like you and me who are sponsored by the President of the National Bank of Cuba, the biggest thief ever born into the world."

Chandee shook her head with another ironic smile. "Well, realistically, only you. I don't think this degenerate Che shares his comfort even with his own family, because he doesn't want anyone to know how he lives. It's possible he told his family, 'Sacrifice, sacrifice for the Revolution,' while at the same time he enjoys for himself the most exquisite food, the best liquor, and those fine Habanos cigars. But the rest of us have to sacrifice for the fine Socialist Revolution."

I smiled. "Don't get so upset, or you'll have indigestion. Even though he doesn't know what I've been doing, I've been making a lot of people happy by seeing to it that the proletariat enjoy whatever they need, using the money I took from his portfolio. That, of course, includes my family, my brother and his wife, and my cousins. They took several dollars that I hope will make their lives wherever they end up a lot easier to start a new life with a better hope and purpose. By the way, how did your father's car turn out after the Roman touch?"

Chandee was looking at the menu. She smiled and held up one hand to signal it was okay. "You were right.

That car's been running like new. Even my father asked me what I had done to it. He caught me by surprise when he asked that, and I thought something else had broken down with it at first. I told him that I believed your father's mechanic changed the oil and did some kind of adjustment or maintenance, but that was all. He said, 'Oh, no wonder. The car drives so much better, so smoothly now.' One of the noises he was used to hearing had disappeared. He said to thank you very much because I told him you'd paid for all the work."

I smiled with my right hand held high. "You tell him he's very welcome. Tell him your car is the last one Roman is ever going to fix in Cuba. He left shortly afterward. I paid him in dollars, and he used that to get his visa so he could get out. Apparently he wanted to dry his hands on the *Bohemia* magazines in Miami. You see what I told you? You should listen to me more frequently."

"I do, I do," she protested.

"Well, you avoided an unnecessary bad time for your father. After all, the car is great, and he didn't even noticed it had broken down."

She reached over the table and took my hand. "Thank you very much for all you did."

I smiled. "You're very welcome, sweetie."

I signaled to the waitress. Chandee ordered a chicken salad sandwich French style and a sugared napoleon. While they prepared the sandwich, I laid out my plans to Chandee for the celebratory party Che was going to throw at his house in Boca Siega. I gave her a summary of what had happened over the last few days and my conversation I had with Che before the public release of the news of the Kennedy assassination.

She shook her head and raised both arms over her head. "I still cannot believe it. I'm still in shock. How did this happen?"

"I told you it would happen—and they made it happen."

"I never believed it. I still cannot come to the realization that the President of the United States is dead. Probably the majority of the Cuban people who wish for freedom and the return of this country to democracy have lost all hope in that dream. It will be very, very difficult from now on, if not impossible." She shook her head again.

I said, "Don't be a pessimist. When a door closes, you can find a window that's open."

She had almost finished her sandwich when my uncle arrived. He came up to us with a big smile. "It's so nice to see the two of you so cozy here." He looked at Chandee's napoleon sitting next to her plate and my half-finished one and said, "Those napoleons look better than the ones they serve in Artemisa."

I smiled joyfully. "*Claro*! We're in the Hilton. Everything has to be superior here."

Chandee started to eat hers and made an appreciative sound. "You're right! These have to have an imported liqueur or something, because it's delicious!"

My uncle nodded his head as he sat down. "OK, OK, OK. You kids have both convinced me, so now I have to order one for me, as well. I cannot let you guys take all the sacrifice by yourselves. I should share in your suffering."

Chandee looked up as she chewed on a bite. She

replied in the same vein, "Don't worry about it. We can bear it all ourselves. You don't need to suffer as well. Don't distress yourself." She pointed at the pastry. "It's not good for your health."

He smiled. "Well, if this is not good for one's health, girl, it will bring great satisfaction to my palate." He raised his arm to summon the waitress. "Will you bring me two napoleons? Sugared ones." After the waitress left, he said, "We'd better take advantage of the government still allowing us Cubans to enter a place like this. I see a future, if these morons remain in power, when our money will be valueless. Then the only ones who can come into this kind of place and can afford to enjoy these delicious napoleons will be foreign tourists with their rubles, dollars, francs, pounds, and marks."

I smiled and replied. "Then you guys have nothing to worry about." My uncle looked at me in confusion, so I continued. "I have a good quantity of every currency you just mentioned. That means we can continue eating our napoleons for quite a while yet."

He looked at me wonderingly but said nothing. Instead, he shook his head dismissively, at least appearing to dismiss my words. The waitress brought his order over, and he started to eat one of them.

After she left, I started to relate to my uncle the conversation I'd had with Che. I gave him the details of what had happened and was planned for next Wednesday with the visitors. After I finished, I asked him abruptly, "Who is JUBATERE?"

He looked at me in surprise and consternation. I had only referred to the spy who had eliminated Yuri in New Orleans and Arzate in Dallas. I wanted to get to the bottom of who was behind that and who was pretending to be the Lightning outside of Cuba, especially since I had no knowledge of who that was. I didn't know if this was done with good intentions to protect my identity or if something darker was behind it.

He continued looking at me in silence as he ate. Getting no answer out of him, I asked him another question. "Did you guys pass the information relating to Lee Harvey Oswald's doubles and their route to infiltrate the continental United States with enough time for counter-intelligence to eliminate them?"

He didn't even finish swallowing. With his mouth still full, he said, "How do you think they intercepted Yuri to kill him in New Orleans?"

I leaned back and stroked my chin. I crossed my legs and replied, "What about the other three?" I didn't wait for an answer. "I still cannot believe, with all the information we sent to the CIA, how this happened—unless you're not dealing with them but with another agency above them. You're the one here who would have the answer. How is it possible that we could not destroy those two subjects before they accomplished their goals today?"

He stopped eating unhappily. He picked up the crystal goblet of water and took a swallow before answering. He raised his left hand up and used it to gesture for emphasis. "You have to get used to the idea that all our hard work, sacrifice, even giving our lives, isn't always appreciated or used in the proper ways. Our job is to accumulate the evidence, put it together, and pass it to them. Even when something horrible like today happens, the bureaucracy doesn't take it seriously or consider it sufficient, concrete, or reliable, and will ignore it. Worse yet, they won't assign all the resources that a good counterintelligence requires to perform a potent offensive and destroy an operation like this before it's complete. It's that they sometimes simply underestimate the magnitude of what they have right in front of their eyes. That is what caused *de magna cagasone*[8], exactly the same shit the North American intelligence have in their hands today. Then they put their feet over their heads to find out who they're going to blame for this fiasco."

    He reached to pull his second napoleon towards him. "Believe me, this is not the first time, nor will it be the last that the bureaucracies in our intelligence agencies will screw up our brilliant counter-intelligence operations. When they already have their shoelaces in their hands, they will forget to tie their shoes. Then they walk around with their shoes untied, trip, and fall to break their noses.

    "I want this experience to be a lesson for you. In this filthy business of intelligence, espionage, and counterintelligence, you can never—and hear me out, *never*—trust anyone completely. Do you know what that means? No. One. Including me. The most important thing for your survival is always to make sure to have a solid insurance policy in your pocket or something to negotiate your exit from a trap or the type of setup Lee Harvey Oswald is going through today. It could come from your enemies, like in this case, but it could also come from your friends. Whether we call it a setup or make him a patsy, it's all the same. You just need to have a

---

[8] The shit hitting the fan

guaranteed exit from the problem. But you already know about this, because I've gone over it with you several times."

He massaged his forehead and shook his head. "I only pray to God that whoever was training Oswald trained him in the old ways, the same way I've been training you guys. I feel sorry for him. Either he will spend the rest of his life in jail for doing something he actually tried to prevent or he can expect something even worse. He might be too dangerous for whatever is behind all of this and so might have to be silenced. Of course, it would be an extreme pity, because that would be part of the plan of our enemies to implicate us inside all of this crap in order to cover up the real crime."

I shook my head and looked at Chandee. "I don't know if I can avoid it. I think so."

My uncle looked at both of us and said, "Wait—what's going on here? You haven't told me about anything yet. You guys are leaving me in the dark."

I replied, "You haven't even explained to me or replied to my question who JUBATERE is. You're leaving *me* in the dark on that. What is his significance, and what is behind all of this?"

My uncle smiled and took a bite of his napoleon. As he chewed, he raised his empty fork up and smiled. "Very well, just as I've taught you. When you don't receive an answer to your question, you ask it again, and if necessary several times until you get your answer. It doesn't have to be truthful, but you can at least compare that answer to corroborate the contradictions that might exist between one answer and another."

Chandee smiled. "Is this now a test? Haven't we

already graduated? Or is it simply a decoy to detour us away from the adequate answer?"

My uncle smiled once more. Gesturing to Chandee with his fork, he said, "Both of you guys are the pride of my work. By the way, you both have the good quality of knowing what it means to work as a team, to surround and entrap the enemy."

I replied, "Let's hope that when we surround the enemy, it's not you. As you've told me thousands of times, even just now, we can never trust anyone completely. Even with all these compliments and glorifications, which are really welcome and appreciated, you still haven't answered my question, and you've almost finished your second napoleon."

This time he could not hold back his laughter, and he had to wipe his lips from the napoleon that had nearly exploded out of his mouth. He used the fine linen napkin to wipe up the crumbs that did manage to escape. He shook his head. "Kids, kids, kids. Stop what you're doing. It's very simple. Every spy has a code name. He may not even know what that name is. It is a code for the people above us to identify that spy. Even though you are freedom fighters and only work out of patriotism, this is only the way to classify your work and who you are. In this way, when a report is sent to the agency, they can determine the source of the information. Based on the track record of that spy, they will assign the importance and priority to the material in that report."

I said, "When did you intend to let me know about this? Or is this like the betrayed husband, who is the last one to find out that his wife is cheating on him after the entire city knows? Am I to be the last one to know my own code name when the entire intelligence community already knows it?"

He finished his second napoleon and wiped his mouth. He dropped the napkin on the plate and shook his head. "This is a recent thing—very recent. Up until now, in order to protect your identity, I've been sending all your reports with my code, mixing the information from other sources with mine and yours, so that I can confuse whoever receives it without knowing where it came from. But after the recent October Crisis, the commander in charge ordered a change in all of this. It's more secure and prudent, but also to make it more efficient in identifying a person like you clearly through a code. They don't know who you are, but they want to know who that source in our circles is. Since your reputation is so solid from the information you've sent in the past—without exception, they ordered me to separate your information from all the others. That way, we can give absolute priority to any report you produce."

"Who is this spy in New Orleans who used my clandestine code?"

"One of the special agents who worked directly with Lee Harvey Oswald. This special agent received his orders only from Oswald. This was done to divert our enemies' attention away from you. This is customary procedure to protect any important source of information. You cannot be in two places at the same time, so they'll follow the trail left down in New Orleans and ignore you. They have no idea who you are or what you physically look like. Today, I managed to make you look like a ghost, and he could be any one of us. It could be me, the General—anyone."

I asked, "How did Che come to know the name of JUBATERE?"

He stroked his chin. "Because we know exactly who most of the double agents working with us are, especially those in service to Che and the Cuban counter-intelligence. Once in a while, we leak information that is real but of no bother to us at all. In this case, we want them to know this information so that they completely exonerate you, since you could not be in New Orleans and Cuba at the same time. We've cleaned you of all suspicions, and it clearly worked beautifully. If Che had any doubts about you right now, he would never have invited you to that party. There's no doubt they've committed the most perfect crime in history, but eventually this will backfire on them.

"Well, if my answers satisfy you, and you have no more questions, can you please lay out your plan to me as to how you're going to extract the information from the debriefing that we will find so valuable? Then we can expose them before the world for exactly what they've done." He leaned back in his chair. "If you succeed, it will be something a lot more fantastic to add to the story of the assassination of JFK. Maybe we'll be able to unwrap the enigma so that it won't be buried in the course of history."

He paused and let me lay out my plan.

Once I was finished, he grew very serious. He asked, "Where do you intend to hide the recorder pen?"

I rolled my eyes and looked at Chandee to invite her to reply. She said, "In the only place where I hope the adult men who will be searching me will not dare to check, considering me a virgin because of my age."

Dr. Julio Antonio del Marmol

My uncle's eyes widened and leaned back uncomfortably in his chair. He stroked his forehead with his right hand. "What if they have a lady to do these kinds of searches? You have to think of every possibility, because this is a maximum security location. You may be entering a carefully calculated trap."

Chandee smiled and replied, "I'm going to be sure that, even though I'm not menstruating, a combination of ketchup, a little mayonnaise, and a touch of fish sauce to ensure that whoever will do that search on me will not take too long or search too deeply."

My uncle raised his eyebrows again. He shook his head. "My girl, I think you will serve them an exotic salad accompanied by a bloody Mary." He smiled then. "I see you guys have thought of everything. This is extremely dangerous, but maybe it could work out after all. I think if we manage to accomplish this, the people in North America and public opinion around the world will force the bureaucracy to invade the island instead of going around in false pretensions."

He gave me a small signal that he wanted to speak to me privately. "Excuse me," he said, standing up. "I have to go to the restroom."

I stood up. "I'll go with you. I think I have to obey the same call from Mother Nature, as well."

Chandee smiled as we left to walk through the lobby and into the restrooms.

We walked into the luxurious restroom and walked over to the urinals, standing next to each other. My uncle said in a low voice—almost a whisper, "I want to warn you in case you don't know. This government has recently declared it illegal for nationals in negotiating to carry any kind of foreign currency. National pesos only. The sentence for anyone in possession of foreign currency is twenty to thirty years in prison. The worst case scenario is death by firing squad if a Revolutionary tribunal determines one is a spy or is assisting the counter-revolution." He shook his head gravely. "Do you know how easy it is to find anyone before a Revolutionary tribunal guilty of any of those charges? As you know, those tribunals are composed of officers in government service from the regular Army."

I smiled. "You don't have anything to worry about. I only make these transactions with foreign currency when it's absolutely necessary—and even then with only a single person who is absolutely trustworthy. Otherwise, I never carry that currency on my person. Most of the time, I use it to save someone's life or to bring that person to safety outside of the country."

"Nobody is absolutely trustworthy," he reminded me, shaking his head. "But I just wanted to warn you. This government is coming up with new hypocritical laws designed to asphyxiate the opposition every day. At the same time, they're trying to convince the rest of the world that we have no political oppression and that all they're doing is applying the normal laws established by this Revolution. But it looks like you know what you're doing."

We finished and went to wash our hands. The attendant gave us the towels which still had the logo "H. H. Hilton" on them. We tossed them into the laundry and smiled. My uncle said, "This government has the money to send assassins and invasions all over the world but none to change the logos on the towels to the hotel's new name."

We left a tip for the attendant and left.

We gave each other a big hug outside. "Say goodbye to Chandee for me," he said. "I'm very late for an important meeting. Between the pleasant conversation and the napoleons, I lost track of the time."

He looked me in the eye. "Remember—be extremely careful, and be aware that the unexpected can crop up at any time, so be prepared to improvise. The same way we're learning to defend ourselves, they're learning how to trap us better. This invitation to that house of Che's could be another trick to entrap the Lightning. Without being paranoid, but with extreme caution, just walk into that place looking at all the angles as if you were diving into a pool filled with sharks. Go into the water without fear, but be prepared so that you're not surprised."

We said our goodbyes, and he left.

I returned to our table in the cafe where Chandee waited with a huge smile on her face. "What did your uncle want in private with you?"

I smiled. "How did you know?"

Without losing her smile, she answered, "It's obvious. He probably made you a signal. He had barely gotten up when you stood. It was only a matter of seconds between the two of you."

I nodded. "He only wanted to make me aware of something for security reasons. He probably didn't want to look too paternal in front of you and embarrass me. So he wanted to do it in private. In reality, what he told me was completely unnecessary, though I appreciate it. His worry is a demonstration of love to me and is also an obvious demonstration of his professional responsibility and experience, which we should take seriously. He's been in this business for a long time. His knowledge is something we should appreciate tremendously."

She reached over the table and squeezed my hand. "Don't worry. I agree with you. I know he loves both of us and wants the best for us. I also realize that blood is a lot thicker than water. You are his blood, and I'm not. I never forget that."

I looked at her seriously. She continued smiling and then opened her eyes wide. "Why are you looking at me like that? You know what I told you is reality." She shrugged her shoulders. "I cannot change that."

"You're not my blood," I said, "but I trust you more than anyone who does have it." I continued giving her that serious look.

She slapped me on the shoulder. "Stop looking at me that way!"

I couldn't hold it in any longer and smiled. "The reason I'm in love with you and I like you so much is because of your intelligence and caring. You're realistic and keep your feet on the ground. That's why you and I get along so well. I have the tendency to be a little optimistic and a bit of a dreamer. But you return me to reality with your questioning and cruel analysis of the obvious reality."

She leaned forward and took my arm. "If you like the way I am, I like much more the way you are an optimistic dreamer. Please, never change the way you are. I promise to continue to be equally cruel and realistic, since I know you like it so much. OK?"

She gave me a tender kiss on my lips. The waiter came in with our bill and smiled at the sight. We noticed him and stepped back.

I hurriedly paid the bill and tipped him generously. I said to him, "The food has been great, but the service was superior."

The waiter smiled and thanked me as he left.

I was filled with joy after the good time I was having with Chandee and in excitement over what we had planned. I hadn't seen her in a while, and life was great for the moment; she had helped me forget the previous terrible moments I had endured as the international situation had evolved. I thought of a way to prolong that temporary happiness, at least for the next few days.

I took her by the arm and said, "I have an idea that you will probably like. My uncle already has the plan of what we're going to do. Tell it to your parents and say that you're coming to Pinar del Rio with me for a couple of days to prepare for Wednesday. Instead of going to my house, however, we're going to Viñales Valley. There's a small hotel in a valley the mountains overlooking rivers and cascades. Not only can we prepare all the details of our plan, but we can relax for a couple of days in the privacy we haven't had for a while and enjoy ourselves."

She squeezed my arm and looked at me in enchantment. With a grin of happiness she said, "I love that idea. You see? Those are the beautiful dreams you always have and know very well to prepare in your mind. Those dreams are the ones that fill my heart with love and happiness. When do we leave for the valley?"

I smiled. "Six o'clock tomorrow morning, really early. I'll pick you up at your house." I pulled some paper and a pencil out of my pocket and wrote a small note. "If you can, please, this is what I want you to bring from your father's toolbox. We'll need them to complete our project."

"OK," she said enthusiastically.

We left the hotel and I walked her to the valet. After a big hug and a passionate kiss, we said our farewells. I returned to Canen's farmhouse, where I found both the guards who were supposed to take care of the security of the premises fast asleep. They were caught by surprise and asked me for silence, begging me not to tell Canen. If I did, they would be sent to exhausting hard work in one of the military camps, and their wonderful life as bodyguards they now enjoyed would end. I promised my silence on the condition that this never happened again. With tears in their eyes, they both promised me that it would not be repeated.

I told them, "If I ever see you sleeping on guard duty, I will have no other choice but to tell Canen not only about that incident, but this one as well. This is not just your security but also that of the entire family."

An old man named Toledo was the attendant on the farm, performing such duties as milking the cows and taking care of the other animals. Machete in his hand, he was the one who told me when I arrived that the guards had been asleep for a long while.

Toledo was a small, skinny man in perhaps his late sixties. He never sympathized with the Revolution, but being a Baptist like Canen as well as the caretaker for the farm's previous legitimate owners, my brother-in-law left him in charge. Since their first meeting, Toledo had been honest with him regarding his feelings. He informed Canen that if his work was wanted, he would work as hard as he had for his previous employers but was not to be asked anything relating to the Communist government. He said he believed in God and would never be a Communist. That honesty in front of an officer in the army completely earned Canen's trust. It took only a short time to establish a mutual respect and a firm friendship. Before taking an egg for himself, he always asked Canen and Disa if it was all right.

When I entered the house, everyone was already asleep. Canen was still up, brushing his teeth in the bathroom. I took the opportunity to tell him I was going to Pinar del Rio for the weekend, since I hadn't seen my family in a while, and I wanted to say hello to Mima. I wanted to use the trip to spend a little time with Chandee. He replied, "No problem. Unfortunately, though, the Buick was already scheduled to have some service tomorrow morning. But you can use one of the Soviet brand Ural motorcycles with a sidecar the escort uses. If you don't mind using it, you can take it. I'm going to have to use the jeep to get to work."

I thanked him for his offer. "No, I don't mind at all. It will be an experience for Chandee."

"Both the helmets and goggles are in the sidecar," he said. He reminded me to be back by Wednesday and not to forget about the party with Che.

I smiled. "Of course. I'll be here in plenty of time to arrive there punctually."

I thought that I shouldn't need to be reminded of something so important, especially given what I had in mind involving the destruction of that political process. I was going to be counting the minutes until then.

After we said goodnight, I went into my room as he headed to bed. My room was next to that of the chauffeur, Paco. We called him *Paco el Flaco*[9]; the truth was that he ate like ten fat men.

When I got into my room, I could hear him snoring like a bear, with small whistles like a freight train. The wall was only thin wood, and was in no way noise dampening. The structure was a very rustic country house. The partition was so thin that even Paco's flatulence could be smelled. I covered my head with my pillow to minimize that stupendous sound. At last, I fell asleep.

The next morning, I called Chandee to alert her that I would be picking her up in a motorcycle. Paco got up at 5:30 with Canen to go to the base. When they got up, I also rose to shower and pack my travel bags. I tied them to the grill of the Ural and left the farm to drive to Chandee's house.

When I arrived, I could see her small suitcase in the open door. I knew she was already up and probably finishing up some last-minute details. I cut the engine as soon as I pulled up so that the noise wouldn't wake the neighborhood. I securely tied her suitcase to the grill of the sidecar. I looked up to see Chandee coming out of the door, tucking her hair into the flowered scarf she had tied over her head. It was multicolored, with flowers of blue, green, purple, and yellow. Knowing I was picking her up in a motorcycle, she wore a skirt that was made of the same fabric as her scarf and modesty bloomers beneath. She also wore a leotard and looked like a Hawaiian girl with a pearl necklace and matching earrings.

I pulled my photo out of my wallet and looked at her. "Oh, my God! You have the same clothes on in the picture

---

[9] Paco the Skinny

as you're wearing now!"

She grinned broadly in satisfaction. "Bravo!" she said as she took the helmet and goggles I handed her. "Your observational skills are getting tremendously sharper. In a little while, instead of calling you the Lightning, I will call you the Razor, because you will cut like a Gillette razor blade on both sides."

I smiled and gave her a kiss. "Something like you?" I wiggled my eyebrows at her suggestively. I then made it obvious I was looking at her breasts and rear.

She slapped my arm. "Ah! You always have to take things so literally!" She finished putting on her helmet. "Wow! This will be super fun—more than I had been expecting!"

"I hope so. With my optimism and causalities of presence that the Lord sent me by surprise and my guardian angel, his Son, Jesus Christ."

Chandee crossed herself.

"To be honest, this motorcycle was not my idea. It was a necessity. Thanks to that, we might have more fun. At the same time, we can prepare ourselves for Wednesday's swimming competition with the sharks, as my uncle called it."

Chandee smiled and jumped into the sidecar. She unrolled the tarp so that it protected her from the wind once we were in motion. We then hit the road heading southwest.

After a while, we stopped in Artemisa. I didn't want to do that, because it brought up bad memories of Unit 3234, which was undoubtedly the most miserable time of my life. But Chandee had an urgent need to use the bathroom, so I changed my plans from plowing through there at high speed to stopping.

While Chandee used the restroom, I ordered some cafe con leche and pastries for breakfast. Since we were there so early in the morning, we found a very short line. We had not only the opportunity to buy pastries to eat there but also some extras for the road.

A few minutes later the line was closed down, and one of the service ladies told everyone still in line that there was no more to be had until the next day. Many people heard that news with long faces, clearly not liking it at all. It was happening more frequently as even the small businesses were expropriated from the rightful owners by the government and staffed with people who had no experience. These people were paid the same no matter how hard they worked, and so productivity declined as laziness set in.

About two hours later we arrived at the beautiful motel in the mountains. There I discovered the manager was related to the family of my father's first cousin, Menelao Mora Morales. The government had put him in this position when they nationalized the place. Because of my near relation to him, he treated us like royalty, letting us stay there in the Presidential Suite for virtually nothing, sending us fruit, flowers, even a bucket of expensive champagne (even though neither of us were old enough to drink).

Naturally, neither of us refused it, and we both got tipsy. He treated us as honored guests. The huge, beautiful bathtub was filled with rose water. The first day we had a ball, concentrating all our energies on completely relaxing. After I took Chandee for a horseback ride around the surrounding area, she was completely absorbed by the verdant tropical wonders of that place, arguably the most beautiful valley on the entire island. For her, it was a surprise and everything was filled with extraordinary wonder. After we made love several times in various locations, we headed back to the hotel. She lost her balance and fell off her horse when her mount was startled by a wild rabbit. She landed in a bed of wildflowers on the prairie.

I stopped immediately and dismounted. I ran towards her, thinking she might be hurt. As I drew near to her, she gasped. "I think something might be broken," she murmured. "Right here." She surprised me by taking my hand and placing in on the breast that had been partially exposed. She grinned broadly.

"Ah, *chinita, chinita*, you are a *diablita!*" I said. But the little *diablita* conquered me and we made love once more in the wet grass amid those flowers, spending all the passion and love we felt for one another.

We were utterly exhausted and drained of all energy. We managed to drag ourselves back to the hotel. After a nice, warm bath, we ordered food up to the room. We were completely satisfied, physically and emotionally. We fell asleep in perfect contentment on that rose-fragrant bed.

The next day, we slept until it was nearly noon. We went down to the restaurant to have brunch and then returned to the room to work.

She pulled out the tools I had requested her to bring. With a small drill I made a tiny hole in a Cuban flag pin, right at the tip of the triangle where the blue stripes joined. It was no larger than the head of a safety pin, the exact size of the lens of the camera pens I had been using all along. We then made a slightly larger hole in my uniform shirt. With needle and thread of the same color of the shirt, I secured the edges like a buttonhole to make sure no stray threads interfered with the lens. I created some small, tight loops inside the shirt to lock and firmly hold the pen. I made it secure so that it would only shift if I maneuvered it around. I wanted to be able to use this without looking at it.

To make certain of my design, I asked Chandee to put on my shirt, and saw that the design worked perfectly. To camouflage the hole, I covered it with the pin, making certain that the hole in the pin and the one in my shirt aligned exactly. I put the shirt on and looked at myself in the bathroom mirror. It was going to be nearly impossible to detect the hole in my shirt unless somebody knew to look for it. As only three people knew what I had planned, that would be impossible.

Chandee asked, "How can you be sure the eye of the camera in the pen is pointing towards the front and not in the wrong direction?"

I smiled. "Come over here and feel it yourself." I put the pin on my shirt. "OK, put your finger over the little, tiny hole in the center."

She did as I directed. I put my hand inside my shirt and moved the pen. "Do you notice any difference?"

She smiled and nodded. "Yes, yes. You notice the difference. You don't even need to look at it. When the eye of the camera is facing front, it's smooth like glass. When it's not there, it's rough."

I made a little reverence with my hand and head. "It's all right, genius. It's all right." She put her hand inside my shirt and pinched my nipple.

I yelled, "Ouch! Let go! That's a very sensitive area!" I reached out to pinch her rear, and she let go to dodge away. She ran out of the bathroom as I said, "*Chinita, chinita.*"

She had already run out, so I gave it up. I folded the shirt so that it would be in crisp military condition and very carefully packed it in my travel bag. We went over how Chandee would extract her pen from her cavity, and then we went over the details of the house plans and possible areas we might be sitting in the room in which the meeting was likely to take place.

One in a hundred would be in different places, but I was fairly certain that Che would have it on the big terrace overlooking the ocean where he was accustomed to receiving his guests. I described to her the large planters with the garden flowers by the balcony. If, in an absolute emergency, she had to get rid of that pen or we had to abort the operation, she would be able to hide the pen there without anyone noticing. I told her, "If you have to get rid of it, do it. Don't compromise your safety."

After several hours of going through various possibilities and asking and answering each other's questions so we could anticipate every possibility that might occur, we at last agreed on a finalized plan. No matter what might happen, the only thing we could not allow under any circumstance to be found on either one of us was that pen. We would then be marked as spies for certain, and this would only lead to death.

JFK: The Unwrapped Enigma

Valley Vinales from one angle

Valley Vinales from another angle

November 24, 1963

It was a beautiful sunny day, a splendid Sunday. After lunch, I suggested to Chandee that we leave the hotel and go all the way to Guane to keep my promise to her to show her the house in which I was born. She embraced the idea completely. We were sitting in the restaurant and decided to return to the room, pack, and leave right at that moment. When we returned to the suite, we heard the TV through the door. Chandee had forgotten to turn it off before we left.

When we opened the door, the first thing we saw on the screen was the news of the attempt on Oswald's life by Jack Ruby, the fat, half-bald friend of Che's. This was a playback, not a live broadcast, and the reporters were analyzing the footage.

Oswald and Ruby

Chandee clapped both hands over her mouth. "Oh, my God! That is exactly what your uncle predicted!"

We stood there mutely at the threshold. I broke my reverie and walked inside to turn the volume up. Then I let myself sit heavily on the small sofa, still a little in shock. The scene of the shooting repeated on a loop.

They did not report whether or not Oswald was dead; it was simply the shooting itself.

Later, they showed him going into the ambulance. I noticed two men in civilian clothes, one in light-colored suit and hat, the other in dark-colored suit and hat. Both flashed badges at the last minute, saying loudly in the midst of the confusion, "Secret Service." They jumped immediately into the back of the ambulance where the wounded man had already been placed. The ambulance then drove at an unusually slow pace up the ramp towards the street, followed by several marked patrol cars. However, no police officers got into the ambulance.

Chandee slowly came and sat down beside me, putting her hand on my shoulder. That snapped me out of my shocked surprise, and I turned to her. I said, "Lee Harvey Oswald is already dead."

"Why do you say that?" she asked. "They haven't said yet what his condition is."

"I know this is part of Che's plan. This was already arranged, and plan B is in motion. He cannot survive this attempt on his life. They will manage to kill him, either before he gets to the hospital or once he's in it. This is the second phase of the plan. They have to dispose of all witnesses, like Che told me, so the public will be in the dark for a hundred years or more, long after he is already dead." I stood up and turned off the TV, full of frustration.

Chandee protested. "Why did you turn it off? Let's see what happened!"

"Listen to me, please. Let's get out of here. That man is dead already. I just told you. There's nothing more to hear. We'll know about it later on, anyway. Let's get out of here like we had planned and enjoy the few days we have left, and not let these morbid moments ruin our joy and happiness or destroy this beautiful Sunday. I can assure you," I continued, touching the travel bag, "as I'm holding this bag, that Lee Harvey Oswald and Jack Ruby are both dead. Lee will be first, of course; that's already in process. Later, the other link in the chain will be Ruby. Sooner or later, they will kill him in jail or maybe make him appear to die of natural causes. Maybe a terminal disease that someone conveniently will inflict on him in some way."

I shook my head, my lips pursed as I carried my travel bags out of the room. I recalled all the times I had met Ruby and his bodyguards, with those bags filled with money that had been transported to the United States, maybe to be used in the development of this plan. I had to ask myself what Che must have promised Ruby that was so valuable that made that man, who was by no means stupid, accept the responsibility to personally kill Oswald in full view of the entire world. It must have been lots of money and perhaps the promise of a prominent position of extreme importance somewhere in the world where he would be safe for the rest of his life.

What Ruby didn't know, because he didn't know Che as well as I had come to know him over the years I spent by his side, was that he would be betrayed, abandoned, and later on killed. This is what Che specialized in, and he knew how to do it to perfection. This was especially true with somebody who had no ideological connection in common with Guevara. Ruby was only a dirty, expendable partner as a representative of organized crime. In a way, this was connecting him with Che's principal enemy: the horrible capitalist. Che detested that system. He'd learned to hate it not just in Argentina but also in Moscow, in the highest intelligence school with his KGB comrades.

I tried to pay the hotel bill, but my cousin wasn't having any of that. I insisted several times, and each time, he insisted in return, saying, "Please—after all, you are a great Revolutionary, just like your father."

I thanked him, and we left the hotel. This time we headed to Guane via the Panamericana del Caribe Highway. This made Chandee very happy to know we were avoiding the mountain route.

The trip turned out to be very pleasant, with the only stop we made in a small town called Sabalo. We had some snacks, chicken croquettes, and mamey shakes. After we emptied our bladders, we finished our trip without any troubles.

As we left Sabalo, I saw a checkpoint set up with several soldiers, a truck, and a jeep. They were searching all the cars coming in and out of town at the time. They took one look at my uniform and the Ural I was driving (which was only used by the high executives for the military or the Revolution), and waved us right through. I still slowed my speed as I passed and saluted them as we went by. They took one look at the divisional emblem on my helmet and the insignia on the motorcycle and abruptly switched from just passing us through to standing at attention and saluting us.

Even as we passed by, they kept their eyes on us until we disappeared. I smiled, since I didn't have with me even a CDR identity badge, which was the minimum identification required by the government. This was demanded from each citizen as a way to intimidate and control every person living there. It was also a good way to detect someone who had clandestinely infiltrated the island.

I thought at that moment that this motorcycle was the best thing for any spy infiltrating Cuba to move around freely without the worry of counterfeiting official documents. Steal one of these, and the spy could move around the island without question. My smile grew broader as I heard Chandee say, "There's no doubt that you have a powerful guardian angel behind you. One way or another, you always manage to slip through. Like hot lava flowing downhill that leaves behind ashes, you left those soldiers behind us completely petrified."

I shook my head at that. I gave Chandee a salute, but I did not reply. I didn't want to open my mouth at that speed and wind up swallowing some flying insect.

I accelerated to a higher speed so that we could reach Guane before nightfall. When we finally arrived in Guane, the sun was setting. It provided us a breathtaking sunset as it sank below the mountaintops.

I drove slowly through the town, pointing out to Chandee the businesses my father had created. Even though many of them had been nationalized, most of them had the original signs with the names my father had created, still listing my father as proprietor. For instance, the clothing store he owned still bore its old sign: *Mi Casa, Propietario Leonardo Marmol Mora*.

I told her the short version of what my father had achieved without money, leaving all his family in the capital and moving himself to a small fishing port in Puerto Esperanza. With extremely hard work and diligent saving, he had been able to establish his first business. A few years later, he was so successful that rather being in direct competition with his own family in that small town, he decided to move his business to Guane. Here he had even greater success because, I told her, God always rewarded those who act in good faith. As his success in Guane grew bigger, he opened businesses in Pinar del Rio, later moving his family there.

Chandee shook her head and said, "It must be extremely painful to somebody like your father who worked so hard all these years to watch a few lazy bandits come in and take away the fruit of his sacrifice and labor. I already told my father that he should close our antique store because our home is in the store. If we lose our business, we'll lose our home, since they are in the same entity."

I nodded. "Let's hope that doesn't happen. What you just said right now, believe it or not, has been crossing my mind like *deja vu* when we were talking about my father and his business. In some instances, they didn't even let him remove personal effects like a typewriter out of the store."

Chandee shook her head in obvious sorrow. "God help us."

Julio Antonio as a toddler in front of Mi Casa

Chapter 6: Resurrection

We arrived at my old house on the outskirts of town, not too far away from the large Cuyaguateje River. I rode up to the house and parked the motorcycle in the front yard next to the building. I started to say something to Chandee but was interrupted by a dog barking.

After we had moved to Pinar del Rio, we had left the house in the care of our neighbors, Agripina and Amparito. It had been empty all this time, and the neighbors had been working for my father. Over the years, I would come back every once in a while, and I had never yet seen a dog in the house.

I turned toward the sound and was stunned to see Kimbo limping towards me with his wooden leg. My beloved dog, who had once saved my life and whom I thought had been killed, jumped on me in the front yard, wagging his tail and moving around me in serpentine fashion. He had recognized my voice.

Following Kimbo was the tall, lovely Agripina, chubby and always smiling, the neighbor who had watched my birth and helped relieve my pain from stomach gas when I was three years old. She and her husband were very happy to see me, and both hugged me joyfully in greeting.

I introduced them to Chandee, accompanied by the howling and jumping of Kimbo, who continued to snake in between my legs in his attempts to catch my attention.

He had it, though he didn't realize it. As a matter of courtesy, I was replying to the small talk of my neighbors.

As we walked towards the house from the front garden, I could not help it any longer. I could barely see for the tears in my eyes—tears of joy at that unexpected reunion. I knelt and took Kimbo in my arms to embrace him. He had grown considerably, but I didn't notice his weight, so overjoyed was I in that moment to embrace him once more.

We walked into the house and sat down on the sofa, Kimbo between Chandee and me. Chandee petted him lovingly and scratched his belly. She said, "Kimbo—how is it possible that you've been resurrected?"

Kimbo answered her by howling and showing his belly. We both enjoyed scratching it and so continued.

"I imagine you must be in shock," Agripina said. "You have to be wondering how he got here. Let me explain that not even your father knows yet that Kimbo is such a survivor. According to what Leonardo told us, he found Kimbo lying among a bunch of other slain dogs at Leocadio's ranch when he went to visit. He was in complete shock and picked up Kimbo's body. He assumed him to be dead, and so put the bloody body in a blanket to transport in his car. He brought him to us, and Amparito buried the body alongside his namesake, the Kimbo your father gave you guys when you were very small."

She turned to Chandee and related the story of the first Kimbo and how his death had so grieved my father that he refused to allow another dog into our home.

Then she turned back to me. "When you found this dog by the river, your father knew you had brought him to Leocadio. He closed his eyes to this so that he wouldn't hurt you. You were being very respectful of his rule, and you did not, in fact, bring him to the house. When he found out you had named him Kimbo, it really got to him. He decided to let it pass, hoping that you wouldn't have a repeat experience. When he got to the ranch and saw with sorrow that history had repeated itself, he knew it would break your heart again—something he had been trying to avoid for so many years. That's why he put the body in the car to take it right away before you saw anything. He wanted to bring it here for burial."

Amparito raised his hand. "You don't even know, my son, what is behind all of this."

Amparito was a short man of English origins. He was always very well-dressed with neckties and matching pocket handkerchiefs sticking out of his suit pocket. He always wore expensive cologne.

He shook his head with an ambivalent smile. "I had the biggest scare of my life. When Leonardo brought me Kimbo and took him out of the car wrapped in that blanket, he told me to make sure I buried it by the small white cross on the patio where the other one rested. You remember—by the beehive, where the most beautiful flowers on the patio grow, and where you kids used to leave flowers.

"That very night, very late, I decided to go and bury him. I was afraid if I left him until morning he would start to smell. I changed my clothes, put on overalls, got a pick and a shovel, and went to the patio to start to dig a hole next to the other dog's grave. After I finished digging, I deposited the blanket in the hole with this gentleman, Kimbo."

My intelligent dog started howling at the mention of his name.

"I saw the blanket started to move as if it were walking towards me. This scared the daylights out of me, and I nearly broke my neck as I stumbled back to try and get out of that hole."

He removed his deerstalker hat and put it on the table. His eyes opened wide.

"*Claro*, I freaked out. I couldn't even speak, I was so frightened at the sight of that blanket coming towards me. I closed my eyes and crossed myself. Even though I know he doesn't believe in ghosts or superstitions of any kind, when he gave me that body your father said to me, 'Amparito, I'm convinced that if reincarnation exists, this dog has the spirit of the one that died many years ago. Or what could be worse, and I resist in believing, that this dog is the same one that died.'

"He told me he had been tempted to come dig up the grave of the first Kimbo, but he hadn't done it out of a fear of finding that the other dog's remains were gone. If the body weren't there for whatever reason, he would freak out, and it would change the way he had thought his entire life and the only reason he had embraced Masonic logic."

Amparito shifted in his chair uncomfortably. He leaned forward towards us. "Your father also told me of the times he went to see him in the clinic when Dr. Raimundo had to amputate one of Kimbo's legs. He said that the dog looked at him as a person, not an animal, like he was grateful for all he had done." He gesticulated wildly. "Of course, this is not possible. But it was very strange when he told me all of this. Imagine what it was like when I saw that blanket moving towards me in that hole! My mind was already predisposed to superstition, and to make matters worse, I started to hear his howling.

"I opened my eyes and started to unwrap the blanket. It was like he was trying to ask me for help. Once I finished unwrapping him, Kimbo lifted his head up and did to me what he probably did to Leonardo and started howling. Getting blood all over my overalls, I picked him up, put him in my car, and drove him to the veterinarian."

As he said this, Kimbo howled once more. He pointed at the dog. "You see? Exactly like that. You can see this isn't a tall tale, something I'm inventing.

"When I arrived at Dr. Vivian's clinic, she removed two bullets, one from his rear paw, and the one that she said nearly killed him from the right side of his chest." Amparito pointed at Kimbo with his right hand. "And there you are—the miracle of Kimbo being alive today. And it didn't take him very long to recover fully."

I asked him, "Does my father know that Kimbo is alive?"

Agripina replied, "No, no, no. We've been waiting, because it will be a huge shock for him. He won't believe it. Dr. Vivian explained to us that Kimbo had probably entered a coma, a shock reaction from the impact of the bullets. He lost consciousness and slipped into that coma. When your father brought Kimbo here to be buried, he departed as soon as he had left his instructions. We haven't seen him since."

Chandee asked, "Leonardo brought him here to be buried and never came back?"

Agripina replied with a sad expression, "My child, Leonardo has more on his plate than he can really handle.

Dr. Julio Antonio del Marmol

Each day he loses another business to government expropriation. He hasn't rested for the last seven or eight months, going back and forth between here and the capital to save from the capricious laws the government creates each day the few businesses he still has. What an irony! Fidel only promised to nationalize those businesses that were run by Batista's followers or the illicit ones, but he never said he would strip away everything we all of us own, including our own property—even those who are great Revolutionaries like Leonardo."

Amparito picked up his hat and put it on. "The last time I spoke with Leonardo was the night he brought Kimbo here. But this dog has more lives than a cat. That same night, before he left this home, he told me he'd just returned from the capital, trying to see his great friend Fidel. The secretary in the office told him that he had to come back in a few weeks, because Fidel was out of town. Leonardo told me that when he went down in one of the elevators in the building, he saw Fidel get out of another elevator not far from him, and their eyes met. Fidel put his head down, pretending he didn't see your father, and walked away.

"Your father told me that was the biggest deception he had even encountered in his life. He knew Fidel had seen him and was hiding from him. He told me, with tears in his eyes, that there was no doubt that Fidel was no different from any of the other corrupt politicians we've had before. He said, 'Yes, Fidel took out the corrupt politicians like he promised us, but just to put himself and his friends in power, who are even more corrupt individually than all the others put together.' He told me how disappointed he is. I told him that Fidel never disappointed me because I never liked him or any of the others.

"But let's not talk anymore about these sad things, because I'm hungry, and you two probably are, too. Let's go eat before our stomachs start howling like Kimbo." Kimbo howled again. "You see? He's hungry, too!"

We laughed and stood up to walk into the dining room. Memory flooded my mind as I thought about us all gathered around that long table, eating the delicious meal Mima had prepared for us. I sat down with an extreme sadness as I thought about my father's horrible disillusionment. I had tried to make him aware of what was going on, but he hadn't listened. I wanted at that moment to go and find him to give him a big hug and tell him how much I loved him. I wanted him to know I knew how he felt, since I'd had the same disillusionment a few years before. The betrayal I'dfelt was small next to Papi's, which must be hundreds if not thousands of times deeper. He had not only embraced the Revolution and brought his brother Masons in, but he had also risked his life as well as those of his family in getting involved in clandestine activities against Batista.

Chandee guessed my feelings, probably through her feminine intuition. She took my hand and squeezed it hard. I looked at her and breathed deeply. I said, "Well, we have to say something good. It's wonderful to be in our home, no matter how beautiful it may be out there in the country or anywhere else in the whole world—I don't know, since I haven't been out there yet."

She smiled. "You're one hundred percent right. Even though coming home can be a little melancholic at times with childhood memories coming back, there's no other feeling as great as being home."

Amparito and Agripina held hands, smiled, and gave each other a little kiss.

Chandee crooned, "Ooohhh," and leaned in to give me a kiss as well.

After we ate a delicious pizza with Canadian bacon, mushrooms, and pineapple, and decorated with anchovies, Cuban style with tongues of cheese, we celebrated Agripina as the greatest Italian cook ever. We had small slices of flan for dessert and then walked out on the large porch. The breeze from the river cooled things wonderfully, and we sat on the same rocking chairs Mima had rocked me in while we watched political parades going by in front of our house as well as the beautiful carnivals that came to town.

Agripina sat near Chandee, and lost no opportunity to tell her about how, when I was about four or five years of age, I would go by myself to her house to have my belly rubbed when I had painful gas. My mother didn't know it at the time, but cow's milk didn't settle well with my digestive system.

It was growing late that night in November, and the sky was filled with stars. Chandee and I, followed by Kimbo, went for a little walk around the riverbank. Chandee collected some wild flowers to bring back as a present for Agripina. When we got back, they were already asleep, so she cut and cleaned them before putting them in a vase of water as a surprise for Agripina when she got up the next morning.

That night, Kimbo slept with us because he didn't want to leave my side. I didn't like the idea very much, but I allowed it as a reward for all the suffering he had gone through. The next two days were passed by exploring every single corner of the town of my birth and in which I had spent my early childhood. Everywhere we went, Kimbo followed us. He never passed up an opportunity to mark his territory. The days were very happy for us, mixed in with memories that were for me occasionally a little sad, knowing that this was no longer our home. However, we created new memories for ourselves with that trip, and that was enjoyable and good.

Wednesday, November 27, 1963

After breakfast, we said our goodbyes with hugs and kisses to Agripina, Chandee and I were invited back whenever we wished, since it was really our house. They had already sold their own domicile and had moved in to take care of the building for my father. When the government had determined that people could only own one habitation at a time, my father told them he was going to make the deed in their name.

They waved to us as we rode off on the motorcycle, with Kimbo howling his own farewells to the couple in the language of dogs. What was completely paradoxical about the dog was that the same burial place of the previous Kimbo lay along the same path Majito walked me when I was born to baptize me in her African protection ritual.

We traveled for a couple of hours with only small stops to answer the call of nature and to give Chandee an opportunity to make herself more comfortable, as she shared the sidecar with Kimbo. We finally arrived in Pinar del Rio, where we made a couple of brief stops. The first was at Leocadio's ranch. The sight of Kimbo coming out of the motorcycle alive nearly sent Leocadio into hysterics. The second stop we made was at Raimundo's clinic, where we surprised the vet, as he also could not believe how Kimbo was jumping around so energetically as if nothing had happened.

He told me, "You had better take good care of this dog. There's something very unusual about him."

After we said our goodbyes, we went to my house, where we had a small lunch Mima quickly prepared for us, in spite of our admonitions not to do any work. She insisted, of course, and we spent a couple of hours relating Kimbo's remarkable story for her to pass along to my father, who was once more in the capital with his attorneys in an attempt to litigate a way to stop the government from taking away all his businesses.

Mima shook her head. "He is only wasting his time and money on attorneys and prolonging his agony. This is all inevitable."

I nodded. "Yes. I agree with you. The only thing that will stop these people is another Revolution."

She put her hand over my mouth. "Don't say that. They'll kill you."

I shook my head and clucked my tongue. "Don't worry, Mima. I would never say that to anyone."

After we said our goodbyes, we left Pinar del Rio around 1:00 p.m. for the capital. It was a pleasant trip without major problems. We made a brief stop for some pastries in Artemisa. Miraculously they still had some. That day the bakery chef had started baking thrice a day, and we got there early enough in the afternoon to catch the full stock. He told us that this was to create the impression they had product all day long. The government told him it's too depressing to see the shelves empty, so he now took his daily baking load and divided it into three smaller batches.

Two and half hours later, we arrived in Havana. When we got to Chandee's house, I spent a little while with her going over our plans. I told her I would pick her up around 6:30 or 7:00, and I left her house to give her some time to rest before going to the party later. I drove to the farm in Santiago de las Vegas, Kimbo's new home for many years ahead. As I drove from her house, I stopped at my uncle's house on Carlos III for a few minutes to pick up the rest of the cigars I had left there following the French operation with French ambassador Pierre Andreus.

When I arrived at the farm, I settled Kimbo in his new home and spent the rest of the afternoon with him. I took a shower and went over the details in my mind, examining the various possibilities in which something unexpected could pop up. I always did such planning while taking a bath or a shower, and I needed to be completely prepared mentally. This could wind up being the single most important thing I had ever done in my life. If I didn't manage to obtain the whole truth, I would at least hear from the mouths of the participants important details of that historical assassination which might become the most enigmatic crime of the twentieth century.

Once I was ready, I sat down on the porch of the house. Canen arrived at 6:00, and I had already eaten something light. I declined the great-smelling chicken and rice Majito had prepared. I knew my digestive system; when I was tense and nervous, it didn't function properly, so I didn't eat when I was faced with such situations. Majito had been around me for so long that she knew me possibly even better than Mima. She brought out to the porch a tilo tea for me. "This will relax you and make you feel better," she said.

I smiled, since my black nanny had once again read my mind. I waited for Canen, rocking in one of the old rocking chairs. I reflected on one thing I had learned in my short time on this Earth: that the one thing I did not like to do is wait for anybody. I grew impatient, and I felt like I wasn't in control and might wind up arriving late for my appointment. I tried to control myself to avoid being rude and rushing my brother-in-law through his meal.

I thought that the idea of Canen coming with me was an excellent way to cover up what I was going to do. Even better, it wasn't my idea; it was Che's. Everything would look more natural and relaxing, since I was only bringing the person he'd told me to bring. I hoped in silence that everything would go as planned.

November 27, 1963
6:45 p.m.

We left the house in Santiago de las Vegas, headed towards Havana to get Chandee and then to Boca Siega and the party to celebrate the success of the assassination of President John F. Kennedy. We picked Chandee up a little earlier than I had predicted, and we traveled in Canen's Buick with his driver, Paco. Canen sat in the front seat, Chandee and I in the back. Canen had left his escort behind, since security was going to be so tight at that party that they would not be needed. Paco was a laconic man, speaking only when he had something to say or was asked a direct question.

Chandee noticed the pocket of my shirt was completely filled with Habanos cigars. Not knowing if I had said anything to my brother-in-law, she just gave me a glance and smiled. She looked meaningfully at the cigars, and I nodded an answer to her. She was dressed in *miliciana* formal uniform of a light blue blouse with a knee-length olive green skirt. At her waist she bore a small pistol. She looked radiant and exotic, the maturity of her body shown to advantage in the outfit, with the skirt highlighting her curves.

Canen had not seen Chandee for a while. He looked at her discreetly, noting the vast physical change time had brought. Before she got into the car, he smiled and said, "My God, you've become a beautiful woman in front of our eyes, and we never even noticed!"

Chandee smiled at the compliment. "Thank you, but I've always been a woman. I was just in a girl's body."

We all smiled. As we approached the house thirty minutes later, we started to notice the strict security half a mile before the safe house. They had closed off every block in the surrounding area. Police, G-2, and other federal government cars were all over the place. The only people allowed past the road blocks were people who lived there, and they had to show identification to prove their residence. Paco dropped us in front of the entryway of the house and went to park the Buick where the rest of the drivers were to wait.

As soon as we stepped out of the car, officers in formal dress approached us with several lists in their hands. They had been separating the groups by those lists into different areas in the residence. Everything had been well-coordinated. All the areas were cordoned off to separate them. Overseeing it all were military personnel, armed with machine guns. This looked like a very segregated following, separated by protocol, clearance, and status. The guards were enforcing these distinctions very strictly without exception.

Our group, based on the names they called, included French ambassador Pierre Andreus and two other gentlemen. I greeted him, and he welcomed me cordially. He was with two tall gentlemen in civilian clothes that I did not know. I assumed that they were either G-2 or military intelligence. One of the officers said to our group, "Follow me, please."

I noticed that Chandee's name had not been called. The officer, however, allowed her to come with us in spite of that. We entered one of the rooms, and they asked us who had come together. They separated us, and had us remove all personal effects: rings, wallets, watches, everything. These were put into envelopes, and they gave us a ticket with an identifying number that matched the one on the sealed envelopes. We were then taken to another room, where we were politely asked to wait. We looked at each other. A short while later they returned. One by one, people were called by name into another room. After a while, the person would come out to where the rest of us waited. I realized this was a strip search, and my name was called.

They brought me inside the room and asked me to remove my clothes and put them on the table. They searched my clothing with gloves on. The man came over and asked, "Would you please bend over and spread your cheeks." I was concerned about this but complied. However, he did not touch me. "Cough," he said. I coughed a couple of times. Clearly, he was making sure I hadn't concealed anything up my anus. I was a little nervous, but I had felt in control up until that moment. I pretended I had forgotten to remove my beret. When I turned around, the guard smiled and pointed at it.

"Oh, I'm sorry," I said. I took it off and held it to him.

"No, no—just shake it out for me." I shook it, and turned it inside out for him. "OK, go ahead and put it back on." He returned my clothes. "Thank you for your cooperation. I'm sorry for the inconvenience, but this is a high security situation. Not everyone here has the privilege of entering the section you're going into."

"I understand," I said.

"After you've dressed, you can return to your *compañeros*."

Since I was the last one to be searched, the only one who had not been checked was Chandee. I hoped that they might not bother her because of her sex. I could not see how a man could do that kind of search to her. Maybe we would be able to get to that section with her without any problem. However, a lady of perhaps fifty with very masculine features whose repugnant, tomato-red face gave the impression of high blood pressure or of being on steroids came forward. She said to Chandee, "Please come with me." Chandee was taken to the same room in which we had been searched, and my heart sank. A few minutes later, the officer took all the men to the part of the terrace we were supposed to go to.

I asked our guide, "What happened to our friend Chandee?"

"Don't worry about it, Commandantico, she'll join you in a little bit. It takes a little longer for women to get dressed again."

We could see that the terrace was filled with people. As we walked to our table, we saw Fidel, Raul, Ramiro, and the rest of the first circle of the government sitting together. I saw someone who looked like Marko, but I couldn't be certain. He had bandages on his face, and his eyes were blackened, as if he had undergone surgery. He saw me looking at him, recognized me, and waved to me. Next to him sat Marcelino, who was likewise bandaged and bruised, and he also waved at me as soon as he saw Marko's action. Both were at a small table separated from the crowd at a podium. Che was also seated with them. He saw them gesticulate and noticed us. He then also waved in greeting.

We finally arrived at our assigned table. Canen sat down, and I took a seat one removed from him, keeping the vacant chair between us for Chandee. The French ambassador sat down between the two civilian men. They looked like G-2. I looked at the empty chair in profound concern, and the worse scenarios flashed through my mind.

About half an hour later, I was about to stand up to see what had happened. I had asked Canen twice already what he thought was going on, and he replied with vague reassurances. My heart returned to my chest when I saw the silhouette of Chandee at the door, waving to us. Next to her was the muscular woman, who escorted Chandee to our table. As she walked past the tables, every man and woman watched her. She caught everyone's attention with her youth and figure. Even Fidel watched her.

JFK: The Unwrapped Enigma

As I stood up to pull out her chair chivalrously for her to sit down, Fidel's eyes met mine as he followed the beautiful Chinese-Cuban girl in fascination. He smiled and raised his arm to wave to me. Raul and Ramiro, seeing Fidel's motion, also looked and greeted to us courteously. Chandee whispered in my ear, "I think that old lady is a lesbian. She wanted to keep me with her in there forever. She was decent enough and didn't perform a cavity search the way she was supposed to. She apologized several times to me. She had to check with Che repeatedly, because my name wasn't on any list. The guards at the entry had told her on the radio that they had allowed me in as a courtesy to you and Canen, but they wanted her to check me out. She apologized again and said that she was only following her orders. Che finally authorized my clearance, and until then I could not come to this particular section, where only those with high authorization could come. She also asked me if I had ever had sex. I told her of course not, I'm still a kid. She decided to ignore that protocol then, especially when I told her I was in the first day of my menstruation. She also said that, if I wanted, I could remain there with her or any other room in the party until you guys were finished; but she could not let me in until Che gave her the OK."

I shook my head impatiently. "How did you resolve the problem? How are you here now?"

She smiled. "Well, I did what I learned from you. After Che said twice that he did not recognize who I am because that stupid man either didn't remember my name or ever know it in the first place, I asked Grisela—the woman in charge of my search—if they ever mentioned to Che that I am the future wife of the Commandantico. Oooh!" She smiled maliciously and nodded. "After I thought everything was lost and would not be able to get in, that worked! And, la! As the future wife of the Commandantico, they immediately let me in."

I smiled and shook my head. The table was about chest high on us with a broad tablecloth. I noticed how she very nonchalantly, inconspicuously had reached under the table and began to worm a little. I touched her shoulder with a finger and whispered, "Be careful of those guys across the table with the ambassador. They have all the signs of being G-2 or worse—they could be KGB agents working with Che. I believe that is why they were seated at our table."

She smiled and looked at me and then the man across from her, who had been staring at her since she sat down. She looked him in the eyes with a straight face. She leaned over to whisper in my ear. She murmured to me, "Don't say anything. Watch this. Look in that man's face as if you're angry."

I knew what she was trying to do, and I started to stare challengingly straight in the man's eyes. I wanted to convey annoyance at his staring, and it worked. A little shamefacedly, he turned away and started a conversation with his partner, pretending that he hadn't actually been looking at Chandee.

It was enough of a distraction to let her work freely and retrieve her pen from its hiding place. An announcement went out requesting silence and stating that Ramiro was going to introduce the program in a few seconds, which provided an additional distraction for Chandee. She picked up her white napkin and put it in her lap, then between her legs. Bringing one hand out, she said to me in a very soft voice, "Could you please with very great discretion take your napkin and pass it to me?"

I unrolled my napkin nonchalantly and nodded. I coughed a couple of times into it and dropped it onto my lap. I observed Chandee use the napkin to remove the pen, smeared with the convincing concoction of ketchup, fish sauce, mayonnaise, and mucus. She wiped it and removed the pen from the protective plastic. She cleaned the pen once more and put it on top of the clean napkin on my lap. Folding the napkin slightly, I took my beret off and put it on my lap. I scratched my hair, pretending I was giving relief to my scalp. She put the pen in my beret and then took the dirty napkin and plastic sleeve and slid it under the tablecloth on top of the table, and then discretely smoothed it down so that the slight bulge was not noticeable.

Everyone was paying attention to Ramiro, who was at the podium to begin speaking. I picked up my beret as if I were holding it before my chest. I used it to cover what I was really doing. Very carefully, very inconspicuously, I opened my shirt enough to gently slide the pen into the loops I had installed inside my shirt and then adjusted it so that the lens was correctly positioned. I then rebuttoned my shirt. Once I had finished, I began to work on my beret. I had already installed a second pen in the rim of it. I had purposefully "forgotten" in my search to take it off. I knew that, as Fidel's favored one, my status as the Commandantico, and my youth would all combine to make my searcher sympathetic towards my situation. I was already considered in his mind to be a trustworthy individual, and then the nature of a beret's construction led him to simply accept that I was hiding nothing.

It had been a great risk, though; had he actually taken it to search, I would have been discovered and would probably have never left that room alive. I had prepared the other side of my shirt, using the Communist pin to cover that lens hole.

Ramiro started to speak just as I had brought my two weapons to bear. He said, "After so many attempts to assassinate our Maximum Leader and to destroy our Socialist Revolution, Mr. Kennedy has finally met his Waterloo. He wound up a loser in the history of the world, without even knowing he consolidated this Revolution, which will last longer than any of us mortals. The Cuban Revolution is immortal. Every single individual who attempts to damage or stop her progress will end up like that imbecile Kennedy, who in his omnipotence began to believe himself to be indestructible, underestimating all of us. But we demonstrated to the world on the twenty-second of November, 1963, at twelve-thirty before thousands of spectators that no one is indestructible. In the same way the head of the serpent fell by the effort and drive of the international proletariat around the world, so also will the Yankee imperialists, every one of them, will be destroyed and brought to their knees, just as was JFK. *Patria o muerte, venceremos*[10]! I now yield the podium to the great leader and the mastermind of what we're celebrating today, Dr. Ernesto Guevara de la Serna, or as we call him in friendship, Che."

Everyone gave him a standing ovation as he rose to go to the podium. At my table, I smiled, knowing that

---

[10] Homeland or death, we will win.

everything in this function was going to be recorded and filmed. I took care to periodically fix my shirt to make sure I was getting the best angle. I wanted to make certain no one disturbed my panoramic view of the podium. Chandee took my hand under the table and we exchanged joyful looks. Our hearts were pounding like stampeding horses.

Che stood proudly at the podium, openly showing his satisfaction as his nostrils flared while he savored the triumph that was attributed to him, shared only by obligation with his cohort Fidel. After a few seconds, he adjusted his microphone, and quieted the noise of the ovation.

When everyone finally sat down in response to his gestures for silence, he said, "I will be very brief for three reasons. First, our comrade, Ramiro Valdez, has already said very eloquently everything I wanted to say. Second, I'm extremely anxious to hear from the lips of our international combatants the details and last-minute improvisations they had to pull off in order to take this enormous and ambitious plan to its successful end without being deterred by any impediments or obstacles—and they encountered quite a few. Some of them very serious. From the little I was able to get from them in our brief talk, they conquered all these wrinkles with tremendous sacrifice. It even cost the blood of one of their comrades and great friends, Yuri, who gave his life in order to bring success to the mission, which is what we are here joyfully celebrating today. For Yuri, I ask all present here to stand up in his memory to give him one minute of silence."

Everyone stood up and remained silent for one

minute. Once we were seated once more, Che continued. "It's really a pity, because I'm anxious to know all the details. I managed to finally speak with Marcelino and Marko only a couple of hours ago. From the moment they finished their mission, as a security measure for them as well as all of us, we have followed the strict guidelines we put into place for this operation. As soon as they arrived here, they were transported to one of our secure medical clinics in Santa Clara, where they submitted to intense surgery, as you can see."

He gestured to them, and they both stood and bowed. We once more gave them a standing ovation.

After the applause died down, Che said, "Today, only a few hours ago, we have been able, against the doctors' advice but under my personal responsibility as a physician, to bring them over here today out of that facility. They're not to have a drop of alcohol, because they are on antibiotics and anti-inflammatory medication. If any of you see them take a drink, you come over and let me know, OK? I'm like their papa now."

He paused while everyone laughed.

"They have asked me how the hell I can bring them to a party without letting them take even a shot of whiskey. I answer that they've already spent so much time in Yankeelandia that they've become bourgeoisie. No whiskey, no luxuries for them. My heroes have become corrupted too quickly!"

More laughter.

"But I promised them that in a few days I will take them to an exclusive beach where Fidel took me several years ago. Guardalavaca in Holguin Oriente. It's the most beautiful beach in the world, even better than Varadero.

Then they can drink all they want for a whole month without anyone bothering them!"

Everyone laughed once more, including Marcelino and Marko, who made gestures of happiness.

"Well," Che said, "my third reason is because everyone here knows it's not a good celebration if you don't have good food. We have great food, and I don't know about you guys, but I'm very hungry!" He patted his stomach. "*Patria o muerte, venceremos!*" He waved to everyone and pointed at the two men. "Let our heroic international fighters tell at least a small portion of their story."

Dr. Julio Antonio del Marmol

Chapter 7: The Enigma's Official Unveiling

Everyone stood up once more and applauded the men for a few minutes. Chandee, Canen, and I exchanged glances as we clapped.

Marcelino was the first one to take the microphone. "Whatever we do, the job is done by a team. Always within the team exists somebody who, for one reason or another, executes the most important roles in that particular mission. To me, it's very important to recognize this. A good Revolutionary is honest, and he has the duty to recognize the effort of that particular comrade. As Comrade Commandante Guevara said when they killed our friend and comrade Yuri, they not only killed an excellent friend and soldier who has been fighting by our side for a long time—they also took one of the most solid legs of the table of this operation. The tasks assigned to him were left in the air.

"Thanks to the extraordinary qualities and abilities that Marko possesses, he managed to complete his mission and at the same time assume the mission elements that were Yuri's with very little help from me.

"I myself almost fell into the hands of the police after everything had been done. I was supposed to leave the book depository to manage one of the most important details that had been Yuri's to handle. As I came down to the second floor and was ready to leave the building, a policeman came in and screamed at me by the side of the soda machine, 'Hey you! Stop right there! Who are you?'

"Roy Truly, the personnel supervisor, identified me immediately, believing that I was in fact Lee Harvey Oswald. I did not even have to speak. He took charge and told the police without allowing me to answer that he knew me and that I was one of his workers.

"The police officer, whose badge read 'Baker,' didn't bother me anymore with a single question. Unfortunately, though, he continued to linger and speak with Roy and other employees, questioning people. I had no choice but to hang around there wasting precious time so that I wouldn't draw attention to myself.

"I bought a soda from the machine and stayed there until the police took off. I was supposed to go to the movie theater, where Lee Harvey Oswald had been sitting for a while, and perform one of Yuri's assignments—to come in the front door without buying a ticket and then immediately leave by the back door, disappearing from everyone's view. I did that successfully, but a little late. Unfortunately, I did not feel this to be a great accomplishment. I should have been there half an hour earlier but for the incident with the police in the cafeteria.

"The day had gone wrong from the beginning, when it started to rain. This could have ruined all of our plans, as the President's convertible would not pass by with its top down. Thanks to destiny, as soon as Kennedy arrived at airport, the rain stopped."

Marcelino smiled and put his hand on Marko's shoulder. "This man is the real hero. Everything went wrong for me on this particular day and on this mission. By luck or whatever you want to call it, Marko saved the situation."

As Marcelino spoke, Marko stood a little behind him, waving his hands in mocking deprecation as Marcelino praised him. Every time Marcelino turned towards him to get some corroboration, however, he stopped his antics and looked serious, smiling and nodding his affirmation. Marcelino seemed to have no idea why people kept laughing. However, he appeared to be enjoying the response.

It crossed my mind that all of this was an act prepared by both comedians beforehand in order to promote each other as heroes without seeming to brag about their own accomplishments. They were professional spies, and professional spies have to be good actors.

Marcelino continued, "From the very start, I had terrible luck. I had to wait in the car in front of the building for over forty-five minutes until Oswald left the building so that I could replace him. He was supposed to receive a phone call from his clandestine case officer, who was to tell him to go to the movie theater, where he would receive information on the whereabouts of Marko and me. Then Oswald would let the dogs loose on us as he had done with Yuri, and we would both have been eliminated. That was Oswald's mission: to frustrate and destroy our operation. He had our decoy plan, but he didn't have the most important detail—that his case officer, his source of information, is a double-agent working on our side."

Marcelino paused and shook his head. He looked back at Marko who had until now remained silent. Marko leaned in toward the microphone and said, "Everything Marcelino has been telling you is exactly the truth—with one exception. I'm not a hero. The true hero is him." He pointed at Marcelino.

Marcelino put his hand once more on Marko's shoulder, smiled, and said, "Everything that went wrong that day happened to me and not to anybody else." Marcelino shook his head. "It went wrong to the point that I even got bit by a rat in the book depository at the exact moment I was squeezing the trigger to shoot my target on my first try."

Everybody laughed, thinking he was joking.

Enjoying the attention of the public, he raised his pants leg and exposed his ankle to the crowd, revealing a bite mark near the heel. "No, no—see for yourselves. Don't think I'm inventing this. The rat almost took a piece of my leg. Of course, I lost the shot, which was a disaster. The noise I made with the shot as it impacted in the street alerted everyone without even touching my target. This blew the element of surprise, diminishing the possibilities of successfully completing the operation. I hit the rat with the butt of my rifle and trained it back on my target right away.

"Then I heard one of the supervisors running upstairs, screaming Oswald's name. This made me lose concentration, and even though I made contact this time, I knew the shot would not be effective. When I heard that man on the stairs, I rushed the shot to abandon my position and hide the rifle in those boxes to avoid being caught red-handed. I knew I'd screwed up, and everything was going to be a fiasco. I could not take another shot without the risk of giving away my position."

He clapped Marko on the shoulder once more. "Thanks to Comrade Marko, things changed. From his key secondary position, he had patiently waited across the street behind the fence on that grassy knoll, where it turned out he had the perfect shot. Marko was positioned to take the last possible effective shot that could be made before we aborted. He accomplished that, and the rest I will let him tell you comrades himself. *Patria o muerte, venceremos*[11]!"

Marcelino stepped back, took Marko's left hand, raised it high, and pointed at him. People stood and applauded frenetically. Marko stood forward, pumped up by all Marcelino's compliments and by how seriously the crowd took his words.

Marcelino moved back to allow Marko to stand before the microphone. He pulled the microphone down a trifle. Only I had noticed until then that Marko was the shortest of the three, by perhaps a quarter of an inch. With a smile, he said, "I'll try to be very brief." He was interrupted by the crowd who started to yell protests, and they wanted to know more.

Marko raised both hands to get people to sit down and quiet down those who were voicing protest. "Well, well, well. As I tried to say before you guys interrupted me, I will try to be brief, since like Commander Guevara, I'm very hungry. But let me start by saying that the only true hero in all of this is Commander Ernesto Guevara. His years of brilliant and extraordinary persistence will inscribe in the pages of history that empires can indeed be brought down."

---

[11] Homeland or death, we shall prevail.

Everyone applauded Che.

It took Marko a while, but he finally got the crowd under control once more. Fidel, Raul, and Ramiro had no alternative but to stand and applaud each time, though I did not think any of them very much liked having Che be the center of attention. I kept my eyes on Fidel to assess his reactions.

"I have to add to what Commander Guevara said about our fallen comrade, Yuri, because he was the best of us. When Jack Ruby brought us the president's itinerary route, which he'd bought from an employee in the Texas governor's office, Yuri was not satisfied. He wanted one from another source to corroborate its veracity. So Ruby brought another, this one from the Dallas Police Department. Yuri was still dissatisfied. Finally, Ruby brought him a copy with the stamp of the Secret Service. Only then was he happy."

Marko paused and raised his hand high, pointing upwards. "That, I call tenacity and efficiency. I want you guys to give a very loud ovation to our great comrade who gave his life to accomplish this mission."

Once more, there was thunderous applause.

"Thanks to that tenacity and efficiency," Marko continued once the applause died down, "Marcelino and I are alive today." He gave a reverence into the air. "Thanks once more, Comrade Yuri, wherever you are today.

"I should also add something with the honesty and humbleness that characterizes every internationalist soldier. When we have to cover one of the assignments required of men who died during the mission, we have the duty to leave everything behind us completely clean and without any traces, just as the plan required. Yuri was to plant some evidence in Lee Harvey Oswald's residence, and I took on that part of the operation. I almost destroyed the work in fractions of seconds when a policeman stopped me on my way to the extraction point as I was leaving his apartment. When I tried to persuade him to not take me to the station for more questioning, he remained dissatisfied with my answers, and I unfortunately had no other alternative but to shoot him on the spot. This policeman could have ruined everything and been a dangerous witness left behind. He, unfortunately, became a casualty of the mission."

He paused for a moment. "I want to clarify one more thing of vital importance. If it had not been for those lost shots of Comrade Marcelino, the president's chauffeur would not have braked almost to a stop. I would not have had the excellent opportunity to take that money shot. Tendering my apologies to Comrade Marcelino, if any one of us, with the exception of Comrade Yuri, is without discussion a hero, it is my great best friend and comrade in combat—Marcelino. It has been the greatest honor to share this historical operation with him, proving to the world what a Socialist Marxist-Leninist country is capable of doing. *Patria o muerte, venceremos!*"

Both men hugged each other as the crowd went crazy. They separated and he said, "OK, everyone. Let's enjoy the sumptuous meal the Revolution has provided us today!"

The applause continued until both men, accompanied by Che, Fidel, Raul, and Ramiro, went inside the house.

The servants started to bring the food out, along with jars of wine, beer, orange juice, and ice water. Conversation buzzed across the terrace, and the food was a typical Cuban meal of white rice, black beans, roast pork, and *yucca con mojo.*

After we finished dinner, I leaned back in my chair and said, "I think I've eaten enough for today and tomorrow."

I took one of two good cigars out of my pocket, with the idea of possibly getting rid of the other men if they didn't like smoke, so that we could speak more freely. However, one man, who identified himself as an officer in military counterintelligence, asked me for a cigar.

"This is from Che's stock," I told him. His friend, who was his ADC, asked for one as well. Both of them received my secretly medicated cigars, and they thanked me. I then offered one to the French ambassador. He looked at me as if he had seen the Devil himself and then at the cigar in my hand. He shook his head violently and shuddered. Clearly, he remembered the last time he'd had one of Che's cigars that I had prepared for him.

He said, "No, no, no. Thank you very much. I'm not a smoker anymore. I quit." He raised his eyebrows. "Ever since that time when last we got together, remember?"

I took the cigar back and leaned back. I replaced the cigar. "Yes, yes, I remember. You got sick from those chocolates. Either you guys ate too much or they were fermented."

Chandee turned away to hide her smile.

Canen said, "I don't smoke, but you know what? Seeing you guys smoking—give me one of those."

At that moment, Che walked up with Marko and Marcelino and introduce them to Canen. Canen congratulated them, and Che asked me, "Are those the cigars I gave you a long time ago? You still have them?"

I grinned broadly. "Yes, I left a bunch in my mother's

house in Pinar del Rio and brought them from there today."

Che looked at me and said, "They should have an exquisite flavor now, because they been cured for so long."

Both men had already lit up and were making comments of appreciation. They raised their cigars on high as if showing off their glory. Little did they know the glory would be short-lived and they would end up soon at the door to Hell with their anuses completely on fire.

Che said, "Would you give me one of those?"

I raised my eyebrows. Nothing would give me greater pleasure than to give that man one of them, but I only had one unmedicated cigar left, and Canen had already asked me for one. Even though I wanted with all my heart to give Che one of the treated ones, I knew that Che had some medical training. It could be very dangerous, because after he recovered from his illness, he might have the residue analyzed and discover the truth. It was a life-threatening risk for me to take.

In those seconds of indecision, Che said, "What about it? You don't want to give me one? I'll give you another box before you leave. I only want to taste one of those cigars that you've had so long because they're so cured."

I made up my mind and handed him the remaining safe one and handed Marcelino and Marko medicated ones. With pain in my heart, I gave Canen the last medicated cigar I had, thinking that as soon as Che and the others left I was going to get it away from him, either by changing it with mine or otherwise getting it out of his mouth. It was unnecessary, since God always protects the innocent. Canen had not even brought the cigar to his mouth.

Che noticed it looked darker and thicker. "Canen, you have the most luck. From that color and thickness," he said, "that must have the best flavor of all of them. I think that because you're his brother-in-law, he picked the best for you. There's no doubt—look at that cigar and look at this one."

Canen was a little embarrassed. He was very proper and well-mannered, and held out his cigar to him. "Che, the truth is I'm not a smoker. I was going to light it just for the heck of it, because I saw all these guys here at the table enjoying theirs."

Che courteously declined. "No, no—I was just joking. It's OK. It's all the same."

Canen insisted and finally convinced Che by saying, "It would really be a pity, Che, if I light this cigar that you like so much, and I'm not even a smoker."

"OK," Che said as he traded cigars with Canen. He lit it, and after a few minutes, the three of them walked inside.

As soon as they left, I said to Canen, "I think it's time to leave."

He had no idea of what was about to happen soon. I was actually very concerned, since I still had my pens, and I did not want to be around if Che decided to have us arrested. I had never told Canen what had happened at meeting in the French ambassador's house.

Canen nodded. "Yes, we should leave, since I have to get up very early tomorrow morning."

After the half hour we had been there, it was easy to see a large number of people were intoxicated. We walked out to get our car, and Paco drove up to pick us up. Two of Che's bodyguards came up to us.

"Commandantico, Che wants to see you inside."

My heart sank. But I said to Canen and Chandee, "It's probably nothing, he probably wants to say goodbye. I'll be back in a minute."

I walked inside following one guard and the other followed behind me, a little more like I was being escorted rather than accompanied. Thousands of possibilities flashed through my brain, and I repented my audacity in bringing those stupid cigars to the party, since I had under my shirt what I needed. It was possible that Pierre had taken his medicated cigar to a lab and kept the news all to himself. Now that he had seen me give out more cigars to Che and the others, he might have given warning. I knew the ambassador was Che's friend and a fellow internationalist. I held my breath and put my hand to my chest, touching the pens I had concealed there. I began to perspire profusely, and my heart pounded like the drums of the firing squad in my ear.

At the end of the corridor the first guard knocked on the door. I heard Che's voice say, "Come in."

As I entered the room, I saw everyone with serious faces: Che, Pierre, Marcelino, and Marko, as well as both officers from the counterintelligence. They stopped their conversation as I walked in. Che looked at me and said, "Why are you guys leaving so early?"

"Canen has to be on base very early in the morning."

Che nodded appreciatively and took a long draw on his cigar, and my stomach heaved. I thought I was about to lose my dinner.

Che stood up and raised it on high. "This is the best cigar I've smoked in all the years I've been smoking." He walked over to the library and took down two boxes. "I'm going to ask you a great favor."

"Sure," I said, more relaxed.

"All I ask in exchange for your present is that you take one of the boxes I'm giving you now in the same place for the same amount of time as before, and bring it back to me."

"Of course," I said. "What else can I do as a thanks for the beautiful boxes you've given me?"

He came over and hugged me, and I immediately felt the pens against my chest. Goosebumps covered my flesh as I thought he could not help but feel the pens, and I began to sweat once more. Apparently, though, he had drunk enough that he didn't notice anything during the hug. He said, "Remember what I told you. I have great plans for you."

"Thank you."

"Go ahead, go. Have a great evening."

I turned and left the room feeling like I was about to throw up at any moment. Chandee looked worried as she waited for me next to Canen. He smiled when he saw the two boxes in my arms. She hugged me and murmured in my ear, "Thank God it's only that and nothing else."

Canen said, "There's no doubt in my mind that no matter what, Che, with all his craziness, looks at you like the son he wishes he had."

I shook my head as we got into the Buick. "Let's hope he doesn't love me like the Devil loves his son—that he loves him so much he pokes his eyes out to carry in his pocket so he has his son with him all the time."

We drove for half an hour and entered Havana. I asked Canen if he could pull over so I could make a phone call. I needed to call my uncle, and with all the excitement about the party I had forgotten. Canen told Paco to pull over the first place he saw a public phone. Paco slowed down, looked around, and finally pulled into a gas station. He used the opportunity to fill the car's gas tank and clean the windshields while I called my uncle. I gave him the emergency code and said that I would meet him at the Club Nautico in one hour. When I got back to the car I saw that Canen was not there. I asked Chandee where he had gone.

"He said he had to go to the bathroom."

"OK, I have to go as well."

I went to the bathroom to find Canen. When I got there, I said to him, "Please don't take Chandee to her house. I want to take her for a walk on the beach. I'm not feeling a hundred percent with my stomach, and I want to take a walk and spend some time with her before the night ends."

He looked at me in astonishment. "God, you just spent a week with her, and you haven't had enough yet? Love, love!"

"Come on, don't bug me, OK?"

"Don't worry about it, but come back early, OK? We'll go to the base in the Soviet jeep early in the morning. Enjoy the rest of the evening, OK?"

"OK," I said. We finished our trip to the farm. Paco and Canen said goodnight to us, and I got into the driver's seat while Chandee climbed in front. We then drove into the Miramar district and our meeting at the Club Nautico.

We didn't have to wait long, as my uncle arrived early. We greeted and hugged each other and sat down. I gave him a debriefing of some of the things we had learned at Che's party. My uncle could not believe we had been able to accomplish not only recording but also videotaping the entire event without incident. We talked for a while, he asked me, "Where are the pens?"

I replied, "The pens? There was only one pen."

He looked at me seriously and asked in surprise, "You didn't make two copies?"

"Two copies?" I shook my head in complete surprise. "It was extremely difficult to bring in one pen—where did you think I would bring my second pen? Up my anus? That's something I won't do, because even a suppository disgusts me."

He said, "Yes, yes, yes, that's true. I'm sorry, I don't even know what I was thinking. I'm sorry, please."

I took one of the pens out of my uniform pocket and handed it to him. "First thing in the morning, I will put this in the courier's hands to deliver with priority to Guantanamo base to get it in the hands of Langley with a request to be seen by the new president, Johnson."

"Very well," I replied. "I believe this mission is completed. Now let's see what the United States government, or more precisely what the Johnson Administration, does with this."

We hugged each other and left. Chandee and I walked towards the beach, leaving the car in the parking lot. We sat down under one of the palm umbrellas. I rested my body against the pole, while Chandee reclined against my chest. Under the star-filled sky we kissed each other tenderly. She said, "Where in the hell did your uncle come up with the idea that you had two pens?"

I smiled. "I don't know, but that kind of caught me very much by surprise. Unless he has somebody in there, another spy, just in case we failed."

Chandee turned and looked at me. "No, that's not possible. Besides, let's assume that it's like you say. He would tell us so that he wouldn't send us to take an unnecessary risk."

I smiled and shook my head with a knowing look. "You have a lot to learn. You don't think that my uncle has the capability to have somebody there without telling us, because that could compromise the other contact in case we're apprehended? In something of such extreme importance that could break this government and save millions of lives?"

Chandee shook her head. "That's not fair. Then why make us go through all this agony and danger without even informing us in case something goes wrong so that we can support each other? I think you're creating things with your supersonic mind."

I smiled.

She asked me, "You wouldn't do that to me, would you?"

I did not change my expression.

She pursed her lips and shook her head in recrimination. Half-jokingly, half surprised, she said, "Julio Antonio Marmol." She continued staring at me as I continued to smile. "No, you could not ever do that to me."

I took the other pen out and showed it to her. She clapped her hands to her mouth. "How did you do that?"

I took the Communist pin and showed her a small hole in it. I said, "The same way we did together the one in the valley, I did the other one while you slept at my house in Guane."

She asked, "Where did you hide it?" She looked at me

slightly disgusted. "Don't tell me you put it.... No!"

I took off my beret and put the pen inside it, and then handed it to her.

She took it and said, "But they searched all the clothes, and I notice this inside!"

I replied, "They never took the beret in their hands."

She put a hand to her mouth. "No? How did you manage that?"

I described to her how I had done it.

After I finished, she said, "Julio Antonio del Marmol! Why did you take such a risk? For what? What do you need another one for? For what purpose?"

"For many purposes. The first one, what if you had to drop that pen in the bathroom like I told you to do? Then I have a spare one. Second, I wanted to have insurance, like my uncle told me to have so many times. This is a secret so powerful and so highly classified that the American government might be afraid it could lead to the end of the world. They might decide not to confront the enemy, even though it would be the most cowardly cover-up in the history of the twentieth century. But in the world in which we live today, it's also an inexorable reality. Now, just imagine for a few seconds—anyone can blow that whistle, but we have it in our hand. You know what that signifies? If one of us is ever in danger or someone tries to destroy us like they destroyed the noble spy and Marine, Lee Harvey Oswald—the only real hero in all this story—all we have to do is blow the whistle."

I brought the pen up to my lips. "Heaven knows—maybe the world will be blown into pieces, or maybe we'll save the world from such an elaborate, gigantic lie."

Chandee hugged me and kissed me tenderly on the

lips. "You are my only and wonderful hero. You always think of me before yourself."

I smiled. "Thank you. But it takes two to dance a mambo, and you are my hero."

We both stayed there, staring up at the beautiful star-filled sky of that Wednesday, November 27, 1963. We stayed there for a few minutes in silence, and I finally broke it. "Blessed are not only those who possess material wealth, but more blessed are the ones who possess important secrets of great scale that can guarantee, under any circumstance, the security not only of themselves but also those others who surround them in the course of their lives in this crazy world in which we live today."

Chandee smiled. "In that case, I feel very secure by your side. We should never be separated."

After a few days, I met with Che at his house in Boca Siega, I heard from the mouth of a not-too-happy horse that everything had not gone as they had predicted. The debriefing with Marcelino and Marko had led us to believe that everything had gone smoothly and satisfactorily. The reality, however, was that they had left out many important details. Che, to demonstrate his confidence in me, shared them.

"Yuri," he said, "not only was supposed to go to the movie theater where Oswald was to be, but to get the attention of the ticket window, he was to bypass the main window so that the person selling tickets would notify the police. That would have given us a record of when the police were called and by whom. He was supposed to go there, kill Oswald with a silencer, and plant a suicide note in his pocket that would make it appear that he was the only one behind the assassination and that he was filled with remorse over it. He was then to leave by the back door.

"In the meantime, the man who'd called Oswald to meet in the theater was already there, maintaining surveillance. His instructions were to wait and watch for Oswald to enter, but later on *another* man who looked the same would come in and enter the theater without buying a ticket. As soon as this man saw that happen, he was then supposed to call Ruby, who would then alert his contact in the police department that the bird had entered the nest."

"What went wrong?" I asked. "Sounds like Oswald should not have been taken alive."

"Unfortunately for Marcelino, he was half an hour late in getting there. By the time he had located Oswald, the police were arriving, and it was too late for him to do the job. He had no choice but to fade into the background and put on his disguise. Unfortunately for us, because Oswald had paid for his ticket, the stub was found in his pocket. When they processed at the Dallas Central Police station, they found it. One of our mysterious agents floating around him made sure to take that and have it destroyed."

Che's disappointment was obvious.

"What about the fifth wheel I met—Arzate? Did you ever find his body?" I asked.

"Arzate was a *great* disappointment to me," he continued. "As it turns out, he's still alive." Che shook his head in disgust. "Can you believe it? He had simply cut himself shaving while in the shower, which is where the blood on the shower curtain and the towel came from. After that, he dropped off the radar, the moron!

"He was supposed to be the most efficient and capable man in the entire group, which is why he was held back as our spare. One of his assignments was to stay in the area where the action was to take place—not too close, but not too far, either. That way, he would be available to respond to anything very rapidly."

"What happened to him?" I prompted. "From your tone, it doesn't appear that he was killed in action."

"Like any human being, though, he isn't perfect. Indeed, he's further from perfection than most people. He is a typical Spaniard with a high level of testosterone, and he ran across a beautiful blue-eyed blonde from Madrid with a monumental figure—an international model in many European and North American magazines. They met the night before in the restaurant of the hotel he was staying at, and after a few glasses of wine he got a little tipsy. He fell in love with her seductive beauty and could not say 'no' when she invited him over to her house. It was far beyond the perimeter within which he was supposed to stay, and so he was about half an hour from any of the operations that he wasn't supposed to abandon.

"He wasn't merely a standby for contingencies. He was also to make sure that the most important detail of the entire operation was accomplished: to be certain that Lee Oswald was not to survive long enough to open his mouth. They called him several times to replace Yuri, but he was unreachable. They left several encrypted messages for him at his hotel. The most important role he had was containment. He was to see to it that what was really going on never leaked out. In disguise, after the job was done, he was to simply leave the theater like any normal person."

The main thing that Che had tried to prevent happening, as it turned out, is what occurred. Before the cameras of the entire world, Oswald was able to leak out the crucial detail that he was only a patsy. I've seen Che enraged many times, and this was the absolute worst I had ever seen with him. The kindest thing he called Arzate was *gallego imbecil*[12]. He had broken intelligence protocol by having contact with a stranger—and one of the opposite sex—within forty-eight hours before the execution of an operation. This could wind up having been a trap set for the agent, which could then result in the destruction of the entire operation. He had also put his own life at risk.

"What about that model? Won't she recognize who he appeared to be and tell people she spent the night with Lee Harvey Oswald?"

Che shook his head and replied, "Fortunately, he did manage to retain enough wits to remember one crucial rule. He was to remain in disguise until and unless activated, so this model won't be able to identify him should she talk to anyone. As they say here in Cuba, an ass and a tit pulls more than a wagon. Evidently that beautiful woman managed to distract our best and most competent agent. Who would ever believe that? A master to perfection in everything he had done before, now completely disgraced. And not just with me—that perfect

---

[12] Imbecile Galician, a regional stereotype similar in America to calling someone a redneck.

imbecile has disgraced him before the entire entourage! Not only did he sleep outside his perimeter, he overslept between the legs of that sculptured, seductive beauty from Madrid." He shook his head in disgust. "That could only happen to a Spaniard or a nigger!"

It was clear to me that this beautiful woman would cost Arzate his life. I didn't want to ask Che what they were going to do with him upon his return to Cuba and the confession of his negligence and subordination to Che in person. I didn't have to, because Che finished the conversation with revealing it.

He said grimly, "Arzate will never, *never* spoil any of our future operations."

I took that as confirmation that Arzate was about to die, if he was not already dead. I knew that Che didn't wait long, and that luckless agent would wind up suffering the same fate as the unfortunate Claudio, with his brains blown out all over the highway. Arzate turned out to be a genuine ghost. Even the other doubles would never see him again.

I asked him, "Why did Jack Ruby break cover like that?"

Che snorted. "He was the ultimate standby. As it turned out, he was a better one than Arzate. He enacted Plan D. Once that was put into play, Jack moved his contacts in the Dallas Police Department so that he could attend to the execution of Oswald personally, as soon as possible. This is by no means the ideal alternative; Marko and Marcelino decided they trusted Ruby more than anyone else to finish the job. Given the emergency of the situation, they had to proceed quickly to prevent further damage. It was the only alternative to provide complete damage control."

I was struck once more by how meticulously planned this operation had been. Che's casual reference to Plan D was an indication how deeply he had planned for contingencies. Another point was making me curious.

"What about Oswald's comment to the press? You could see the news of the president's death came as a shock to him."

"It will remain in history a lingering puzzle," Che answered. "No witnesses exist that can corroborate what he said, and both sides of the intelligence network will protect their own interests, preferring to bury the truth in the same coffin as Oswald. For completely different reasons, each side will try to convince the public that Oswald was the sole assassin involved in this act.

"This tremendously embarrassing failure for American intelligence will leave a large black stain in the pages of their history due to the incapacity and negligence they are the victims of. They underestimated the efficiency of their enemy, and it has cost them the life of their Commander-in-Chief."

A few days after this conversation, I walked along the beach close to the Boca Siega house. I was waiting to share a ride home. On my way back, I saw a group of curious people surrounding something that looked like a fish or perhaps a dolphin. A large, dark object lay on the sand in their midst.

The small group included a young mulatto wearing a life guard T-shirt. He was trying to clean the marine algae and seaweed off of the object. As I got closer, I realized it was the body of a man. He was wrapped completely in a fishing net filled with vegetation, as if it had been in the ocean for several days.

The lifeguard was able to use his knife to finally cut the remaining threads on the net. As he pulled, the body rolled over, revealing the face of the corpse. The lifeguard jumped back in surprise. Everyone in the crowd could see that the man lying there had been horribly mutilated in the face. His nose had been cut off, along with the upper lip. The lower lip hung on by a thin shred of flesh. Half of the scalp in the front was missing, revealing the bare cranium.

After the young man recovered from his shock, he continued his attempts to remove the seaweed from the body. As more and more of the corpse was revealed, it looked quite desiccated, as if it had been dropped into a vat of acid. He pulled once more, and the corpse turned face down, exposing the neck.

Close the hairline along the neck, I could see a small tattoo, black, blue, and red. It was a Chinese dragon. I had noticed it before on Arzate when I met him. I was not surprised by any of this, as it validated my suspicions. I was reassured beyond doubt that he was yet another victim in the long list of crimes Che dragged in his diabolical shadow around the world. However, in spite of my lack of surprise, I felt chills all over my body and an uncomfortable sensation in my stomach. My discomfort rose at the thought of how close I had been to such a sadistic man, who was not content to merely kill an enemy, but to utterly destroy any trace of his existence by mutilation of the corpse and dumping it in acid.

I looked up and saw in the distance police cars approaching. With them were other government security vehicles, and I decided that it was time for me to leave. I walked towards the house, thinking how accurate I had been in predicting Arzate's murder. Che probably shot him in the head, and left the rest of the work to his assistants. They probably took him out in one of the yachts, wrapped the body in the netting with heavy weights, and dropped the bundle into the deep ocean. Perhaps they hadn't secured the heavy object enough, and the motion of the waves caused it to drop out, allowing the body to surface. I thought it ironic that the tide would bring it in so close to the safe house used by the criminals.

I hoped that no one brought this news to Che's ears. If that happened, the assistants would be revealed as being insufficient to fulfill the job to Guevara's level of expectation and so would wind up sharing the same fate of having their mouths filled with seaweed like Arzate, their partner in crime. I remembered at that moment a passage in the Bible that read: "Those who live by the sword will die by the sword."

Chapter 8: The Lady of the White Rose

Hotel Miguel Angel

As I later discovered from the lips of some of the participants, another story was developing at the same time Marcelino and Marko were meeting with us at the debriefing party Che held at his house. It took place in Madrid, Spain, in the grand banquet room in the elegant, luxury hotel called Miguel Angel. This was neither a military, political, nor intelligence celebration; it was an award ceremony recognizing excellence in international journalism, modeling, and other categories. The awards were given to the prominent magazines from around the world, not only for their political articles but also for the beauty and design for their front and back covers, as well as their artists, models, and writing. The winners received a gold statue and great recognition as well as a large check in compensation for the excellent work they had performed throughout the previous year.

The spacious banquet room had been rented for the event, decorated with the most refined taste required of an event at this level. The organizers wanted their names to shine in the reporting in the various periodicals of the ceremony.

"The winner this year for Best Cover in the International Awards is Natacha Sausa," the emcee announced. "She is the pride of Madrid. Give her a huge round of applause."

The audience rose to their feet. The beautiful, statuesque, blue-eyed blonde beamed as she walked to the podium. She wore a black evening dress cut in the back down to her rear, highlighting her tiny waist and shapely hips. Two gentlemen helped her up the stairs as the ovation continued unabated. Everyone cheered her accomplishment save for three women sitting in a side corner table.

They each had their own exotic beauty. They were dressed to the hilt with the most elegant, fashionable clothing Europe could provide and accessorized with jewelry likewise designed by the most famous jewelers in the world. All of their faces, while impeccably made up to enhance their beauty, nevertheless displayed something uncommon in most female faces: coldness, dangerous confidence, and harsh insensitivity. These characteristics were certainly seen far more often in men than in such beautiful women, especially at that time.

These three women were Tanya, Sonya, and Yoska, Che's elite international squad of assassins, tasked to take out anyone Guevara identified as an enemy of the Revolution or his ideas. They looked at each other as they listened to the compliments being showered down on Natacha. They raised their eyebrows unsympathetically. No words were needed to share with each other their opinions. Their expressions were smugly superior.

Natacha gave a brief speech of humble appreciation to everyone supporting her through the ups and downs of her career. She was teary eyed as she invoked God's blessing on those who were too numerous to mention in the brief time allotted for her speech.

The public, very touched by her graceful acceptance, gave her an even more thunderous ovation. It was almost more than Che's agents could take. They rolled their eyes mockingly at each other, and one of them tossed a napkin on the table to display her disgust.

Tanya muttered to the others, "This is a bimbo's award."

After finishing her emotional speech, Natacha stepped away from the podium and walked down the red carpet. As she sat back down at the large table with her group of friends, she wiped a few tears from her eyes. The ceremony continued on as more awards were handed out in other categories. The spectators continued in suspense as they waited breathlessly for the announcement of each winner. Their glasses of champagne bore the beautiful logo of the hotel, and each table held bottles in ice buckets to maintain a proper chill for the beverage.

Occasionally one could hear a scream of joy as some

nominee was announced as the winner. That person would cheer as he or she stood up and walked rapidly to claim the award. As all of this went on, Che's three Amazons never took their eyes off of Natacha. They followed her every movement. They could not help but compare Natacha's beauty to their own, and it was evident that she was at least equal to the three of them combined. They watched her laugh as she celebrated with her friends the greatest accomplishment of her career. She had not a single care in the world, and the sweet naivety shone in comparison to the cynical, hard-bitten expressions each of the Amazons wore on her face.

Natacha stood up, saying something to the others at her table. She walked towards the bathrooms.

The three assassins opened their purses completely in unison, as if they were performing a dance they had practiced extensively. They covered their action with napkins. Reaching into their purses, they each took small Russian Makarov pistols in one hand while they carefully screwed silencers on to the barrels with the other. They stood up and followed Natacha.

As they walked into the hallway, Natacha greeted well-wishers and thanked them for their congratulatory statements. The three women watched as Natacha entered the women's bathroom in the lobby. Like a well-trained Special Forces team, Tanya used hand signals to command Sonya to follow her while Yoska stood guard by the only door. With practiced precision, the three women moved out to carry out their orders.

Sonya followed Tanya very closely. Both women kept their right hands inside their purses. The bathroom was vast, with stalls lining both walls. Tanya signaled for Sonya to check the right-hand line of stalls, while she took the left. Using her free hand, each woman methodically went down her line, checking the stalls one at a time.

Like the rest of the hotel, the bathroom was luxurious. It was also completely empty. Tanya and Sonya finished going down their respective lines without finding anyone. They looked up at the vast mirror in surprised confusion. Wordless, Tanya pointed for Sonya to check one utility room while she headed to another.

Tanya reached her door first, as it was the closer of the two. When she opened her door, she had the biggest surprise in her life as a hand reached out from the darkness and sprayed her in the eyes with some chemical substance which stung badly and blinded her at once. She grunted in pain, something unusual for her.

Blind as a bat, she reached inside her purse for her weapon while she wiped at her eyes with her sleeve. Sonya turned and headed to the assistance of her comrade. Both had been taken by surprise, but Sonya was able to recover in order to react, pulling the pistol as she turned. With catlike speed, Natacha jumped out of the closet barefoot. One shoe in her hand, she charged Sonya and impaled her hand with the metal spike of the heel. She then sprayed Sonya with the same chemical as she had Tanya.

Sonya gasped in pain as she clutched at both eyes, dropping her purse onto the ground. The half-cleared pistol clattered onto the floor, the weapon discharging with a quiet pop. The injured hand streamed blood from the puncture wound left by the heel. Also blinded, she tried to check her hand, squeezing pressure points in an attempt to alleviate the excruciating pain there. The bullet from the shot went through Tanya's left ankle.

Now both women were injured as well as in pain. They had been caught completely by surprise. They could not comprehend how this bimbo could do this to them—three highly-trained professionals. Tanya stuck two fingers in her mouth and whistled shrilly, signaling to Yoska their distress. Neither of them could see what was going on. Sonya adopted a pose of self-defense as she attempted to discern where her assailant was. Tanya blindly trained her pistol around the room. The pair of them looked more like something out of a pantomime than any real threat.

Save for Tanya's whistle, all of this happened in virtual silence. No word had been spoken on either side. When Yoska approached them, she found both of them dancing before the mirror in that ridiculous fashion. As soon as Tanya had whistled, Natacha slid into the alcove by the entrance, slipping past Yoska as she burst in and quietly leaving the bathroom undetected.

Yoska rushed to pick up Sonya's purse. She went over and took Tanya's pistol and put it back in her purse.

Sonya said, "That woman—she attacked us. Didn't you see her?"

"No," Yoska replied, "I came in as soon as I heard your whistle, but she's not in here."

As Yoska helped them wash their eyes in the lavatory sink, Tanya asked in frustration, "How did you not see her? You were by the door the whole time!"

"I told you, Tanya—I walked in as soon as you whistled. She could have slipped out when I came in here."

Tanya exclaimed, "I can't believe this happened to *us*! I can't believe it!"

She grew more agitated, and the other two women

worked hard at calming her down.

Tanya said to them, "One thing you have to promise me—Che must *never* know about this. This will be a huge blow to his confidence in us, and he'll never trust us again. This has to be buried right here and now."

Sonya handed Tanya some paper towels. Mistaking where Sonya was, Tanya turned and hit the wall full tilt with her head.

Yoska said, "Tanya, you have to calm down. We have to get you and Sonya to a doctor, make sure that whatever you got sprayed with doesn't permanently take away your sight."

When Tanya heard that, she and Sonya bumped into each other in their blindness. Yoska grabbed them each by an arm.

"You have to walk in a straight line with me," Yoska said. "I can see, you can't. Now let's go!" Yoska carefully led the two women out to the car. She got into the driver's seat, and they drove off.

A few hours later, they were examined by one of the doctors used by their intelligence forces. He informed them that the blindness could last for anywhere from a few hours to a full day. He gave them something to put on their eyes and then treated their wounds.

He cautioned, "Do not let anyone in Madrid see that bullet wound. They are bound by law to report such injuries to the authorities and could lose their license if they don't comply."

Tanya was extremely upset. "I can't believe we're incapacitated for twenty-four hours. Yoska, you have to remain here to protect us. This is the most embarrassing, ridiculous situation I've ever been in my entire life!"

Tanya's protests continued until they reached the hotel where they were staying. It was apparent that the blonde who had managed to distract Che's most trustworthy, reliable agent Arzate had turned out after all to be more than just a pretty face. She had not only handled the attempt to assassinate her very well, she also had managed to temporarily put out of business two out of three of Che's elite Amazons. Skillfully, she had walked out of that trap without a single scratch, right in the middle of the public.

The information I later obtained of these developments revealed that Che had sent these women out of pure, hateful revenge to kill that blonde model merely because she nearly had spoiled years of work spent developing the operation to assassinate John F. Kennedy.

Initially, it never occurred to Che that this woman was a spy planted intentionally by his enemies to do exactly what she had done. He questioned that Arzate had simply fallen asleep, as the hapless spy had confessed to him during debriefing. Che suspected that some professional spy had drugged Arzate's drink that night in the hotel where he had been staying. The sole object would be to distract him and make it look like a casual meeting between a man and a woman, all the while protecting her cover.

Immediately following the successful assassination, Che had wasted no time in sending his investigators, who conducted a meticulous investigation and spoke to everyone in the hotel, including the bartender and desk employees. Not one of the employees had ever seen the blonde inside the hotel itself. However, they corroborated having seen her in Arzate's company for several hours, having a good time in the hotel bar. They also established that they had later left the hotel together.

That is when Che reached the conclusion that this was no casual meeting; she must have been a plant. When Che briefed Tanya, Sonya, and Yoska, none of them believed Che. They took the mission to eliminate the woman in the most discreet way, making certain her body was never found. However, they also thought it would be an easy walk in the park, that Che's paranoia had created all the drama, and that this was just an empty-headed bimbo, a pawn of the real enemy.

Instead, Natacha took all three of them completely by surprise. That night, the Amazons discussed the situation and decided that Che had been correct after all, his paranoia notwithstanding. At least they had discovered for a fact that the model's reality corresponded with the scenario Che had described and was indeed a professional spy. After many hours of frustrated conversation, the women said goodnight to each other. Tanya and Sonya's eyes were still very irritated, but their vision was gradually returning, although everything was shadowy, as if seen through smoke.

They had followed the doctor's instructions exactly. Indeed, the compresses they were supposed to apply every four hours they applied every two.

Eventually, they fell asleep in defeated frustration. Though their temperamental mindsets would not allow the sharing of a room, their three rooms were all adjacent, with adjoining doors connecting them. They were staying at one of the most luxurious hotels in all of Madrid, even more expensive than the Miguel Angel, which was not up to their standards. To maintain their cover as political assassins, they had to maintain the appearance of a certain level of lifestyle and so always used that excuse to stay at the most expensive hotels available. After all, they were completely financed by the Cuban government, all the while the ordinary citizens had to work all night just in order to buy a loaf of bread. This is the hypocrisy of socialist ideology.

Even though the three rooms connected with one another, the interior doors were locked for privacy's sake. They would have to knock in order to enter another room, just as if they had gone into the corridor outside. The presidential suites they occupied were normally taken only by visiting heads of state due to the high daily room rate.

By around 3:00 a.m., all three women were sound asleep. The ninth-floor window overlooked a beautiful panoramic view of the city of Madrid, with a few cars still driving in the streets. On the small balcony of one of the suites appeared a silhouetted figure which descended a blackened nylon mountaineering rope. Using a master key, the form opened one of the glass doors and very slowly, to minimize noise, opened the door.

As the double door opened, it jammed against the chair set up against it. A hand reached in carefully and quietly to slide the chair to one side so that the door could fully open. It was Yoska's suite.

The silhouette was dressed all in black. A black cloth wound all about the head, leaving only slight gaps for eyes and mouth. The cloth wound down around the neck and was tucked inside a tight black suit with a belt containing several pouches. The overall effect was reminiscent of a ninja.

The figure carefully shut the door after entering the suite, opened a compartment on the belt, and lightly bit down on something from inside. Slowly, very carefully, with hands held out in combat preparedness, the prowler crossed the floor, one step at a time, cautiously looking for traps along the way.

The figure approached the bed and leaned forward to make sure that Yoska, who slept with a black face mask, was not a dummy.

The silhouette stepped back and reached into a pouch, pulling out a small syringe, then leaned over Yoska, needle at the ready. Yoska was sleeping with several pillows, and it was difficult to immediately spot the precise spot on her neck where the injection had to occur. The figure located the right spot, leaned in a little more, and raised the arm holding the syringe.

At that moment, Yoska moved rapidly, pulling her hand out from under the covers as she dropped her act of sleeping. She held a large Arabic janbiya dagger, twelve inches long, and very sharp. She slashed at the intruder's upper chest, cutting it slightly. The figure jumped back, even as Yoska slashed again, this time missing.

Yoska screamed, "I've been waiting for you, bitch! How do you like this?"

The invader spoke not a word but took one step back. White flesh gleamed in the darkness from the cut in the suit, and a red line of blood seeped down the front. A hand immediately clapped onto the wound to apply pressure. Yoska reached under her pillow, obviously going for another weapon, fully exposing her neck. The figure sharply compressed an arm against its abdomen and spat out a dart, which flew with extreme accuracy and embedded itself in Yoska's exposed neck. Clearly this was an emergency plan B.

Yoska was taken completely by surprise. She halted in her reach. Knowing she had been hit by something and that it did not bode well for her, she reached up and grasped at her neck, removing the dart and looking at it. She shook her head.

"*Carajo*, bitch—I didn't expect that one," Yoska said.

Her right hand was still holding her dagger, but the strength seemed to drain from it as it fell limply on top of the covers of the bed. Yoska's eyes grew glassy. She weakly shook her head and with effort looked up at her adversary.

"You're...a lot better...than what we...were expecting," Yoska said with an effort.

The silhouette replaced the syringe in the pouch it had come from. With one hand, the assassin plucked at the top of the turban that covered her face, and began to unwind the garment. Natacha's long hair was wrapped around her head under the cloth. She regarded Yoska, who looked up groggily with a look of resentful spite. Yoska's hand clutched weakly at the dagger, but she lacked the strength to lift it.

"Remember one important thing before you go to your proper place in Hell," Natacha said. "There's a first time for everything. The only difference for you is that this is not just the first time for you to be caught by surprise, it's also your last one. Bitch.

"The drug running through your veins right now will paralyze every muscle in your body, including your heart, which will be your end. Your autopsy report will give your cause of death as a heart attack. It's a much more compassionate death than the one you three had in mind for me."

She waved a hand. "Bye-bye, daughter of Satan."

She left Yoska on the bed and went into the bathroom. She unzipped the top of her suit and removed it over her shoulders, fully exposing her torso. Due to the tightness of the suit, she wore not even a bra. She removed something similar to a staple gun from one of the pouches. From another she removed an antiseptic pack and applied it to her wound. She held the device over the wound and closed the superficial wound with surgical staples. She put some more antiseptic on the wound, and then bandaged it up. From another pouch she removed an antibiotic injector and jabbed the needle into her arm.

When she was finished, she raised her left breast to examine it with her right hand. Something was bothering her there, and her examination revealed a small scratch, bleeding but not deep, perhaps an inch or an inch and a half below her breast. Apparently, the hooked point of Yoska's dagger had caught her there as she had stepped back. She likewise cleaned that wound with antiseptic and bandaged it.

She explored her suit with her finger until she found the small hole made by the dagger point. She re-dressed and thoroughly cleaned all signs of her presence from the bathroom. She walked back into the room. Yoska was still sitting in the bed, her hands lying open on the covers. However, her head was bent onto her chest, as if unconscious. Natacha arranged the pillows and replaced the dagger under the pillow to restage the room as it was before. As she did so, her hand touched an object, and she discovered the pistol, silencer still attached.

Natacha breathed deeply as she realized how close she had come to losing her life. Had she failed in her aim with the dart, she would most certainly have been shot. She made sure the pistol was left as it was.

Even though she knew the unconscious Yoska could not hear her, she said, "Your instructors should have taught you that there's always someone better than us—no matter what profession we're in and no matter how great we are."

As she spoke, she arranged Yoska into a more natural sleeping position in her bed. When she was discovered the next day, the subsequent medical examination would lead to the conclusion of a heart attack, no matter what suspicions others might have.

Using another master key, Natacha managed to open the door that connected with Sonya's suite. With extreme care, as she had done before, she walked stealthily across the room towards Sonya's bed. She knew the other two women were partially incapacitated in terms both of vision as well as minor injuries. She likewise knew the law of the jungle: that a wounded animal is most dangerous when it feels trapped. She moved very slowly, not only to carefully survey the room for potential booby traps, but also because she expected at any moment a surprise similar to the one she'd had with Yoska.

She cautiously listened for the regular, deep breathing of someone fast asleep in the bed, once more to be certain that a dummy had not been placed there instead. As if to make the determination easier, Sonya shifted in her bed, muttering slightly in her sleep. Natacha stopped and observed to see if there was going to be any further motion.

Satisfied, she approached the bed. Taking care to not disturb the sleeping occupant, she searched under the pillow for weapons. She found the small Makarov pistol and slipped it out. She pulled out the magazine and removed all the cartridges. She double-checked the chamber to make certain that it was also unloaded. She then put the gun down on the nightstand to the right of the bed. The ammunition she deposited in her belt pouch.

She reached into another pouch on her belt and pulled out what appeared to be a glasses case, only a little wider. Inside were two wrapped bundles. She took one out and carefully unwrapped it, revealing a white rosebud. Once fully unwrapped, it opened beautifully into a blossom. She closed the box and replaced it in the same pouch from which she had removed it. She then pulled out a small notepad and wrote, "*Cultivo una rosa blanca/ en junio como en enero/ para el amigo sincero/ que me da su mano franca./ Y para el cruel que me arranca/ el corazon con que vivo,/ caldo ni ortiga cultivo;/ cultivo una rosa blanca.*[13]"

It was a poem by the patriotic poet Jose Marti. It was meant to be a warning to them, not a death threat. It was instead another chance for them to live. The message to back off was clear, lest they suffer the same fate as Yoska.

Natacha walked over to the nightstand with the pistol.

---

[13] I cultivate a white rose/ in June as in January/ For the sincere friend/ Who gives me his hand frankly./ And for the cruel person who tears out/ the heart with which I live,/ I cultivate neither nettles nor thorns;/ I cultivate a white rose.

She placed the note on top of the gun and the white rose on top of the note. She then walked carefully to Tanya's suite. She opened the door as she had before and repeated the procedure. Once again, she used the right nightstand to leave her message.

Very carefully, she removed the chair by the balcony door and placed it next to the adjoining door which led to the corridor between the suites. She did the same in the other two suites as she made her way back out. She wanted to leave a sarcastic message that exposed their vulnerability in spite of their precautions.

Once in Yoska's suite, she reached under the pillow and pulled out the Marakov. Once again, she unloaded the ammunition—this time, however, she replaced the pistol under the pillow next to the dagger. The cartridges she arranged in a circle on the right nightstand. Then she went over to the closet and began to search through it. She picked through different dresses until she found one she liked—the same one Yoska had been wearing at the awards ceremony.

She put the dress on over her stealth suit. She went into the bathroom to check the fit in the large mirrors in there, turning left and right. She nodded in approval, and unwrapped the black head covering. She draped it over her head like a scarf and put on a pair of glasses with smoked lenses, not too dark for nighttime use.

Dressed as she was now, she would look enough like Yoska as to confuse any employees that might see her as she left. It was the perfect cover. Should Tanya and Sonya decide to report the incident to the police, they would wind up being implicated as suspects themselves. She knew the odds were slight, as she was fully aware that the women were spies, but she wanted to take the added precaution.

    Natacha smiled in satisfaction and walked to the door to the hall, leaving the room as if she owned the place. As she closed the door, she saw one of the hotel attendants at the far end of the hall with a small room service cart. The attendant nodded in greeting. She smiled and nodded back wordlessly. The man continued towards the room that had ordered service, and she walked towards the elevator. Out of the corner of her eye, she watched the attendant to make certain he actually was delivering someone's breakfast.

    The first elevator arrived, empty as one would expect at such an early hour. She entered and pressed the button for the lobby. The elevator stopped on the fifth floor, and an aristocratic-looking lady entered, carrying a Yorkshire terrier dog.

    She greeted Natacha in Spanish. "*Buenos dias.*"

    Natacha made certain to reply with a Cuban accent. "*Buenos dias.*"

    When the elevator arrived at the lobby, she allowed the older woman to leave first. The lady smiled, and they exchanged farewells. Natacha walked over to the internal telephone by the concierge.

    "Room service," a voice answered.

    She answered as Yoska, gave the suite number, as well as the names of Tanya and Sonya, and ordered a breakfast large enough for the three of them. Then she left the hotel and disappeared into the crowd that was starting to flow in the street with the earliest workers starting their day as the sun started to break over the horizon. A new day was dawning for everyone—except

Yoska, who had concluded her final mission as an international assassin.

Approximately forty-five minutes later, three breakfast carts filled with fancy food and expensive Dom Perignon champagne arrived outside the suite. It looked as if, to everyone else, a celebration was going on or that the women were expecting company. Almost at the same time, the three attendants rang the buzzer on each suite, each one with a big smile on his face in anticipation of a fantastic tip.

Tanya was the first one to wake up. She stretched in her bed.

"Who the hell is ringing the bell so early?" she asked of the darkness. She got out of bed in the darkened room. Though the sun was up, the thick curtains over the windows effectively blocked all the light.

She turned on the lamp on the left nightstand. She raised her hand up with a happy smile on her face.

"Oh, yes!" she exclaimed. "I can see everything!" She looked at her hands. "Oh God! Thank you!"

Her happiness was of short duration when she reached under the pillow for her pistol, only to discover it wasn't there. She lifted each pillow to look under it, without result. She looked around in utter confusion. Something on the other side of the bed caught her attention. It looked like a flower. Her eyebrows shot up in surprise, and she crawled to the other side of the bed.

Her surprise turned to panic after she read the note. As she read, her eyes widened more and more. She now knew for a fact that someone hostile had visited her. She heard from the other room Sonya answering the repeated ringing of her doorbell.

"Will you please hold on?" Sonya asked. "I'll be there in a few seconds."

It sounded like either she hadn't seen a message or had not received one. Tanya sat down in bed and struggled to get out of bed.

She yelled with all her might, "Don't open the door, Sonya! Come over here immediately—you have to see this!"

Tanya snatched her pistol off the stand. She checked it and saw it was unloaded. She held it with her right hand, while in her left she still held the white rose. She managed to get out of bed and limped towards the door. As she did so, she continued to call out.

"Sonya! Did you hear me? Come here!"

As she reached connecting hallway, Sonya was coming out the door to her room, and they met in the hall. She noticed the chair sitting by the door as she limped past it. They both looked at each other, and then wordlessly looked towards the terrace.

Panic grew in both women as they realized beyond doubt that someone had not only been there to move the chairs, but both held pistols in their right hands and white roses in their left. Sonya held her note up first, along with its accompanying rose.

"Do you have one, as well?" she asked. "What does it say?"

Tanya replied, "It's a poem by Jose Marti, 'The White Rose.' What does yours say?"

"The same."

The bell on the door to Yoska's suite continued unceasing. Sonya ran into Yoska's room and shook her leg. She yelled out, "Will you please wait a minute?" Without waiting for a response, she ran back to Tanya.

Tanya was looking through the peephole in the door. She said to the attendant, "I didn't order any breakfast."

The attendant replied, "No, *señorita* Tanya. *Señorita* Yoska ordered all three breakfasts."

Sonya and Tanya looked at each other in surprise.

Tanya replied cordially, "Please, will you charge it on my card that you're holding at the front desk? Leave all three breakfasts by each door. Come back later, and we will give you your tip. None of us wants to face you as women just waking up, with no makeup on our faces, OK?"

"You are always welcome," he said. "You can leave your gratuity at the front desk in envelopes with the names of each of us serving you today."

"Thank you very much for your understanding. I will remember your courtesy when I deposit my gratuity in those envelopes."

"The pleasure is mine, and *bon appétit.*"

"Thank you very much again."

As soon as the conversation ended, Sonya ran to Yoska's suite, Tanya limping along as best she could. So far, Yoska had shown no sign of waking up. Sonya went over to the bed and began to shake her.

"Come on, Yoska, wake up! What's wrong with you?"

Sonya turned on the light and paused at the sight of the circle of bullets. Tanya limped in and went over to the curtains to let the light in. She looked at the lock on the terrace doors. With a confused look on her face, she went through and checked everything. She paused when she saw Sonya, who was pointing at the bullets, this time without a note like they had received. She checked for a pulse both on the neck and wrist.

"She's dead," Sonya said, her voice trembling with fear and consternation. "My God! Yoska's dead!" Sonya started to nod. "It makes sense. Why leave a note for a dead body, which cannot read it."

Tanya massaged her forehead. She limped to the other doors on the terrace, making certain that they were locked.

"How did you get in, ghost poet?" she muttered as she opened one of the doors.

She looked around, searching for any dirt or disturbance to provide a clue as to how this had happened. Not finding any trace, she came back inside the suite and closed the door.

Tanya said, "Completely undress Yoska."

Sonya looked at her in puzzlement. There was no doubt, however, that Tanya was the group's leader, and Sonya knew better than to question a direct order. She began to undress the lifeless corpse. As she did so, Tanya walked over to the closet. She began searching through Yoska's clothing to see if anything was missing or was not right. After shifting the dresses around, she wordlessly shook her head.

She went out onto Sonya's terrace to verify that the doors were still locked. She then went out onto the terrace, looking down at the street and up towards the sky. As she looked down, she could see the cars driving along the busy road. She stayed there for a few seconds, squeezing her chin in thought. She studied the situation carefully, thinking about how she would have done the job herself, looking for the most inconspicuous and inaccessible area possible. She also thought about how she might enter a suite without leaving a trace.

After she finished her inspection, she went back inside the suite, closing the door behind her. She went to examine her own terrace. After checking outside once more, she gave up. She went over to her door and peered through the peephole. Verifying that the hall was empty, she quickly opened the door.

She checked the cart for explosives or any other danger, and then brought it inside, closing the door behind it. She limped over to Sonya's suite and repeated the search before bringing it inside as well. Then she returned to Yoska's suite, doing her cart check once more.

This time, she said to Sonya, "Don't touch anything on these carts, not even the water. For the first time, *we* are the marks. There's a strong possibility that these notes with Marti's poem is nothing more than a distraction to see if we help them finish the job. They might be thinking that eliminating all three of us at once could create too much noise, something no one, including us, wants."

Sonya nodded approvingly. Everything Tanya said made sense to her. Tanya looked at Yoska's body, which still had undergarments on. She looked sharply at Sonya in annoyance.

"What part of removing all her clothes did you not understand?" she demanded.

Sonya, a little stung, replied, "You didn't tell me to remove her bra and underwear as well."

Tanya shook her head in disgust. She went over and did the task herself. Sonya understood Tanya's irritated demeanor, and tried to assist in removing the underclothes by holding the body for her. Tanya looked at her and realized that her nervous state was not her normal behavior and that she had not really spoken appropriately in reprimanding Sonya.

After they finished, she said, "I'm sorry. I've been a little distressed, but we have to be completely sure before we leave these suites how Yoska was assassinated. This is the only way we can be prepared for them when they come back for us. I'm ninety percent certain that they will, no matter who it was who entered our suites. This is probably a direct retaliation for our failed hit yesterday. They left us alive for some reason, but I don't know what that is yet. Those notes might have been left to terrify us. That's why we have to be clear and together, more united than ever. We have to act with extreme caution, or we will not leave this country alive. They might be watching us right now, giving us some rope in order to gain time.

"Whatever reason they have for letting us live, once it no longer exists they will proceed to the kill, like they did with Yoska. That's why it's so important to discover *how* they killed her, so that we can defend ourselves. There's no doubt in my mind that this is a well-planned hit, because Natacha, when we approached her, was already waiting for us. My question is, how was it possible for her to know our plans ahead of time? More than anything else, how was she able to identify us as her killers? How could she have identified our faces, unless somebody provided her with our pictures and a description of each of us? The only conclusion, you know as well as I do, is that somebody at very high levels has sold us out to our enemies."

As Sonya examined Yoska's body for some sign of violence, replied with panic-stricken eyes, "I don't think we will get out of Madrid alive." She took a deep breath. In a convinced tone, she continued, "I knew one of these days we would face it, but I never imagined it would be so soon!"

Tanya stopped what she was doing and grabbed Sonya with both hands. She shook her a little to snap her out of her near-hysteria. In a commanding tone, she said, "How the hell can you say that? No, no! That is what our enemies are looking for—that we should act in panic, so that we will not think clearly. That makes us easy prey for them. We have to get out of Madrid as soon as possible. At the moment, that is our top priority."

Sonya spread her hands. "What about our mission? If we abandon that, Che will be very angry with us. Heaven knows what he will do. For us to fail for the first time in our careers at something he sent us to do...."

Tanya yelled, "To *hell* with Che!" This time, she shook Sonya by the shoulders more violently. "The moment Yoska died, this mission was aborted. Our lives are more important than any mission Che sends us on, OK? If we don't have our lives, we have nothing!"

Tanya took a deep breath to calm herself down before continuing. "Who the hell cares what Che thinks anymore if we're dead?" In a calmer voice, she said, "I promise you, Sonya, that if you don't fail me by panicking at the thought of our enemies or Che, we will get out of Madrid today. Just as we had planned before."

Sonya looked at little more reassured. She tried to smile, but it didn't really come out the way she had intended. Tanya was examining the neck of Yoska. She noticed a small dot on her neck.

"Ah, ha!" she exclaimed. "This is the point of entry by

which they introduced the poison that took the life of our *compañera* Yoska."

Tanya left the bed and limped towards her suite. Once there, she took out a bag and removed a long wallet with a zipper. She limped back to Yoska's suite and Sonya. She noticed Sonya double-locking the door in panicked anxiety, as if she were expecting someone at any moment to kick in the door to finish them off.

Tanya said, "Just think about it, Sonya. If they wanted us dead, we would already be dead by now. They had plenty of opportunity, and that door won't hold them. That's why we have to move fast, before our time runs out."

She opened the zipper and removed a jeweler's loupe. She carefully examined the wound on Yoska's neck. She smiled and nodded, proud of finding the point. She said, "The redness around the point cannot be seen by the naked eye, but if you look at it under magnification, the poison irritated the skin. If we're very lucky, there will be some residue of the poison on the surface."

She pulled out a glass vial with a needle attached to one end. She took a sample from the corpse, removed the needle, and stoppered the end. She shook it up and noticed that the blood a yellowish color.

"There's definitely poison here," she said as she put the sample away in the wallet. "After we send this to the lab, they will let us know what kind of poison they used to kill our friend Yoska."

Sonya asked, "What are we going to do with the body?"

Tanya looked at her sadly and shook her head in resignation. "Nothing. Absolutely nothing. Unfortunately, this is completely out of our hands. After we leave the hotel in a little while, I will call agents who specialize in this sort of thing. They'll communicate this to the highest levels in Cuba—probably Che and the others in counter-intelligence—and they will decide what to do with Yoska's body. They might smuggle it back to Cuba, or they might send it to the crematory. I advise you, before we leave, that you say your final goodbyes to her now. We probably will not see her again to say them later."

Sonya shrugged her shoulders uncomfortably at the thought that the body might have been hers. Mental confusion, fear, and distrust combined to make her ask Tanya a surprising question.

"Do you think Che had anything to do with this?"

Tanya looked at her, caught completely off-guard. Her eyes flew wide with astonishment.

"What are you saying?" she demanded. With a stern face she continued, "What the hell is wrong with you? Have you gone crazy? Che involved in the assassination of Yoska?" She shook her head. "Where did you get that stupidity?"

As they re-dressed Yoska's body out of respect for their slain partner in crime, Sonya remained silent. Tanya realized again that she had overreacted and treated Sonya unfairly. This particular behavior was very out of character for Tanya, and up until today they had formed the perfect trio. Tanya knew best how much each of their lives depended on the efficiency and loyalty of the others. She took a deep breath.

"I'm sorry. I know we're both very stressed. That's only natural for us as human beings. But we can control it. I'm sorry again. It was not my intention to attack you, Sonya."

Sonya replied, "I'm trying to control myself and not blow up in your face. But all of the things that have happened in the last twenty-four hours have been too extremely strange and coincidental. I'm sorry, and forgive me, but that is the reason I doubted Che."

They finished dressing the body without a word. Tanya, however, was ruminating on the word "coincidental." It stuck in her mind, and so her curiosity increased. Finally, she asked, "Is there something I don't know, Sonya? Something you know that you've been holding back out of fear of hurting me? 'Coincidental'? Why did you use that word?"

Sonya sighed and waved her right arm dismissively. "Please, Tanya. I can't take any more of your screams and frustrations. As you said before, the most important thing is that we get out of Madrid alive. This is not the moment or the time. Let's wait, and we can discuss it later."

Tanya looked Sonya directly in the eyes. She sighed and said very calmly, "I will give you my word right now that whatever you say, I will not raise my voice again. I ask you, please, if there is something that happened between you guys and Che, and you have *any* thoughts that Che has put our security at risk, our lives today might depend on you telling me that so that we can leave Madrid in safety or change our plan for extraction. I don't want to be taken by surprise again. Remember, our lives have been linked for many years; but now, if one of us dies, the other will as well. I don't want to die for something I don't even know about. Remember, I have my own contacts, and they are loyal to *me*, no buts about it.

"I don't tell Che everything, you know that. Even though I love and respect him, I also know he's not reliable. His narcissism can sometimes turn him into a monster who will destroy anyone he has by his side, like the Devil destroys his own family out of pure personal satisfaction. I tell you this in complete confidence, so please repeat this to absolutely no one."

Sonya raised her eyebrows in surprise. She raised her hand to hold off anything more. With more assurance, she replied, "Whatever I have to tell you is also completely confidential. If you tell anyone what I'm going to tell you, as soon as I get to Cuba, they will put a bullet in my head."

Tanya looked at her with even more concern than before. "Is it that serious? Come on, help me to do something we have to do before we get out of here, and we'll talk for a few minutes before we leave."

The two women went to Yoska's closet and took out her suitcases. They folded up her clothes and packed them up. They rolled her luggage into their suites and cleaned every trace of anyone having been there in order to facilitate their cleaner's job. They walked over to Tanya's suite and Sonya sat down in the breakfast nook at the table there.

Tanya took out of one of her suitcases a small bottle of imported distilled whiskey. She took out two glasses and poured them both drinks. She sat down facing Sonya. They clinked glasses, toasted for health and long life, and Sonya took a long sip.

She said, "Do you remember, a few months back, when you told me that Che had shared with you the extremely sad news that his daughter, your niece and adopted daughter, had been killed? That she had tried to sneak off of the island with a group of lesbians?" Tanya nodded wordlessly. "You told me also that Che had said that the Coast Guard had tried to stop them, and they had to open fire, leaving the Coast Guard no alternative to return fire, and everyone was killed?"

Two tears rolled down Tanya's cheeks. Sonya's eyes filled with sympathetic tears. She took her glass and downed the rest of the whiskey in one gulp. Tanya tried to refill it, but Sonya prevented her.

"No, no more." Sonya leaned forward. "All of that story was a lie—as we say in Cuba, a Chinese tale, created by Che to clean himself of the guilt for what he did."

Tanya massaged her forehead with the fingers of her left hand. "How do you know that it's all a lie?"

Sonya leaned back. "Yoska is the one who killed Maggie." She hesitated, and when she spoke her voice cracked with emotion. "She was under Che's direct orders." Two more tears escaped her control.

Tanya put her glass down in astonishment. She poured herself another shot. This time, Sonya wordlessly extended her glass for more. As she poured Sonya another shot, Tanya asked, "Why? Why did Yoska tell you all of this? If this was supposed to remain secret, why tell this to anyone?"

Sonya looked at her in a pained expression of assurance. "For the same reason that I'm not to repeat this to anyone. Now, after these strange events of the last day, I decided to share with you the secret that Yoska entrusted me with. Her main reason for telling me was because she wanted to have a witness if her life was ended in a strange way, as has indeed happened today."

Tanya was frustrated but now completely convinced. She sank her face into both hands. "What a son of a bitch that miserable man is! Maggie, after all, told me several times, and she was right. This man doesn't love anyone. He killed my sister, Maggie's mother. There's a very great possibility that he killed my sister's husband, Aldames, who was an honest and good man. My question now is, why Maggie? What did she do to him? What danger did she represent to that degenerate?"

Sonya took another deep breath. "According to Yoska, Che told her that Maggie was the hand who executed his most trustworthy, loyal man, Fausto. According to counterintelligence, Maggie was working for our enemies on the side of the gringos. She had provided to Lee Harvey Oswald vital information to destroy Che's plans to kill Kennedy."

Tanya shook her hand and sank her face into her hands once more. "May God forgive us today for being so ignorant and stupid, letting us be manipulated by Satan's hands. I know our souls haven't the remotest possibility for salvation for all the crimes we've committed, but please—have mercy on our souls. Today, my eyes have finally opened, and I realize the monstrosity of Your enemy that my friends and I have until today served with blind loyalty and willful ignorance. This ends today. No more—I promise you, no more. Amen."

Before Sonya's astonished eyes, Tanya crossed herself. Until now, her religious feelings had been repressed, and for a long time Tanya had never shown them to anyone. With tears in her eyes, Sonya also crossed herself and repeated, "Amen." This time, her smile was genuine.

The two women stood up and embraced. Tanya said, "Thank you. Thank you very much for your confidence in me. Until today, Sonya, you've been one of my great and trustworthy friends. From this day onward, you are my sister, and I will defend your life with mine, if necessary."

Sonya smiled in genuine pleasure, the kind of beautiful smile that comes from the soul. She replied, "And I will be thankful to you and to God for giving me today the strength to tell you the truth. I will offer up my life to save yours, as well, if necessary. My only regret is not telling you this before."

Tanya shook her head. "It's never too late. Now everything makes complete, logical sense. Che didn't send us here to kill Natacha. He sent us here in order for Natacha to kill Yoska. He probably sent his accomplices to alert Natacha about what we were there to do. If we both got killed in the process, then oh, well. He doesn't care about anyone else's life, so why would he care about yours and mine? After all, he might wish from the bottom of his heart that we would be killed as well. That way, if for any reason this confidence between us is revealed, no one is left to tell.

"He knows very well a human being's weakness. There is no doubt in my mind that he's a son of the Devil, and only evil runs in his veins. The fact that we are so close to each other drives him crazy; that's the one thing he resents most—friendship and loyalty between others. He has a spiteful envy for those who achieve it. After all, maybe Natacha, with the opportunity to kill all three of us with impunity, decided at the last minute by herself to give us fair warning. I can guarantee you that the idea of the white rose and the Marti poem had too much beauty and talent—it's something Ernesto Guevara de la Cerna completely lacks, so it's certainly not an idea of his."

Tanya shook her head again as if trying to rid her mind

of a bad thought. She added, "This is a great day for us. From now on, we should not let evil hold our hearts ever again. Let me make some phone calls and get out of here as soon as possible."

She got up and went over to the phone to place her calls. Everyone she spoke to she gave a timetable of thirty minutes. They packed a small handbag. Tanya said, "Put in here only what is absolutely necessary. The rest they will send to us."

She took out of one of their bags two passports and two airplane tickets.

Thirty minutes later, two elderly women, each holding a handbag, walked out of the suites towards the elevators. When one of the elevators opened, they saw the same elderly woman with the Yorkshire terrier Natacha had earlier seen.

The lady greeted them, "*Hola.*"

They both answered in kind. Once reaching the lobby, they left the hotel and hailed a taxi. While they were on their way to the airport, Sonya held Tanya's hand.

She said, "When we get back to Cuba, I can take you to where Maggie is buried if you want."

Tanya nodded her thanks. She squeezed Sonya's hand. She put her other hand on Sonya's shoulder and said, "Sister Sonya, you don't know how happy you've made me today. I have such a great comfort in my soul. I feel free of guilt."

Sonya replied, "You're welcome. If you are interested in punishing him, I have some great information that could perhaps serve that purpose. It would give him a good setback and maybe teach him a lesson that without loyalty or friendship, a man or woman has less value than a running cockroach in a tropical outhouse."

Tanya nodded. "Unfortunately, Che has no idea what those two words really mean. He has all his life been a perfect cynic. He will one day discover that life is a lot more than lying, killing, and all the other evil things he concentrates on."

JFK: The Unwrapped Enigma

Political Correctness or Dishonesty?

If people stopped saying things to please others and begin to say what's really on their hearts and minds, the world would become a better place for everyone to live in.

Dr. Julio Antonio del Marmol

Chapter 9: The Amazons Repent and Retreat

Tanya and Sonya's taxi arrived at the Madrid-Barajas Airport at last. As they got out, Tanya removed from her handbag both passports matching their disguises and their tickets for Cuba. She handed one to Sonya and then proceeded to pay the taxi driver. In addition to being part of her disguise, her cane served a real purpose to aid her as she walked on her injured ankle.

They entered the terminal of the airport. An elegantly-dressed man of medium height with white hair and a beard approached them. He wore dark glasses and a Spanish beret, and he had a pipe in his mouth. After greeting them, he handed an envelope to Tanya.

He said, "Here is the ticket for your luggage. The rest is taken care of. We will deposit the package in an appropriate place. Your guys in Cuba declined to receive it and ordered us to destroy it and make all traces vanish. We decided, in honor of our friends that we've worked with for so long, to deposit it in a peaceful place where you or her family can later claim it."

Tanya patted his shoulder in sincere gratitude. "Thank you. We will see each other soon."

The man bent down slightly and kissed her on the cheek. He nodded and walked away, rapidly disappearing in the crowd. Both women walked to the check-in counter at the airport. A small line of five or six people were waiting there.

Behind them, a small family with two boys between six and eight years of age and a little girl of around four or five, all olive-skinned with large green eyes, played with a small ping-pong ball. The parents paid them little attention as the children continually pestered everyone in line as they ran in between everyone's legs, laughing and shoving each other. Occasionally they tripped and fell at the feet of those standing in line.

No one said anything, enduring all of this patiently, only rolling their eyes at one another. A few minutes passed, and the line moved a little as the next person was called forward. The children continued playing their little game of soccer with the ping-pong ball. More people arrived, and the line grew in length. More time passed, and finally Sonya and Tanya moved up to the desk, very happy to get away from the children.

The pretty young clerk at the desk smiled at them sympathetically through her glasses. She was a redhead with freckles. She said, "I'm sorry. Some people should never have kids if they have no idea how to discipline them."

She checked the tickets to see that everything was in order and assigned their seats. She asked them if they had any more luggage, letting them know that the handbags could remain with them and which gate they needed to report to.

After they said their farewells, they were about to turn around and leave. The small ping-pong ball rolled up near Tanya's left foot, the injury on which was camouflaged by her disguise. The largest boy ran towards them as they turned. When Tanya moved, she tapped the ball with her foot, and it moved slightly.

The boy simultaneously reared back to kick the ball. He missed, and kicked Tanya in the ankle. To make matters worse, he was wearing a cowboy boot, and the reinforced, pointed toe dug into her bullet wound. Tanya screamed in agony and fell to the floor.

Sonya tried to help her, but Tanya was unable to stand. The white cotton circulation sock was drenched in blood, and it started to drip on the tile floor. The kick had reopened the wound. Everyone in line looked at the old woman on the floor and her bloodied leg as she screamed in pain.

Tanya screamed, "Damned kids! What is wrong with these people? Oh, my God! These unconscious parents!"

Sonya leaned down and tried to put some pressure on the wound. She took a handkerchief from her travel bag in an attempt to stop the bleeding. She said to Tanya in a quiet voice, "Calm down—we don't want to attract attention. We don't know who might be watching us right now."

The young clerk came around from behind the desk with a box of tissues in an attempt to help. She returned to the desk and picked up the phone to summon assistance. People from the airline and some executives started to arrive, along with security. With Sonya's help, Tanya was finally able to get back onto her feet. A janitor arrived to swab the floor of the blood. The executives went over to speak with the negligent parents, who were extremely ashamed. The mother made the boy come over to Tanya to apologize, and the three children were now behaving like angels.

Tanya had recovered from the pain and accepted the boy's apology. She said, "I'm sorry if I was a little harsh, but I had surgery yesterday on that ankle."

A very tall man, dressed tastefully in a tailored suit, apologized to them on behalf of the airline. He suggested to Tanya that she come with him to be examined by their staff doctor.

Tanya raised her hand. "Thank you very much, but it's not necessary. My friend will accompany me to the bathroom to help me change my bandage. I had surgery yesterday to remove a malignant polyp from my ankle. As soon as we bandage it back up, it will be OK. There's no need to see a doctor."

Sonya agreed. "Don't worry about it, sir. She's OK. Once we change her bandage, it will be all right." She took Tanya by the arm. "Let's go and get that done before we board the plane."

They turned to leave, but the man stopped them. "I'm sorry, but this will be a problem. The airline is responsible for the health of everyone we carry. I cannot allow you on board that plane until the doctor checks you out and gives you the OK to fly, especially since this incident happened right here in our check-in area. This could create a serious problem for the airline's insurance."

Not knowing how to answer that, both women looked at each other with long faces after hearing the executive's ultimatum. They knew that only a person with greater authority within the airline could reverse that man's decision. They kept silent, but they were extremely concerned about to what to do.

In the midst of their mental turmoil, they heard a female voice behind them say to the executive, "Don't worry, Enrique. I will take full responsibility. As you heard from Maria's lips," she added, using Tanya's assumed name, "she is OK."

This was odd, as the only person who could possibly have known what name Tanya was traveling under was the redheaded lady behind the ticket counter. Her next comment further increased their anxiety.

"As her friend Soraya said, the wound will be dressed, and everything will be as it was before this incident. You will be a witness as an airline executive, and I will be able to make sure all of this appears in my report to our insurance company."

The woman turned to the elderly travelers and said, "Ladies, I think you should go to the bathroom and change those bandages as soon as possible. We have only twenty minutes to board the plane. I'm certain you two are anxious to return to Cuba."

Tanya and Sonya had been frozen until that moment. This incident had increased their paralysis to full mummification. They looked at the woman and were shocked to see that it was Natacha, wearing Yoska's dress. They knew it was hers without a doubt; but they also had no idea how on Earth she could have known their travel identities. Not even Che knew these IDs existed. Tanya had formed them with a completely trustworthy contact in the Cuban emigration bureaucracy as a standby in case they needed a way to get out of trouble should they be compromised. Tanya wanted an identity that absolutely no one in the world would know. It was the only way to avoid being tracked by anyone in a life-or-death situation.

This time it was Enrique who snapped the two ladies out of their paralysis. With a pleasant smile, he said,

"Well, ladies, you heard her. She's in charge of our insurance policies. If she says she assumes all responsibility for this incident, I have nothing else to say. But you had better hurry and change that dressing. I don't want to be the one responsible for you missing your flight. Go, go, go!" With his pleasant smile, he gestured for them to leave.

Both women thanked Natacha with forced smiles and rushed as best as their disguises and Tanya's limp would allow towards the bathroom.

Remaining behind, Enrique asked Natacha, "What is your reason to go to Cuba?"

She smiled and replied, "An extremely special mission. I have to perform a very detailed investigation into the policy the Cuban government held concerning the ship *La Coubre* that blew up in the Havana harbor a little over three years ago." She grimaced. "They haven't a hope, even though the international law firm contracted by Cuba filed appeals against us. When our company declined the claim, I expected to have to return soon. This is just a dirty game the Cuban government is playing without any basis, since we have incontrovertible evidence of the fraud committed by them. No judge on Earth is going to give them a penny. I have to go over there to convince these imbeciles to drop their claim."

"This doesn't look good at all," Sonya fretted in the restroom. "Natacha knows who we are, yet she got us out of trouble. What could be her motive to get us on board that plane? I hope it's not to drop us somewhere over the Atlantic! She certainly has a personal interest in wanting us to leave Madrid without a problem."

Tanya looked a little more relaxed. "Maybe her interest

is based on a personal need," she replied. "Perhaps she wants to recruit us to the other side." Tanya massaged her forehead with her fingers. "If there's anything I'm absolutely sure of is that she is the one who visited us last night and killed Yoska. That dress she's wearing is the dress I liked most in her entire wardrobe, and I noticed that it was the only dress missing. She has good taste, given that it's the only one she took."

Sonya flushed Tanya's bloody sock down a toilet and helped her put on a fresh one from her handbag.

"Keep your eyes open, but relax," Tanya said in a serious voice. "I don't think her intention is to hurt us, much less kill us. At least for the moment. But let's see what happens when we arrive in Cuba. There, we will be on *our* patio. There's no doubt that she has guts. Up to a certain point, she's taking a great risk to travel with us to the only place where she knows we can really hurt her."

Tanya stood up from the chair she had been sitting before the bathroom vanity. She nodded. "You never know. We might have a thing or two to learn from Natacha. Let's see what the wind blows to us in Cuba."

They started to leave the bathroom. Sonya shook her head in sad resignation and said, "Well, at least she got us out of a problem with the airline representative. You never know—our enemy can, in the end, wind up having more compassion for us than our own supposed friends, who sold us to our enemies without any compassion and left us to our own devices."

They walked towards the gate where their flight was due to depart. They handed their tickets to the attendant at the booth and walked down the jetway to the plane. At any moment they expected to spot Natacha. When they arrived at the door to the plane, they were greeted by the pleasant smiles of the flight attendants. They were young, pretty girls in their picturesque uniforms.

One of the girls had pale skin, black hair, and long eyelashes, typical of a native of Madrid. She gave them a souvenir bag with the airline logo on one side and the seal for the city of Madrid on the other. The pilot and copilot gave them small bags of chocolate bonbons as they welcomed them onto the flight.

Tanya and Sonya walked down the aisle looking for their seat. As they did so, they took advantage of the moment to scrutinize the seats on both sides, looking for Natacha. They reached their seats near the tail of the plane without spotting her. The attendants helped them stow their carryon bags in the overhead compartment. Both breathed deep sighs of relief once they sat down.

One of the attendants got on the public address system. "Please, everyone return to your seats, fasten your seatbelts. We will be departing shortly for our destination in Cuba."

Shortly after the announcement, Natacha appeared. She still looked radiant and tastefully dressed. She had changed into more tropical attire—a dress with a floral pattern and a white hat with a matching bandana. Her attire enhanced her beauty, making her look like a movie star.

As she approached the old ladies, she said *"Hola."*

As if the greeting wasn't enough to raise the hairs on both women's necks, they noticed that Natacha sat down in the row behind them. That completely spooked them.

Sonya said, "I have to go pee." She started to get up.

Tanya held her down and said, "No, we're about to

take off." She took Sonya's hand. "You can hold it, sweetie. A few minutes after we're in the air, they'll signal that you can go." She gave her a brave smile. "I told you we would leave Madrid alive."

The plane's engines grew loud and they felt the invisible hand of gravity gently push them back in their seats as the aircraft accelerated to take off speed. Sonya nervously shushed Tanya, jerking her thumb agitatedly over her shoulder at where Natacha sat immediately behind them.

Tanya said, "Relax, relax. She can't shoot us right here."

Sonya looked out the window at the city, rapidly shrinking beneath them as they gained altitude. She put her hand on her chest and breathed deeply. She crossed herself and said with a small smile, "Thank you, God. Thank you, Tanya, for keeping your cool in the midst of this whole ordeal."

Tanya nodded and said, "You're welcome." She smiled. "Let's see what other surprises we have when we reach Cuba. I will tell you in detail the version of the story I want you to repeat, the one that we will both sell to Che and the others. It must be only our version, the one that will favor both of us. You understand?"

Sonya smiled and nodded. "Of course. I understand completely. I will only say what you tell me to say, nothing more."

Tanya smiled and nodded. She patted Sonya on the shoulder. Both women looked at each other in silent, complete, mutual agreement.

Around ten hours later the airplane's wheels touched down on the runway of the Jose Marti International

Airport in Rancho Boyeros, Havana, Cuba. The plane taxied to the terminal, and the passengers started to deplane.

   Natacha passed the other passengers and waited outside the terminal. A tall, skinny black man opened the back door of his white and mint green 1958 Edsel. With a polite gesture and a big smile, he said, "Welcome to Cuba, *señorita* Patricia. I am Chopin. The Masonic brothers sent me to place myself at your disposition for as long as you wish."

   Natacha looked him up and down distrustfully. "The Masons don't believe in God," she said a little harshly.

   Chopin replied, "That is a complete misperception—mostly negative propaganda against the Masons. If it were true, who do they refer to the Supreme Architect of the Universe?"

   Natacha recognized the code. She smiled warmly and extended her hand. "What a pleasure to meet you, Chopin. I am Patricia Flores."

   He helped her into the back seat of the car, closed the door, and put her luggage into the trunk. He got into the driver's seat and they drove towards the city of Havana.

Club Nautico Edition
Miramar Community

   My uncle, the General, and I were at the beach sitting around a rustic wooden table under the permanent umbrella. They were debriefing me on the intelligence community's new plan that had been given priority implementation.

   "At this moment," my uncle said, "the most important

subject on our table is facilitating the intel to our contact. According to my information, this person is already in Cuba. The contact needs all the details to eliminate every single person involved in the assassination of Kennedy. The main priority, initially, will be targeting those who were directly involved in pulling the trigger. Once we accomplish that, the others will follow in order. The rest of the group associated with this act, one by one, are to be punished. Right up to those who planned it. Intelligence wants to send this message to anyone who might in the future attempt something like this. We cannot, as a civilized world, allow such a horrendous act. We will not stop until we bring to justice every single one of these people.

"Everything should be done with complete efficiency and utter discretion. This has been authorized by the new President, but he doesn't want anyone to know how or why those men die. He doesn't want a confrontation with the Soviet Union; he in no way wants to rock the boat. He wants to maintain peace and preserve global stability.

My uncle pointed at me. "You will be a tremendously important factor, because you will facilitate transmitting the vital information that our contact needs to be able to pinpoint the exact location and new faces of these individuals. According to your last intelligence, they are the only two assassins who have survived this venture. You said both of them had plastic surgery to change their appearances, yes?"

I nodded. "I haven't seen them since the debriefing at Che's house. Like I said in my report, their faces were almost entirely covered in bandages. Since I've met each of them, though, it won't be too difficult for me to identify them, no matter how much they've changed their features. It doesn't matter how many surgeries they have on their faces, they cannot change the length of their arms, the details of their hair—"

The General put up his arms and interrupted me. "No, no, no—we don't want you to get too close to them and take unnecessary risks. You might be suspected in their disappearances or death. All we want you to do is get the information of their exact location at this moment, today. Then we can form a plan with no room for error that later we can put into the hands of our contact to give the necessary details for the trigger to execute the plan and put these two murderers out of combat."

I leaned back in my seat. "According to my information, which I included in my report, both of them are resting on a beautiful beach on the Oriental side of the island, in Holguin on the Playa Guardalavaca." I stroked my chin and continued, "However, it's not unusual for them to change places. If you can give me a few days to verify this, I'll find out if they're still in that place."

The General raised his arm with a big smile. "That is exactly what we want. However, don't compromise your cover. Do not in any way put yourself in jeopardy, because we don't want you getting too close to these guys."

This time, I was the one who smiled. "Thank you for worrying about me so much and trying to protect me. However, Kennedy did not really live up to our expectations as President of the United States. He was a great disappointment, not just to our people but also to the democracies around the globe. But as the leader of the free world, he represented our principles and ideology, and he didn't deserve to die like a dog with his brains blown out. It wasn't just the way he died, but the way these guys did it in front of his wife. Besides, he was a religious Catholic like my Mima. He had to have a good heart like hers, at least. That tells me that even if I have to blow my cover in order to bring these murderers to justice, I will do it with infinite pleasure. No man deserves to die like that."

My uncle nodded in agreement. "I agree completely with everything you say, but remember: you are extremely valuable for us. You have to remember how important you are to our cause, to us, and to every Cuban. I hope you will do this with the same intelligence and tenacity that you have used in the past in fulfilling all of our requests and missions for you.

"You've learned from the bad times and extremely difficult situations you managed to get out of alive, and you've built on those experiences. You've managed to complete this assignment without putting your security or life at risk. Remember, you're not an assassin. You haven't been trained for that. So far, you've been a great spy. Leave the shoe repair to the shoemaker and the bread making to the baker.

"We each of us have experiences and skills, like you do, but when you spoke of Kennedy, I saw something in your eyes which scared me. Don't even think of doing anything that goes beyond simply collecting information. Leave the other work to those experts, and keep your emotions out of the assignment."

I shook my head with a big smile. "I believe that both of you guys are breaking your own rules that you've repeatedly taught me. You've gotten too close to me and perhaps look at me as an adopted son that you don't want to lose."

I leaned forward and put both elbows on the table. "I never said anything about my killing those two assassins myself. Let me make this clear: I don't like any idea that involves taking the life of another human being, if I can avoid it. But certain men are filled with hate, evil, and darkness, and I believe that in the eyes of God and the rest of the world Earth would be a better place if these individuals cease to exist."

I paused to look into each man's eyes in succession. "Remember, both of you, that the game we've decided to play doesn't place much value on our lives. We all die of something—even mere citizens who are not involved in this particular game, which holds the highest risk of mortality. No one lives forever."

They looked at each other. This time, my uncle shook his head in disagreement. "I was afraid that all the things you've been doing will eventually damage your personality. Remember what we do is for freedom, democracy, and justice in this country. But don't become a cynic. Don't let these bastard, degenerate thieves fill your heart with resentment towards life. Life with freedom is beautiful. Maybe I will not live to see the freedom of our country once more, but you will."

I looked at him. "I don't know what freedom is. I was born under a dictator who dropped bodies in the middle of the street, pulling eyes and nails out of people to make them talk, and now we have an even worse dictator who puts people in front of the firing squad just to take their property or harvest their organs. I've read about it and heard from Papi and you how beautiful freedom is, but I don't know it for myself."

"My nephew, you are very smart and brave. You have many great qualities, but you also need to have hope. If you believe in God, as I think you do, please believe me that with freedom comes all the splendor that will fill your life. On the day you find yourself no longer living under a tyrant, remember your old uncle telling you how beautiful it will be. It's like falling in love, and I believe you already know about that."

I smiled, and he continued. "If you remember that feeling, you will multiply it by thousands, if not millions, when you live in freedom and in love. Don't give these communist bastards the gift of your life." He pointed at me sternly. "Take care of yourself, *carajo!*" He smiled then. "Life is the most precious thing we have. God forbid something should happen to you—your father would skin me alive!"

I had never seen him express himself like a typical *isleño relloyo*[14] Cuban in that way. He had always been refined and well-mannered, but the thought of what my father would do to him if something happened to me brought the Cuban in him completely out into the open.

I scraped at my arm. "It must be very painful, taking the skin off like that while still alive." Both my uncle and the General laughed loudly at my joke.

My uncle said, "Let's get back to business." He pulled out a folder and removed from it two photos of a beautiful woman, one from the profile, one full on. "This Spanish beauty is the professional trigger that you probably should not meet. The information you will pass

---

[14] Island Creole

to us, either through one of our contacts or directly either to me or the General. But in case of emergency and you need to improvise, it will be good for you to know who you're dealing with. Memorize these pictures. Keep them in your mind. It's possible that somebody might mention something about her, and you would then be able to warn her so that she can withdraw.

"After all, you have the obligation to be prepared in case she gets made so that you can retreat yourself. Her name is Patricia Flores—that's the name she's using right now." He nodded knowingly. "You know how it is. If, for any reason, you have to contact her directly, your name will be Sebastian Almendares, and your code is, 'The people of Madrid are as sweet as the sugar cane in Cuba.' Her reply will be, 'Ha! I like the sugar in my coffee so much that I keep pouring until the spoon stands straight up in my cup.'"

I said, "Who in our group is working with her that you know of?"

The General said with a grin, "Only you and your good friend, Chopin."

I nodded. "Well, if I need anything else, I will communicate with you guys at once. So far, I think we're done, yes? I want to get moving so that I can get that information as soon as possible."

We all stood up, my uncle first, then the General, then me. My uncle put his hand on my shoulder. As he drew his finger across his throat, he said, "Maybe I sound like an old man, but remember, the individuals who do this kind of job, even though they're cleaners and hunters on our side, always have long tails like dragons. They've done this before. You have to take into consideration that somebody could be hanging on to that tail, following their steps. At times, we can wind up getting caught in a crossfire and wind up the innocent victims of another entity that has nothing to do with what we're doing. Be careful, my nephew. I want to keep my skin intact. Have you ever seen your father angry?"

I smiled. "To be honest with you, I've never seen him angry in all my short life until the day I tried to tell him the truth about what I've heard from Che and Fidel and their morbid plans to steal the Revolution from Papi and all his big money friends. Unfortunately, I couldn't keep it in any longer and put it on the table, point by point, and told him how I felt about it all. I finished by letting him know that there would no longer be a democracy in Cuba but a Marxist regime. Castro and his gangsters would take Papi's businesses and those of all his friends and leave them, as we say here, *como la gallina culeca sin plumas y cacareando*[15]."

My uncle and the General shook their heads and laughed. The General said, "No doubt about it, kid, you have big balls. I would have loved to have seen the explosion after you said that. We don't like to accept the truth when presented to us, even after seeing the lies after a while. But to hear it from you of all people, who was considered the paragon for the Revolutionary youth, the Little Commander. Even though he might have had his doubts about these bandits, his surprise must have been humongous. His explosion must have matched that in size."

I smiled and nodded in agreement. My uncle also

---

[15] Like a broody hen without feathers and clucking

smiled as he said, "I remember that day very clearly. If I hadn't stopped you when you came to me, I don't even want to think about what crazy thing you would have done. You told me that you were ready to steal a plane at gunpoint and that you wanted to get out of here to be reunited with the friends who had left before you. The tears in your eyes and your conviction is what brought me to the determination to do something I had never done before. You convinced me of your sincerity, and that is why I decided to stop you and propose that you come to work with us. It wasn't just that I knew you would be extremely valuable to us in what we're doing, but also because you've always been my favorite nephew. I didn't want to see you waste your life in such a miserable way."

I smiled and nodded again. "Thank you," I said. "You're completely right. If you hadn't recruited me in that way, I can guarantee that one of two things would have happened. Either I would have died, or I would have successfully pulled it off and been far away from these communists, and Heaven knows where God would have taken me today."

The General smiled and raised his right arm. "I have to thank your uncle, too, for his talent, vast experience, and courage in determining at that moment that you weren't a traitor. I'm certain it crossed his mind that you had been sent by the G-2 to entrap him so that they could bring him to the firing squad. Believe me, I know your uncle must have thought very, very carefully before he shared his secret with you. Thank God he picked up the phone and called me so that I could corroborate what his instincts told him. I told him to not waste the opportunity and to grab it, and that's how a diamond was discovered."

"Thank you very much," I said modestly.

"Don't thank me," he said. "You've been a tremendous asset and have surpassed all of our highest expectations. If anything, *we* have to thank *you* for all of your great work."

I grinned. "Thank you, anyway. I have to let you guys know how grateful I am for the training you've given me and for guarding my back, diligently preserving my identity these past years. Like I read in a book, gratitude is a great virtue."

Both men stood up and shook my hand before embracing me. We left the beach table, each heading off in different directions. I got into my Soviet GAZ-69A jeep. It belonged to Canen for his duties in the main HQ, and it had the encircled star of the Cuban army on both doors. He let me borrow it frequently, since he usually traveled to and from headquarters in his chauffeured car, which was more comfortable. If he needed the jeep because he was headed out on military maneuvers, he would let me know to use the car instead.

I thought about the debriefing as I drove back to the farm along Rancho Boyeros Avenue. I tried to form a plan that wouldn't catch anyone's attention, especially Che's, and allow me to retrieve the information they required in order to execute the new plan. The first thing that occurred to me was that I could stop by casually at Che's house in Boca Siega and see what information I could get from him or perhaps one of his escort.

I was completely absorbed in my thoughts as I passed by the Café El Parador. I looked to my right and caught out of the corner of my eye what I took to be Chopin's Edsel parked in the lot. I slowed down and entered the parking lot for a livestock feed factory. I made a U-turn and returned to the café. If that was Chopin's car, I wanted to not just say hello and catch up with my great friend, I also had a curiosity to see if he had yet made contact with the trigger from Madrid.

When I entered the parking lot of the café, I could not see him inside anywhere. I parked and walked a few short steps to the Edsel. I could see the small hula dancer doll on the dashboard, and knew beyond doubt that this was his car. I smiled.

I decided at once to enter the café to find him. I looked around the high-backed vinyl booths in my search. There was no sign of him. I thought that he might have left the car there for some reason, and I headed back to the main door. As I passed the bathroom, though, I saw a very beautiful woman in elegant clothing with a large hat, the kind no longer seen in Cuba. When I looked at her face, I recognized her at once. It was the woman in the photo I had been shown, and I realized at once that I should not be there. Instinctively I looked her up and down to note the details. She noticed, and did the same thing to me.

As soon as she did that, any remaining doubts were gone. In the intelligence business, this is the first thing they teach us. If we see anyone looking at us too closely, we immediately memorize their features, gait, approximate height and build, and any other identifying marks in order to recall them if necessary later on.

I knew Chopin was working with her and realized that if she had come out of the bathroom, he might be in the men's room. I hastened to continue out of the café. My uncle and the General had both suggested I not get too close to the trigger unless an emergency arose or I had a dire need of it, and neither situation was currently present.

As I passed by this exotic woman, I caught the scent of her exquisite perfume. We looked at each other once again, and she gave me a slight smile. I returned it and nodded my head slightly out of respect. I was almost at the door, my right hand on the handle of the door. I heard behind me the familiar voice of Chopin.

"Commandantico? Is that you?" I had no other alternative than to turn to him and saw my good friend grinning broadly from ear to ear. His arms were open and outstretched to give me a joyful hug. "Brother! It's nice to see you!" He gave me a vast bear hug. "What are you doing here?"

I replied, "I was just on my way home to Santiago de las Vegas, and saw your car. And la! Here you are, my friend."

"I'm glad you stopped," he said. "I haven't seen you for a while, and I have a little problem I need your help in resolving. I didn't know if you were here in the capital or in Pinar del Rio with your folks."

"No, I've been around here all this time," I replied.

The lady had been standing close by to us all this time, observing us. Chopin realized it and said, "Oh, I'm sorry, *Señorita*. Patricia Flores of Spain, this is one of Fidel's most favored here in Cuba and my great friend."

She smiled and said in the accent of Madrid, "A great pleasure to meet you, Commandantico." She extended a hand to me.

I took and kissed it. I replied, "The pleasure is all mine, *Señorita* Flores."

She smiled. "Oh, wow! He kissed my hand. The

Commandantico is a perfect gentleman. That is very rare today, and that is very important to me as well as to many other women I know. But please, to my friends only—Patricia. I've heard many good things about you. You are an international figure, because you're around Fidel Castro and Che Guevara at all their speeches on television."

I smiled. "Well, I'm not sure if that's all true. I'm just an insignificant piece in the puzzle of this Revolution."

She winked at me. "I think we're going to be very good friends. Is that not true?"

"Absolutely. For me, it will be a real pleasure and a great honor. Thank you for your offer of friendship." I winked back at her and bowed to her. "It's very curious, because I believe I've heard a lot about you, too, not too long ago. We might have mutual friends in the same places. Besides, from the first moment our eyes met, I had the strange feeling that I've known you for a long time."

She smiled in a flattered way. "I'm glad you feel that way." She looked me up and down, from my military boots to my olive-green beret. "Why do they still call you Commandantico? I don't see any stars on your uniform."

I smiled and chuckled. I massaged my forehead with my fingers. "That is a long story I will tell you later on as we know each other better. As for my stars, I returned them to the military headquarters because they started to be a little too heavy for my shoulders."

We all exchanged knowing smiles, though we were all probably thinking of completely different ways of interpreting my answer. It was also possible that we had the same thought. Her stomach made a loud rumbling noise. She put her arm over her stomach in embarrassment.

"I'm sorry. My stomach is complaining. It didn't like the lousy food they served in the airplane, and it's been over ten hours since I've eaten anything."

I smiled. "You're in luck! This particular place makes the best *media noches* in all of Cuba."

"What is that?"

Chopin smiled as he replied, "The best sandwich you'll ever eat in your life! Do you dare to try your luck?"

Patricia smiled. "With the hunger I have and the noises my stomach is making, I'll dare to try anything! Why not? We're already here. We stopped only to use the bathroom, but since your friend suggests it, let's do it."

We walked a few steps further in and took the booth closest to the door. We sat down and a friendly waitress came to take our order.

Chopin winked very briefly and said, "*Señorita* Patricia has a very important assignment here in Cuba: an investigation into the insurance policy the Cuban government is trying to collect over *La Coubre*. You remember? So many innocent workers on the pier lost their lives."

I nodded. "Uh, huh," was all I said.

I was taken completely by surprise. Neither my uncle nor the General had mentioned anything about this. I hadn't even needed to meet her, but so far everything had gone well. It had been very casual, and I was Chopin's friend. I had a perfectly legitimate explanation should anyone later question my presence. I didn't give it too much importance, as this could only be the cover for her mission. The reality was that everything was likely related, prepared by our side of intelligence in case the Cuban counter-intelligence ran a routine check on her. All they would find then, in reference to her trip here, would be that story. At least, that is what I assumed at that moment.

A few minutes later, the waitress brought our order. As she put the plates on the table, I noticed several cars entering the parking lot at the same time. The waitress left, and we started to eat. I took another glance at the cars and saw that they were the kind of vehicles the G-2 customarily used.

Several men got out of the first car and started to peer in through the window, as if they were looking for someone. The others went over to Chopin's car. I nudged Chopin with my foot under the table.

"I think we have visitors, and they look like State Security. They have several cars." I was seated facing out, as I had been taught, while Chopin and Patricia sat opposite me.

Chopin put his sandwich down on his plate. Around his bite of sandwich, he said, "These bloodsuckers aren't just going to screw up our middle-of-the-night snack, they're going to screw up the *whole* night!" He nodded. "Truly, where we are, close to the bathroom, we're out of their view. These planters behind us with the Malanga vines help conceal us from view, and our location further obscures us."

Without appearing concerned, I said, "Well, if either of you guys has anything to worry about or at least don't have enough time to be detained for questioning by these imbeciles, then I think this will be the most appropriate moment to execute a Houdini before they come in here. My Soviet jeep with its military markings is in the parking lot. It might be a good hideout for somebody."

Patricia said, "I believe I know the reason behind this, if it's what I've been thinking." She pointed to Chopin. "We've never seen each other and don't know each other, OK?"

Chopin nodded. "OK."

She leaned down over the table and wrapped up the *media noches*. She knelt down to a half crouch. She rapidly moved at that half crouch into the hallway, disappearing from view there. All I saw was the flash of the men's room door as it swung open and immediately closed again. Without hesitation, I scooped up her empty plate and put it under mine. She had ordered a sugar cane juice to drink, so I took her glass, emptied it in the planter behind me, and concealed the glass in the vines.

The G-2 agents entered the front door. Some of them remained by the door, keeping an eye on the area and ascertaining that it was the only way in or out. Four other agents split into pairs, covering each line of booths. As they did so, they asked each occupant who they were and what car they were driving as they scrutinized faces.

By the time they approached our table, we had already paid the waitress. She had taken away our plates and thanked us for the generous tip we left her. We stood up to leave in an attempt to avoid them, but one of them came up to us. They noticed my uniform and greeted us courteously.

One agent said, "Good evening, *compañeros*. What kind of car are you driving?"

I answered for Chopin by saying, "The Soviet jeep with

the Armed Forces HQ logo out there."

They both looked at us carefully, and the one who had been asking the questions this time directly asked Chopin, "And you, *compañero*?"

Quickly, to prevent my answering, Chopin said, "An Edsel, mint green and white. Is there a problem, *compañero*?"

The G-2 man was tall, skinny, with dark skin and a mustache. He shook his head and said, "No, no." He had a leather dispatch satchel slung over one shoulder. He reached inside and pulled out a picture, which he showed to Chopin. "Do you know this woman, by any chance?"

Chopin nodded and then shook his head. As he did so, he said, "Yes. And no. As for really knowing her, no. But about half an hour ago, she asked me for a ride from the airport, and I brought her to the resort in Rio Cristal. So, yes, I know her as a passenger." He smiled. "She was very beautiful—you know? But she didn't even allow me to enter the resort. I wasn't even to pull in. As a gentleman, I did as she asked me. By the way, she was extremely generous. That beautiful woman tried to give me a fifty dollar bill—can you believe it?" He shook his head again. "Of course, I couldn't accept that, not even from that beautiful woman. Besides, I was just coming this way to meet with my friend the Commandantico, so it wasn't a hardship for me to bring someone part of the way with me."

He patted me on the shoulder. "He wanted to meet me here, because he wanted me to go with him and Che tomorrow to Santa Clara on some official business."

The two agents looked at each other uncertainly at that, rendered speechless by his startling announcement.

I thought I smelled them soiling their pants. Che's murderous reputation was known not just within his inner circle, but even outside in the broader governmental circles. Everyone knew that Che would send someone to prison for fifteen or twenty years without provocation and do so with the same level of importance as he would watch drops of condensation run down a glass. No one would have the power to stop it. Perhaps someone else had witnessed one of his hysterical attacks of paranoia as I had and spread the word around.

At that moment, one of the agents watching the door walked in and entered the men's bathroom. Chopin and I exchanged glances. To divert their attention, I asked the agent, "*Compañero*, what is the problem with that woman?"

The agent smiled and said in a slightly embarrassed voice, "I don't actually know what's going on with her. All I can tell you is that they sent us with the recommendation of being very careful. We were to pick her up at the airport because they wanted to question her at Villa Marista. Unluckily, the plane arrived half an hour earlier than scheduled, and she slipped through our fingers. We questioned one of the parking attendants at the airport, and they told us that she had left in a green and white Edsel driven by a black man. We just got lucky; as we were passing by on our way back to Havana, we saw a car matching the description, and we thought maybe she could be here."

Chopin smiled and shook his head. "*Compañero*, I believe I'm not the only black man in the whole city of Havana who has an Edsel of that color."

The agent smiled. "You're right. We were just lucky.

Thank you for your information. We should hurry up and see if we can still find her in the resort you dropped her off at."

They said their goodbyes and began to walk out of the café. The agent in the bathroom emerged when they called out for him. He appeared at the door with a paper towel still in his hands as he dried them.

Chopin and I exchanged relieved looks and breathed quiet sighs of relief. It appeared that Patricia had managed to execute the planned Houdini.

As soon as the last car left the parking lot, I got out of the booth and walked outside to be certain they didn't leave anyone behind to watch the restaurant. As I did so, Chopin went to the men's room to let Patricia know the coast was clear. It was evident that Chopin's story was good enough to convince the G-2 agents as being solid, or perhaps it was because of their rush to catch the famous woman at the resort. Either way, they left no one behind.

The only problem was that the resort was about five minutes away. As soon as they failed to find her there, they would turn around and come back to the city. As this was the only highway that connected the airport to Havana at that point, they would pass by the café again. We hoped it would take at least half an hour for them to search the resort.

Chopin came out of the restroom with an expression of bafflement. He spread his hands in confusion and called to me from the door, "I don't know where that woman went! She really disappeared. I looked at her in both bathrooms and all over the restaurant, and she's not anywhere to be found."

I called back, "Where could she have gone? We've got

to get out of here. Those guys could come back at any time! I didn't think she would take the Houdini reference literally."

I heard Patricia's voice loudly say from the rear window of the jeep behind me, "If you two don't stop yelling at each other, you're going to call the attention of someone inside the restaurant, and they'll come out to find out what's going on in the parking lot."

Chopin heard her voice and came out. He crossed himself in relief as he grinned. A little impatiently, he gestured towards his car. "Let's go, let's go! Let's get out of here before these bloodsuckers come back."

I raised both arms high to stop him. "Wait—I don't think it's a good idea. Even though I don't like it myself to get involved in this, from what I just heard that agent say, if you guys both get in your car, I don't think you'll get very far before you're stopped by another G-2 unit or the authorities."

Patricia had by now joined us. She said, "Thank you for your help. I agree with you completely. I think it's better for each of us if we say goodbye here, and I'll take a taxi. You guys go, and I'll handle it from here."

I smiled. "Taking a taxi is like playing Russian roulette here in Cuba. I think that's the worst idea of all. The taxis belong to an organization controlled by the government, and they all have radios. The company name is ANCHAR[16], and many of these drivers have been

---

[16] *Asociacion Nacional de Choferes de Alquiler Revolucionarios* (The National Association of the Chauffeur Fleet of the Revolution), the taxi drivers' union

recruited by the G-2 as informants. Others are formal G-2 who are pretending to be drivers. You'd be taking a huge chance."

Patricia looked at me. "Don't worry, kid. I've handled much bigger fish than this."

I smiled. "Excuse me, Patricia, I don't want to be condescending to you. Yes, you're older than me, but you're on a strange patio. This is not a democratic country. This is a totalitarian communist country with a much different game of chance. The rules don't exist for them, only for us. The odds of the house winning here are multiplied by hundreds, if not by thousands. To add a little bit of salt and pepper to it, you're a foreigner, and they can smell that miles away by the way you speak and the way you dress. You couldn't even walk ten feet here and remain undetected."

I turned to Chopin. "The only way Patricia won't wind up in the hands of the G-2 is for us to protect her from now on. It's evident that her cover has been blown out of the water."

I turned back to her. "See if this makes sense to you, Patricia. Given that you're a foreigner, the G-2 must have a very strong reason for wanting to interrogate you. This country jealously guards its image with the rest of the world. You are the ones who provide the support to the very weak economy this country has. The order for the G-2 to take you in for interrogation must have come from very high levels, even from the leaders of this government. The charges must be very serious for them to take the chance of an international scandal. They should wait to accumulate evidence rather than send these agents to pick you up as soon as you step off the plane."

Chopin looked at me grimly. "You're goddamn right. This must be very serious. Patricia, you should leave with him. You'll be in good hands, that's all I can tell you."

Without speaking another word, he went over to the trunk of his car. He opened it and began to remove Patricia's luggage.

A little irritated, Patricia said, "Wait, what are you doing, Chopin?"

Chopin ignored her and continued transferring her luggage from his car to the jeep.

Her irritation grew. "I don't even know this kid! I'm not going anywhere with him!"

Chopin spread his arms. "Believe me, he's only trying to save your life, and at the same time trying to help you complete whatever work you've come here to Cuba to do. He's giving you the best possibility to get out of here in one piece, the same way as you arrived."

Patricia's irritation was growing by the second. She repeated, "I don't even know who this kid is. He's practically a baby, for God's sake! Please take that luggage out of the jeep. I would rather take my chances with a taxi. Look me in the face, Chopin! Nothing annoys me more than someone ignoring me."

Chopin threw his hands up in disgust. She yelled at him, "What kind of help are you? You're supposed to be my assistant here! Are you deaf or just stupid? What do you know about my work? You only know what I've told you, nothing else!"

Chopin had one of her bags in his hand and he threw it down in anger. Indignantly, he looked her up and down. "I know more about your work here than you know, lady."

He shook his finger in her face. "I cannot believe in a hundred years that a woman so beautiful would so completely lack the most essential principles in a human being: class and respect for others!" He pointed at me. "The only part of his body that could be called 'baby' that I or any of his friends know of, is between his legs! You should respect him the same way you respect each of us. The only thing he's trying to do is save your life, lady, all while putting his own life on the line!"

Things were getting out of hand, so I interceded. I held out my hand to her with a smile. She looked at me incredulously. I said, "It's a pleasure to meet you, Mrs. Patricia Flores. I am Sebastian Almendares." She looked at me as if she had seen a ghost. Her face paled, then reddened, then paled again in her confusion. "The people of Madrid are sweet like the sugar cane of Cuba."

Her expression of astonishment deepened from looking like she was seeing a ghost to seeing an entire army of them. Dropping all pretense, like an automaton she mumbled the proper reply. She went over to the still angry Chopin and embraced him, giving him a kiss on the cheek. "I'm sorry, Chopin. Can you forgive me?"

Chopin growled angrily. "Let's make this very clear. I'm not stupid, and I'm not deaf either."

She smiled. "Yes, I'm sorry. But for a moment there, I thought you were betraying me by putting me in the hands of this kid and into the hands of assassins. Please forgive me."

Chopin nodded as he picked up the bag he had thrown down. "OK, apology accepted." He glared at her and pointed at the jeep. "Now get in that car before I kick your ass into there!"

"OK, sir, OK," she said jokingly to diffuse the situation. She scurried into the jeep, shutting the door behind her quickly.

After she got into the jeep, I said to Chopin, "I will call you at your house in the morning. It's very possible that I may need your help with what I'm going to do. We don't have time now to talk about your little problem, so we'll discuss it then. I have to get out of here before those guys get back from Rio Cristal. The last thing we need is for them to see this woman with us."

Chopin pointed to where she sat in the seat and growled. "Be careful. The pretty cat just showed us her nails for the first time."

Chapter 10: The Precise Hunt

Chopin and I smiled and got into our respective vehicles. We drove out of the lot and headed towards the city. After we drove for a few minutes in silence, Patricia said, "I'm sorry. It was not my intention to offend you. How in the hell did you get into this business so young?"

I smiled and glanced at her. "That is another long story that I'll tell you when we know each other at little better."

"I'll hold you to it. That's two long stories you owe me."

"OK," I replied with a smile. "You don't have to apologize for calling me a kid. Besides, that is part of what this government has stolen from me: my childhood and youth. Don't worry, you won't ever see me angry over that in any way or form. Even though I stopped acting like a kid a few years back, when I actually *was* an innocent boy, it's what I really am, based on my age: a kid playing adult games. It's not by choice; it's my moral duty to my country, an obligation circumstances placed on me."

She shook her head. "You're definitely not a kid. Kids don't talk like that." She smiled at me.

"Thank you," I said with a small smile. "As you know very well, in our circles, the less we talk about ourselves, the less information we give our enemies concerning our personality and character. Our silence might delay giving them the kind of information they can use to put us down."

Patricia was the one to nod this time. "You're right, my friend Commandantico. If you keep your mouth shut, there's no way a fly can enter it."

"We in Cuba have the same saying but in a different way."

She smiled again. "Those sayings have many passports. They travel from one continent to another and all around the world. They only change the wording and structure." We glanced at each other and smiled.

We passed a public telephone and she said, "Please stop. I have to make an urgent call to the Belgian embassy. At this hour, there's probably no one there, but I need to leave a coded message for my contact. After what just happened, I don't think I can put my feet back in that building without getting intercepted by my enemies."

I smiled. "That is a good idea. I also have a phone call to make to *my* contact. You'll probably spend the night there, and tomorrow morning I can find the information you need to complete your work. After that, I'll bring you as close as I possibly can to your marks."

I looked her over. "The greatest priority at this moment is to change your appearance and your clothing. There's no longer any fashion or good taste in dressing here in Cuba. Anyone who has just lived in Cuba for the past few years can easily identify a foreigner ten miles away, because of the clothes you guys wear. That's why you were identified so quickly today and your exact description given to the G-2, who was simply showing around a photograph. From this moment on, the best idea is for you to change yourself into a simple, common Cuban woman, with no details that would attract attention from anyone. Do you understand?"

"Of course I do. You might consider yourself very good at what you do, but humbly speaking, I've been considered the best in the world at what I do."

"Good," I replied. "Then we'll have no problems."

She nodded her agreement. "I only see one problem. From what I've been told, everything in this country is rationed. How will I manage to get a new wardrobe, and what will I do with the wardrobe I have now? The way I imagine I'll have to leave this country, I won't be able to take it with me."

I replied with a small smile, "As for the first question, that is one of the reasons for my phone call to my contact. That will resolve that for you. For your second question, my contact is a woman, and will probably enjoy greatly your wardrobe."

We had already passed the large La Fuente Luminosa. A few blocks later, I saw a phone booth in the lot next to a coffee shop, and I pulled over. The lot was darkened, as a few of the street lights had burned out. I parked in the darkest corner and handed a few coins to Patricia. She went into one booth while I went into the one next to hers to call Chandee.

Chandee answered, and I asked, "Are you asleep?"

"No, I've been waiting for your call."

"Well, I'm not home yet. A little cat crossed in front of my jeep and I had to stop so that it wouldn't get hurt. I'll be there in a little while."

"Oh," she asked, "are you coming to my house?"

"Yes," I answered, "I have something extremely important to share with you, and a great surprise. You're about to get a new wardrobe of the latest European fashion."

Her voice was teasingly insinuating as she answered, "Oh—and what exactly is that going to cost me?"

"You can't even imagine it," I replied.

"Come on," she pleaded, "tell me."

"Well, I'll give you an advance. It'll be a huge sacrifice, something you probably won't want to part with," I teased.

"What?" she demanded.

"Probably a couple of your *miliciana* uniforms."

"Wow!"

"I'm not coming by myself," I cautioned her in preparation. "I'm bringing a woman, and it might be a good idea if she spent the night at your house."

Her tone was teasing. "For you, anything. The house is empty, since everyone else is gone on a trip."

"Be ready at the alternate entrance. I don't want anyone to see us coming in."

Still teasing, she said, "Oh, I guess I have to share you tonight, eh?"

We finished our conversation and I hung up. Patricia's conversation had been shorter, and she was already in the jeep waiting for me. As I got into the vehicle, she was removing her hat and covering her hair with a kerchief. We left the parking lot, and I drove towards Chinatown.

After a few minutes, we arrived outside the antique store. As always, Chandee was waiting on the sidewalk. She gestured for me not to stop and went around to open the gate for us. As soon as I had passed by her, she closed the gate.

I parked and got out. Chandee and I embraced and she kissed me on the cheek. I introduced Patricia to her. I asked Patricia, "What do you need most from the car?"

"The handbag, please," she answered.

I got the bag for her, and we followed Chandee through the maze of passages into the store. Patricia looked at me with an impressed expression. We opened the secret door and walked into the house.

Chandee said to Patricia, "My mother and sister have gone on a trip with my father to the town of Guantanamo to avoid suspicion. The persecution of those who drive by themselves has been increasing, especially in the last few weeks. The authorities are more lenient with someone driving with family—they're less likely to assume someone is engaged in counter-revolutionary activities."

When Chandee offered us refreshments, I declined. Patricia agreed, saying, "Yes, please. My *media noches* was exquisite, but the toilet wasn't the most hygienic place to dine." Chandee looked at her curiously, and Patricia said, "I'll tell you later."

Patricia asked Chandee if she could use the shower, as she wanted to refresh herself after her trip.

"Of course," Chandee said. "This is your house from now on, Patricia. Whoever works with him works with us. You have our full trust."

They exchanged some small talk for a few minutes, and Chandee prepared the bathroom for Patricia, who asked me if I could bring in the remainder of her luggage. "I need a few things for my job," she explained. "Chandee can pick from the rest for herself or to give to someone else—whatever she wants."

I went out to the jeep and brought in the rest of the luggage. After Patricia left to take her shower, I took the opportunity to bring Chandee up to date on what was going on. I outlined the plan I had in mind to enact over the next twenty-four hours and what clothes I wanted Patricia to be dressed in from now on.

A few hours later, Patricia was given Chandee's room. Cuban custom was to give the guest the most comfortable place in the house. Chandee walked me out to the jeep. We kissed for a while, and then I advised her to not leave Patricia alone for a single second.

"Even if she wants to go someplace, go with her. No matter how she's dressed, if she opens her mouth, she'll reveal herself to be a foreigner. That's the last thing we want anyone to notice. No matter how well she can imitate a Cuban accent, the new slang created by the Marxist government is very difficult for a foreigner to pick up on unless they spend a great deal of time here."

As I left Chandee's house, I had in mind to return to Santiago de las Vegas to spend the night, but I changed my mind. I decided to try my luck by changing course and drive towards the safe house at Boca Siega.

I arrived at the house about thirty minutes later and drove through the gate. I found a strange thing there. Several cars were parked around the driveway. Something big was going on.

Two soldiers of Che's escort were on guard at the entry and saluted me. One of them asked me with a smile, "Hey, are you coming to the big party?"

I nodded. "Yes. I hear there's a lot of pretty *señoritas* here. Is that true?"

Both guards nodded. One made an hourglass gesture with his hands and then kissed his fingers as he made a sizzling sound. I said goodbye and continued up the drive, looking for a space to park. It was difficult, but near the end on the edge of the grass I found a small corner space where I could leave the jeep without obstructing anyone who might be leaving.

I walked to the main door of the residence. I could hear the loud music of a live orchestra from outside. As I approached the main door, the trumpet broke out in a solo as the group played Caribbean music. I smiled at my good luck. I had not been expecting to hit the jackpot at that time of night. But my decision to swing by might yield some excellent results, especially as the party would likely put Che in a good frame of mind. He might even be a little tipsy, and after a few drinks his personality tended to mellow in its paranoia and become friendlier as he told everyone tales of his heroic past conquests and his plans for the future.

I greeted the door guard and entered the house. I walked through the corridor, maneuvering through the crowd of wait staff. I noticed one with several bottles of Bacardi and imported Scotch whiskey, similar to the kind I had bought at the Café Labiada not too long ago. I knew from experience how expensive those bottles were. It told me that there was someone of great importance at this party—someone Che wanted to impress.

I excused myself as I moved through the crowd. Some were dressed in military uniforms, and many were very elegantly dressed civilians. I saw a huge table near the kitchen, around which lines were forming. The table was loaded with various kinds of seafood, meat loaf, pâté, and a wide variety of fruits and vegetables. The centerpiece was a Cuban roasted suckling pig with an apple in its mouth.

A tall, distinguished man dressed in white with a chef's

hat was slicing small pieces of the roasted pig and serving them to an exotically beautiful woman. Next to her was a woman of equal beauty, and both were very well-dressed. I recognized both of them at once: Sonya and Tanya.

Tanya looked at me as if she wasn't sure whether she recognized me. I waved to her, and she was able to place me. With a broad grin, she waved me in. She put her plate down and began to gesture to me with both hands.

I excused myself as I maneuvered through the line that was waiting around the table. The suckling pig looked so exquisite that everyone wanted a piece of it. In spite of the splendor of the other food on the table, everyone in line was waiting for their share of that pork.

When I reached her, Tanya surprised me utterly by kissing me tightly on the lips. Of all the greetings I might have expected from her, this was the least likely, especially in front of all these people. When she let me go, I smiled in embarrassment.

Smiling as if there was nothing wrong, she said joyfully, "I wanted so much to see you! I tried to get in touch with you several times, but every time I called your parents, I never had any luck in getting through to you. You were either out of town or they had no idea when you were going to come back. After our last conversation at my beach house, many things have happened. What Maggie told me and you later corroborated made a lot of sense. But I never had the opportunity to speak to you again."

I replied, "Fidel, Che, and other wild beasts in the jungle haven't left me time—not even enough to take a deep bath, which is what I love to do. I've had to content myself with quick showers."

She smiled and said, "I hope you haven't gotten contagious with Che. At least reserve enough time to douche yourself. You are a handsome young man and very different from the rest of the crowd surrounding you. One of things I've always liked about you is that you smell very pleasant."

I returned her smile, getting her message. "Thank you. The sentiment is mutual; you always smell lovely."

Sonya was still in line and had been served. She came over to us and kissed me on the cheek. After saying hello, she said, "Oh, my God. I love your military haircut. You look so macho, so manly. And you're so big now! You're growing up."

"Well," I said, "it's been a couple of years since we last saw each other. Thank you for the compliment. I hope I haven't stopped growing."

We walked over to the large dance floor, which was set up with several tables for people to eat, while still reserving some space for those who wanted to dance. We selected a small corner near the wall with a partition. We set our drinks down on the wide ledge and our plates on the table. This allowed us to keep a good view of the room, whereas sitting down would have obstructed our view.

"What is the reason for this party?" I asked Tanya.

"The new European faction in town, Marko and Marcelino. Che's throwing them a welcome party. They've returned from Guardalavaca, but for security reasons they cut short their vacations. Che has been very paranoid about them, so he brought them today to stay here in this house. He thinks they'll be more secure here, and he decided to throw this party all day long today."

Sonya interrupted to tell me, "If you want to speak with Che, be very careful. He had one of his hysterical attacks today. We weren't bearers of good news for him from Madrid. Even if you see him smiling and apparently worry-free and happy, inside he's in Hell."

Tanya threw Sonya a warning glance. It was apparent that Sonya had been there for a while and was a little tipsy. Certainly she didn't take the hint very well. She looked at Tanya, spread her hands, and said, "So what?" She put a hand on my shoulder. "One of the things your niece told me in confidence before she died was that this young man is solid like marble. He honors his last name very well. He doesn't let anyone intimidate him, no matter what the circumstances. She said this with absolute assurance. He also won't open his mouth to get people into trouble; he only opens it to get them out of it. So stop looking at me like that. I know I'm a little tipsy; I won't deny it. But that has nothing to do with my wits. You know I'm not stupid." She plucked at her hair. "I don't have a single stupid hair on my head. Now, if you'll excuse me. I need to go to the restroom. I have a tickling in my bladder that I cannot hold any longer."

She smiled and put her plate down on the partition. She walked away, swishing her hips seductively. I admired her as I watched her go. Tanya smiled and asked, "You like mature women, eh?" I only smiled without answering.

She took my arm in a friendly way. "Uh, oh!" She grinned. "Those military exercises have made you a muscular man. Look at those biceps!" She squeezed my arm. "I agree with Sonya. That military haircut does well with you, because it exposes the angles of your face, accentuating your masculinity. The long hair you had before hid it."

I smiled. "If you keep telling me these things, I'll eventually believe it. Stop it, please. But let me tell you something in confidence. Even though I came back with these muscles and a tan, it was the worst experience in my life."

"Really?" she asked in surprise.

"Imagine it—after being the Commander of the Commandos for a few years, I suddenly was reduced to a simple recruit in the Army that everyone pushed around. Believe me, there are a lot of those who like to push others around in the Army! I think it is an experience that I will never forget for the rest of my life."

Tanya smiled again. "Just remember, to us you will always be the Commandantico—the most favored Commander of Fidel. I hope you understand this: everyone fears and respects you just because you're so close to Fidel. They don't want you to whisper anything negative to the Commander-in-Chief. Remember also that revolutions throughout history leave us one day at the top of the world, eating the best meals. But the next day we're down at the bottom, eating dirt like animals. Unfortunately, revolutions devour their own sons as Satan does."

She raised her head and saw that Che was approaching with a group of men. "Uh, oh—speak of the king, and the king walks into his kingdom."

My back was to Che, and I was puzzled by the suddenly harsh expression on her face and the change in complexion. I turned around and saw them on the other side of the room. Che was walking in our direction with Marko, Marcelino, and several men in his escort.

I turned back to Tanya and said, "Since the last conversation we had, I've noticed that you've changed a lot. By the way, I'm very sorry about Maggie's death, may she finally find peace. I know that even though she was disturbed and very rebellious towards you, she loved you very much, just as I know you loved her. She revealed to me some very intimate secrets. One of them I will tell you now. She told me that she loved you more than her own mother, because she had never bonded with her mother as she had with you."

Two tears rolled down Tanya's cheeks. Sonya was returning to us. The restrooms were on the opposite side of the room from where Che was. He and his group had stopped in the middle of the room to speak with some of his guests. Sonya came up to us, and she noticed Tanya's emotional state. She handed Tanya a handkerchief and put an arm around her friend's shoulders.

Tanya gently pushed her arm off her shoulder, but held on to her hand. As inoffensively as possible, she said, "Thank you, but look at who is coming."

Tanya gestured with her head, and Sonya looked. Tanya said, "I don't want to show him any kind of emotion or sensitivity. He'll take it as an absurd weakness that is no good for the work we're supposed to do for him. I don't want to hear any more bullshit from him."

Sonya nodded. "Why don't you go to the bathroom? We'll excuse you to him."

"OK," Tanya replied. Very quickly, she turned and headed towards the bathroom.

Sonya looked deep into my eyes. "We both are going to be at the beach house for a few days until Tanya recuperates from a wound she has on her ankle. If you manage to come and visit us, it would not only be very pleasant for us but maybe you can learn a few new things on the menu that you could use in the future for your own security. I'm sorry, but I cannot say any more. Remember, in here the walls have eyes and ears."

This time, I looked at her a little concerned. I leaned against the partition, wondering what was going on here. "OK," I said with a nod. "I might do that, because I really enjoy your company, too. Besides, after all the work they put me through in the Army all these last months, I think I've earned a small vacation."

Che walked towards us again. He finally got close enough to recognize us. I could see from the shape of their eyes and noses that he did indeed have Marko and Marcelino with him, even though they no longer looked like each other.

A little jealously, he said to Sonya, "I hope you're not offering oral sex to the Commandantico." Sonya threw him a look that could kill. Without letting her answer his disrespectful remark, he asked in irritation, "Where the hell did Tanya go in such a rush? When she saw me, she didn't want to look me in the eyes after the tremendous shit you guys left in Madrid."

Sonya breathed deeply and gave him a small smirk. She said firmly, "Sorry, Commandante Guevara, but the pile of shit, to use your own words, doesn't belong to us. It belongs to whoever betrayed us. Not only was our personal information sold to our enemies, but our actual identities as well. It put our personal security at risk to such an extreme that we were almost killed."

Che leaned back in surprise. He glared at her hatefully. Sonya, however, met his resentful stare. It was clear he did not want to hear this. To everyone's astonished eyes, Che whipped out his pistol and cocked it. He leveled it at her—and, indirectly, towards me. Everyone froze, expecting the worst. Sonya did not even blink; she only smiled.

Tanya was returning from the bathroom and saw Che pointing his gun at Sonya. She took in his maniacal expression and rushed towards us. She yelled out, "Ernesto! What the hell are you doing?"

Che whirled and trained his weapon on Tanya. Suddenly, his grim demeanor changed as he erupted into maniacally laughter as he lowered the gun. "What's the matter with you guys? You lose your sense of humor in Madrid?"

He walked over to hug Tanya, but she stopped him. "Did you unload that pistol?"

Still laughing, he complied and then hugged Tanya. Then he brought the embrace over to Sonya and hugged, her as well. "These two women are the most loyal and efficient internationalists I have ever had." He raised his arm and pointed at Marko and Marcelino. "Of course, after you two guys."

Marko and Marcelino were still in shock at what they had just witnessed. Che turned and saw the plate still full of food on the partition. He asked, "Whose plate is that?"

Sonya said, "It's mine. Why?"

"What's the matter with you? Is our food no longer good enough for you? Or do you prefer the European high-class food and dessert?"

Sonya shook her head in obvious discontent. "No. I've only been deprived of my appetite because of the flavor of treason in my throat that I brought back with me from

Europe."

Che looked at her once more with that nasty, spiteful stare. This time, however, he left his pistol in its holster. He picked up a piece of yucca from the plate and pointed it at Sonya. "Boom, boom," he said, and then ate it.

Then with a smile he started to eat some of the pork. As he did, he pointed at me in an attempt to distract from the situation. He took me by surprise with his question. "What the hell did you put in that cigar you gave me in the briefing with Marko and Marcelino? It put me on the toilet for two days. No medication was strong enough to stop the diarrhea that dehydrated me and nearly sent me to the hospital."

I looked him in the eyes with a genuine expression of surprise. He bored into my eyes, either in an attempt to intimidate me or study my reactions. The color rose in my face. The last thing I needed was this man to discharge what he had in his personality or his distress with those two women to pull out his weapon once more and shoot me in the head like he did Claudio a few years ago. I controlled myself with an effort.

With all the calm I could muster, I said, "I'm not the one who manufactured those cigars, and *you* were the one who gave them to me, when I went to the French embassy. I don't know anything about cigars. Remember, I smoked one, right in front of you at the table with Marcelino, Marko, and my brother-in-law. Not one of us got sick."

I allowed a little anger to creep into my voice to let him know he had outraged me. "Why are you shoving this off onto me, eh? Why don't you take the residue from the cigar to a lab for analysis? I told you this once, and I'll tell you again: this is the problem you have. You don't trust anyone—not even yourself!"

Out of the corner of my eye I could see both women smiling in enjoyment. Che tried to stare me down, but I maintained full contact with his eyes, letting him see my discontent. Suddenly, he started laughing once more. "What's the matter with all you guys today? Have you really lost your senses of humor?"

I shook my head, still showing my anger and disgust, even though my knees trembled a little. I knew that what I had contemplated doing could have cost my life. I said loudly, "You'll have to excuse me, but the problem here is that you are the one who has lost his sense of humor—not us!" Tanya and Sonya both nodded in agreement. "How morbid is your humor that you try to intimidate and scare your friends? I don't think you would like that kind of humor if it were pulled on you."

I pulled my pistol out, cocked it, and pointed it at him. The escort immediately reached for their weapons. Che threw up both hands and said, "OK, OK, you got me." I noted that none of the escort had actually pulled their weapons.

I unloaded my pistol and holstered it. "Ha, ha, ha," I said sarcastically as I shook my hands in the air. "That is not humorous for anyone. Then you have the nerve to accuse me of giving you poisoned cigars, trying to make me feel like a shitty traitor, somebody who put his own body in the middle of bullets to protect your life!"

My face by now was as red as the hammer and sickle flags which decorated the room. The adrenaline from his threats to Sonya and Tanya combined with the insult to me personally produced this effect, not even counting my own fear for my life. I was always warned by my advisers how unstable Che was. It made him feel superior to kill other people. According to the best psychiatrists we had on our team, he suffered from a tremendous inferiority complex from his earliest years due to his continued illness with his asthma and inability to play normally like other kids his age.

    I stared him down in silence, waiting for the worst. Che, however, stopped eating and leaned against the wall. He looked at me in a strange way that was for me very familiar; it was the same one he gave me the day at the Pinar del Rio regiment when he asked me about Lenin and Marx's books. I was, however, still thinking about why no one had actually pulled their weapons, not even Marko and Marcelino. Perhaps they actually wanted him dead. We continued our staring contest.

    Che continued looking at me proudly, almost in ecstasy. I remembered how that look was the same admiring one he had given me on that highway in Santa Clara, when I was trying to get my nerves under control and he asked me if I was all right. My diverting answer about the Ford had amused him and created a sense of admiration at my apparently cold-blooded reaction. It didn't matter that I was still badly shaken by the fact I was still covered in the bone fragments and brain matter from the man he had executed in front of me a few minutes earlier.

    I thought about how he had screamed at his entire escort that day as he declared me to be a true Revolutionary. It was the same way he now said loudly before the crowd, "I'm sorry. First of all, to you, Sonya. Second to you, Tanya. And finally, and especially,

Dr. Julio Antonio del Marmol

Commandantico, for reminding me that I'd broken my promise to never doubt your loyalty." He raised his glass. "This is what happens when we drink too much of this stuff. I will only believe you guys will sincerely forgive me if you will now come up to me and give me a big hug of forgiveness."

He opened his arms as he stepped over to us. Tanya was the first to embrace him, but not before whispering something in his ear. From his grimace, it must have been nasty, but he limited himself to nodding as she stepped away.

Sonya was next to hug him, but her smile was still forced. As she backed away, she shook a reproving finger at him. Every time someone hugged him, the crowd applauded.

I hugged him, and he murmured in my ear, "Come with me to the terrace. I have something important to tell you." He put his left arm around my shoulder and pointed at me as he said loudly to the crowd, "This young man is my adopted son. He is the son I've always wished to have!"

As we walked away, Tanya gestured to me to call her later. We left Marko and Marcelino with Sonya and Tanya. As we walked onto the terrace, Che said, "I'm not going to tell you this to justify my conduct, but I've been having a dog's day."

I looked at him and in an attempt to show him a little sympathy and leave the incident behind, asked, "Something bad? Something I can help you with?" I tried to show him I had no hard feelings and that our relationship would continue to be friendly as always. Apparently, it touched a nerve; he put his arm around my shoulder.

"I feel very guilty and remorseful," he said. I knew that was a lie but thought he might have said that as a trick he had learned from the KGB to make me feel like he was human. "I haven't really drunk a lot of liquor. I'm very depressed, in spite of our tremendous success. We had a bad setback, and it's worried me a lot."

"Why do you feel this way? After all, the plan towards JFK was a complete success, and you've received high commendation from Fidel."

We reached the doors to the terrace, and he asked the escort to remain inside. We sat down, and he lit a cigar. "I was actually joking with you only to distract attention from those two bitches. After all these years without failing in any mission I sent them on, they not only failed but left behind them a big pile of shit this time. It's something they should not *ever* let happen. They both think I'm stupid, because they tried to convince me that a superwoman—an invisible poet superwoman—wounded Tanya, killed Yoska, and slipped through their fingers." He comically rolled his eyes. "And after the whole thing, she left a white rose for each of them!"

He threw his beret onto the table in disgust. "I don't know what the hell movie they watched in Europe to bring all this crap drama to me. They also told me that this 'superspy' disappeared in Madrid. According to their information, this woman returned to Langley, which is why they decided to return to Cuba. Tanya was in no condition to continue tracking this woman around the world—so they say. What neither of them know is that our counterintelligence found out that in disguise and under the name of Patricia Flores, our mark not only remained in Madrid, but was also assigned by Langley to come to Cuba on the very same plane they used to return. She is using an identity as an adjuster for the same insurance company that we dealt with during the *La Coubre* incident."

I leaned back in my chair. If what Che was telling me was the truth, why had the two Amazon killers not provided Che their full account? I could only assume that both of these women, being real professionals, were intending to return here. Even if Patricia was in disguise, no matter how good, they had the skills to detect her. I stroked my chin with my right hand as I prepared to drop a bomb Che wasn't expecting.

"Have you considered the possibility that these women were actually telling you the truth about everything? I don't know with what motive, but Cuban counterintelligence might have received orders to misinform you in order to destroy your internationalist group? After the tremendous success you had with the American President, they might be jealous of you. Remember, these internationalist men and women are loyal to *you*, not to Fidel or Raul."

Che jumped as if someone had given him an electric shock. He looked at me in surprise. He shifted in his chair and raked his fingers through his hair. He looked deep into my eyes. "Do you know something I don't know? Have you heard something said behind my back you haven't told me yet?"

I stared him in the eyes, as well. "What I'm going to say to you is completely confidential, and under no circumstance should it go beyond the two of us. You understand—for no reason?"

He nodded. "I understand. Of course, that is our agreement we've always had."

"Yes," I answered, "but in the situation with Piñeiro and Ramiro Valdes, when they were trying to entrap me at the auction, you weren't completely honest with me. That's why I want to give you a warning. This information, if Fidel or Raul call me in to question me, I will deny ever having said, because this conversation never took place. You understand?"

"Yes."

"Very good, just so it's completely clear between us. The reason I repeat it is because it doesn't just involve me; it involves other people."

Che said, "But you have to remember that I defended you against Piñeiro's accusations in Fidel's office. Later, I apologized to you for all that happened. Do you remember?"

I didn't think he liked my words too much, but he also didn't want to argue with me out of fear of jeopardizing the information he wanted to get from me. I noticed his impatience—his eyes were wide open, and his pupils were dilated. I leaned forward and lowered my voice.

"On the birthday of my nephew Frank, Fidel and Raul came to my brother-in-law's farm. After dinner, they sat down on the large porch of the front patio. Majito served them coffee while I got dressed in my room. They must have wanted privacy, because they went to the corner of the porch that was right outside my window. I was dressing to leave, and Canen came to my room to see if I wanted to go with them to the military unit. He was planning to show them a couple of things.

"When Canen walked in, I put my finger to my lips and

motioned him to come in quietly. The walls of that old ranch were made with very thin wooden shingles, so I could hear everything being said outside. On top of that, because it was summer, my window was open—just the curtain was drawn. My lights were off, so they didn't realize anyone was in the room. Raul repeated to Fidel that he had to put the brakes on you very quickly. He said you would be the kind of man to steal the power away from Fidel. Fidel asked Raul how it could be done discreetly. Raul said the only way they had would be to take away all of his command, dismantling it piece by piece and bit by bit.

"His analogy was to draining a body of blood, and the life force slowly ebbs away." I shook my head and leaned back in silence to observe his reaction.

Che also leaned back in his chair and took a long puff on his cigar as he thought. With the cigar in his right hand, he pointed to me. "Is your brother-in-law disposed to corroborating this conversation?"

I smiled. "I've been thinking about that ever since we overheard that extremely private conversation between the Castro brothers. I asked him if he wouldn't mind testifying about what we both heard to anyone. Canen replied to me, 'Only to Che, for his eyes and ears only.' Raul is the chief of the Army, and so is Canen's boss. He's not afraid for himself, but he knows that if he says a word, his family would disappear, and his family is my family."

Che violently knocked the ash on his cigar off against the table. "That is the reason Camilo died, for his indiscretions and the threat he represented to them. All these fuckers are the same. Camilo told everyone that he's no communist and wanted no association with any

Marxist. But then he lacked the *cajones* to say that to Fidel's face. When Fidel asked him about bringing socialism to Cuba, Camilo said right in front of me that he was *fidelista*, and that whatever Fidel decided would be OK with him."

Che spread his arms helplessly in discontented disgust. "What kind of coward has no convictions of his own but follows another unconditionally? That's why the brothers decided to eliminate him. When they consulted with me, I told them that a man with no backbone is not trustworthy and could wind up becoming at any moment your worst enemy."

I couldn't believe it. In the midst of his depression and frustration, spurred by his indignation with the Castros, he confirmed the wide-held suspicion that the leaders had killed Camilo Cienfuegos. The innocent and naïve Camilo had told everyone, including his good friend Huber Matos, that he disliked a communist system for Cuba and that some of the other commanders—feigning friendship—had told Fidel and Raul what Cienfuegos' feelings really were. That betrayal cost him his life.

"Canen is a very brave and decent man," I said with a frown. "He has doubled bones in his back. His *cajones* are twice as big as anyone else's. But above all, we have to respect the decisions of others. Especially when they're actually doing us a favor and entrusting us with something that could put their lives on the line. Do you know why I asked my brother-in-law if he had no problems with repeating this to you?"

My frown changed to a smile, and I let the conviction show in my face. "Because I know you. I know you are an extremely trustworthy man. If you provide me with information and I have some doubts, I don't need you to prove anything to me. I say 'thank you,' I take the information, and I corroborate if I have any doubts. But if I have *any* doubts in respect to anything you tell me, I have to keep it to myself. That is called courtesy towards your friends and comrades, if you want them to be loyal to you."

Che moved his head in nervous confusion. He had no answer for what I had said. For the first time, I saw him at a complete loss, so I went in for the kill. "The most important thing in this life is not the value of bravery or the size of your *cajones*—it's your brain, your intellect. If you don't dedicate some time to cultivate it, you'll wind up like my good friend Camilo—in some country, manipulated by these two conniving brothers who don't leave any space in their power for anyone that could be in any way a shadow for their future ambitions. You take it or leave it, do what you want. I only have the loyalty and confidence that you asked of me at the beginning of our friendship. I hope and expect that you respect my loyalty, confidence, and friendship as I've respected yours."

Che looked at me appreciatively. For the moment at least, I had obtained his complete trust. He knew I had crossed the line when I told him what I had about the Castro brothers, and in doing so I had given him a pledge of unswerving loyalty. Without saying it, I had communicated to him clearly that I did not sympathize with the methods employed by the Castros towards both friend and enemy. They made no distinction between the two when they thought their power was in any way threatened. They would use intimidation, extortion, even murder. Che was no stranger to these methods, being a practitioner himself—but now the shoe was on the other foot, and he took the perceived threat very seriously.

Perhaps because of the extreme confidence I had shown, Che seemed to feel an unusually close bond with me at that moment. He said something then I did not expect, perhaps in repayment of my trust. With the maniacal gleam of a professional assassin, he leaned forward and stroked his beard. Smiling diabolically, he said, "The Castro brothers are tremendously jealous of me. They can't even sleep at night. It's been eating them away like a cancer, because there is another master plan in the works to kill another Pope."

I opened my eyes in shocked disbelief, my eyebrows shooting into my hair line. Pope John XXIII had died in June of that year—purportedly from stomach cancer.

Still staring me in the eyes, Che pointed at me with his left hand and smiled as he continued. "You have exactly the same expression on your face that Fidel had when I laid out the plan to eliminate Kennedy. He told me, 'Che, that plan is too ambitious. I don't think it's possible. But you can count on me if you need anything.' That hypocrite!" He scratched at his beard cynically while he waved his cigar in the air. "I know for a fact that when Fidel said that, he had no doubt that I would fail. It reached my ears from more than one person I trust that not only he but also Raul made such comments behind my back.

"I told him that tomorrow Marcelino and Marko will leave the country to work with our associates inside the Vatican and continue my international masterpiece of a scheme. Fidel knows that what I sight, I put the bullet in. He has an internal conflict, because the more I succeed, the more glory and respect I take from him. Inside all of the official circles, everyone knows who the strongest man in the Revolution is."

He tapped his chest with his left hand with a small smile. I looked at him in awe, but inside I was filled with disgust with this display of braggadocio for something that even a common criminal with the slightest conscience would try to hide. The assassination of a Pope and the plan to kill his successor—it made my mind reel in loathing and revulsion. In all the time I spent around Che, I had grown to know his darkest feelings and knew he was capable of doing anything to anyone, anywhere. If I'd had even the slightest sympathy for him and the hope that he could be changed, it vanished. If he was not Satan incarnate, he was certainly his spawn.

It took an extraordinary effort to conceal my real feelings and the nausea that filled my stomach. I continued to smile and pretend to feel things I did not believe. I rubbed at my eyes with one hand to conceal any chance indication of my true feelings; Che was still boring into them, and I didn't want him to see anything amiss.

I said, "I don't have any doubt that your plans will succeed; if you've already managed to kill Pope John, it shouldn't be too difficult for you to get to the current one. Especially if Marko and Marcelino are going to be the primary triggers to execute your plan. But I have a question, and I want to ask you to excuse my ignorance: what is the object in killing the Pope? He's not a political figure, just a religious one. I don't see any value in risking great assets like Marko and Marcelino in a mission with no value. I have to apologize again for my ignorance; I don't yet know that much about politics."

He smiled and leaned over to pat my shoulder paternally. "You are extremely intelligent, especially to ask that at your age. Remember, many educated adult men die without knowing the answer to such things. Simply put, they are politically ignorant. Let me explain to you that religion is the opiate of the masses—especially the proletariat. Through the fear they put in people's brains about God's punishment, the Devil, and all that stuff, the people continue in ignorance and adore the images that are sold to them. Using God and the Devil, these people enslave the proletariat, obligating them to work for miserable wages and condemn them into poverty for the rest of their lives. Once they become too old to work and are no longer productive, then society puts them in the corner like old, unused furniture to die without any dignity."

I raised my right arm in affirmation as I nodded. "Yes, I understand all that. I read that in the works of Marx and Lenin, but I have to ask again: what does all of this have to do with the Pope? What benefit does this assassination bring to the internationalist movement?"

Che raised the hand with the cigar up to make me pause. He had assumed the mantle of being my political teacher and "underarm intellectual" that he believed himself to be. He looked at me seriously, and said, "To your first question: the Pope is the most important religious figure in the world. Even though there are maybe hundreds of thousands of different religions, eliminating him, or the next one or the one after, will remove the bandage from over the eyes of the ignorant people in the capitalist world. It will destroy the religious meat that church represents. That doesn't even count the disruption this will create. The impact this represents to those ignorant people who adore the capitalist system will show to them the corruption that exists inside that system. With this act, we'll force the masses to look at our new, good ideas. That will be our opportunity to introduce in the midst of the social unrest our Marxist philosophy."

I stroked my chin and nodded to show him my understanding and approval. He smiled and took a long drag on his cigar. He exhaled the smoke and asked, "Who do you think has been helping us kill these Popes and making them look like natural deaths? From within the Vatican itself?" I raised my eyebrows, and he understood the curiosity in my face.

He leaned forward and said in a low voice, "The cardinals. There are disputes between them and different personal ideologies as to how to run their affairs. We're looking for the right one.

"For your second question about the benefit to our internationalist movement: the value will be tremendous. When we replace all the elements from the right wing from the highest positions in all the established institutions and replace them with our people, who have Marxist ideologies, we will eventually find the Pope who will be the closest to our ideals, if not completely Marxist, he will at least give us our support. Later, we'll be able to completely destroy the Catholic Church, followed by all the other churches in the world. Every institution in the capitalist system will be replaced, one by one, with our communist institutions."

I replied with a forced smile, "Then we will be the owners of the Ford factories in Detroit."

He laughed uncontrollably. Finally, he replied, "You never stop amusing me. It doesn't matter what subject we've been talking about. But yes, we'll not only have the Ford factory, but also Chevrolet and all the others."

Behind the forced smile I kept on my face, I determined to cut this conversation short so that I could get out of there as soon as possible. I needed to let the trigger know that she needed to complete her work immediately, or Marko and Marcelino would be lost in the Cuban international intelligence network in the greater world. Our international espionage bureaucracies were so complex that by the time they got their hands on this information, another Pope would wind up sharing the fate of Kennedy. One, apparently, already had. They might not be meeting the violent end the young President had, but the final result was and would be the same.

The other part of my brain told me to stay a little while longer with Che to see what other information I could glean from him in his current depressed emotional state. My information about the Castro brothers should certainly make him feel down.

My brain didn't have to battle for long. Che came over to me and gave me a hug. "I'm leaving tonight for Algeria. We have something very good going on there. But I want to bring you with me on my next trip to Europe." He squeezed my shoulder. "You are all man, and you proved it to me with this last confidence. I know now for a fact I can count on you without hesitation. Enjoy the party and eat. We have plenty food in there, and you look a little skinny."

As we walked back into the house, I smiled and replied, "I look skinny because I'm growing up. I really eat more than I should."

He noticed that I was fixing my beret as if I were about to leave. "You're not going to stay at the party?"

"You know I'm not big on parties. Besides, I have to go back early to Santiago de las Vegas. I don't know if Canen will need the jeep early in the morning. I always make it a routine to return as early as possible to ask him before he goes to bed if he'll need it the next day. I don't want to create in any way a conflict in his military schedule."

He patted my shoulder. "You're too much! How many times have I told you that you can have any car here? You don't have to return it. Go home now and tell one of your friends to bring you back here tonight. This party will probably continue all night long, even though I'm about to leave now. Take whatever car you like there. Please— you will make me very happy if you do that. Keep it, *carajo*! I don't care if you junk it; if you do, come and get another one. You are too proper and too considerate. That is an old-fashioned, capitalistic trait."

I nodded, not wanting to start another discussion with him. "I will take your word this time, and I'll make good on your offer. It's a little embarrassing for me that I'm not only staying with my family in their house, even though they have me there with great pleasure, but also using their vehicles."

Che smiled. "It will give me very great pleasure if, when I get back, I see you in one of my cars. I'm sorry, but my plane is going to leave in a couple of hours, and I have something to attend to in Havana before I leave."

He gave me another hug, and we said goodbye. He left towards the stairs that led down to the garages with his escort behind him.

I looked everywhere for Tanya and Sonya, but they were nowhere to be seen. It looked like they must have left the party at their first opportunity, no longer feeling comfortable there. I saw Marko and Marcelino sitting at one of the tables, eating in the company of two pretty young women. Both of them waved to me as walked past them on my way to the front door.

Dr. Julio Antonio del Marmol

This Is Your Last Call: America, Wake Up!

The United States has been invaded, slowly and silently, by our enemies under the disguise of political correctness. The American people have for a while been intimidated by it and made to feel guilty, forcing them to silence their own feelings and keeping their mouths closed. The true purpose behind it all is to coerce our people, destroy our institutions and our nation, and rob us of our freedoms for which so much blood has been shed. They are taking our country, trying to bring every American under the boot of extreme Marxist-Leninist ideas in a way only comparable to the Nazi's fascist boot of Hitler's legacy. When are we going to scream "Stop!" to these bandits? Don't let them get away with this any longer. Say, "This is it—enough is enough." Without fear of political correctness, scream instead at the top of our lungs what we really feel in our hearts. Throw all these traitors to our nation in prison, and have the courage to elect some decent ones.

Dr. Julio Antonio del Marmol

JFK: The Unwrapped Enigma

Chapter 11: The Extraction and the Ultimate Conclusion of the Enigma

I left the house and walked towards the jeep. I saw Che and his escort driving towards the main gate as I came out. I got into the jeep and drove off with only one thought in mind: to find a telephone at once. A short while later, I saw a gas station. I slowed down and parked. I walked over to the telephone booths.

My first call was to Chopin. He answered after a few rings, still half-asleep. I told him that I had to meet with him immediately. "Now?" he asked in surprise.

"Yes," I said, "it's extremely important. It's an emergency—every minute counts."

We arranged where to meet in thirty minutes and hung up.

The next call I placed was to Chandee. She was also half-asleep when she answered. She said, "I thought you were sleeping already. What are you doing up so late?"

"There's not much I can tell you over the phone, but wake your guest up and tell her the table is set, and we have a buffet. Both of you get dressed as I told you before, and tell her to bring whatever is necessary for the job. She will probably return to her place of origin afterwards. Be ready—I will be there in no more than forty-five minutes."

We hung up and I called another number. This one took longer, and a very raspy, friendly voice answered the phone. "This is Captain Hector Garcia. This must be very important for everyone interested in this conversation. What can I do for you?"

I smiled and replied, "This is the Commandantico."

"Oh! How are you doing? It's a pleasure to hear from you—what new is cooking?"

"I need an extraction. It's extremely urgent."

He replied, "When?"

"Now, as soon as possible."

Surprise filled his voice. "Negative and impossible, unless you guys deliver the package to our coordinates. We normally would need twenty-four to forty-eight hours, minimum, given the proximity to the capital."

"The package is in the capital—very close to it. But it's extremely heavy and fragile. If we move it too fast, it might break."

"OK," he said, "I understand. Always the same with heavy packages." He grunted in discontent. "Give me the exact coordinates, and we will make it an absolute priority since you are one of the favorites of the Commander-in-Chief."

I smiled. "Thank you." I removed from my shirt pocket a small notebook and read the coordinates to him.

"OK, we'll be ready to pick up," he said. "Good luck to you guys in preparing the package."

"The same to you in transporting it," I replied. We hung up.

I got back in the jeep and drove to the underground parking structure at the Havana Libre. Chopin gestured to me when he saw me, and I parked close to him. I locked the jeep and got into his Edsel. We drove from there to Chinatown.

On the way there, I briefed Chopin as much as I could in that space of time about my conversation with Che, especially the new information I had acquired.

As we came close to Chandee's, I asked, "What is the little problem you wanted to talk to me about?"

He said, "It's a personal thing. I don't want to talk about it in front of the women. We'll talk about it later on."

"OK," I answered, respecting his preference. "Go around to the alley," I instructed him.

Chandee was waiting by the gate for us. We pulled in and put some of Patricia's things into the trunk of the Edsel. Then we left for Boca Siega. I used the driving time to bring the three of them up to date on everything that had happened, and I outlined the plan we should follow. I gave them the sheet out of my notebook with the coordinates at which we were to meet in case of separation. I let them know that this was where Patricia was to be extracted to safety. Patricia did not like the timeline of 24 to 48 hours. She shook her head sadly but kept silent.

"I'm sorry," I assured her, "but there's nothing else I can do."

After a while, Patricia broke the silence. In her characteristic accent, she said, "Thank you very much for everything you've been doing. I never expected from you or the others anything more than information. This is a lot more help than that."

I smiled and nodded. "Yes, yes. That is exactly all that I

was supposed to provide you with, and I was advised to not even get closer to you than several miles unless it were an extreme emergency or if your cover got blown. As you know from my debriefing, Che and the G-2 have not only your name but also your description."

I smiled again. "As you can see, I'm only adhering to my instructions. Don't worry about it. Complete your work, and make us proud. Let's make sure that no more Popes die and that these assassins pay for their previous crimes. In the process, let's hope we also prevent future crimes, OK?"

This time, her smile was ironic. "Don't worry about that. Leave that to me." She leaned forward to hug me from the back seat and kissed the top of my beret. "Don't worry at all. I'm as good at what I do as you are at what you do. But, again, I give you my thanks, because you've made my work extremely easy—much more so than I normally expect."

I reached back and took her hand to squeeze it to reciprocate her friendship. Still holding my hand, she turned to Chandee and took one of her hands with her free hand. "Whatever you do, you guys should never allow yourselves to be separated. I can tell that there is a beautiful, true love between you two. That is very difficult in the world in which we live today."

Chandee smiled and leaned over to Patricia to hug her. "Thank you. Those words mean a lot to me."

I opened the visor to fix my beret, which had been slightly set askew by her gratitude. Based on what she had just shared, it was clear that, in spite of her work, she had a loving heart. We had no idea if any of us would get out alive from the mission we were planning to execute that night.

We arrived at the safe house, pulling up about a block away. I pointed out to Patricia the lights of the beautiful mansion. Patricia said to Chopin, "Stop the car right here behind those in the street." She pointed to the overflow parking.

Chopin pulled over as she directed. She leaned forward and took my shoulder. She said, "I will get out here. I'll get in by myself. I know this isn't a part of your plan, but as you said, these people have my description and pictures of me. I don't want to put you at any risk. I know the possibilities of any guard identifying me in the darkness inside the car is minimal, but when you're playing with the Devil, you have to be very careful. Remember, even though the Devil himself is not present, these guys are his disciples, if not his sons. OK? I don't want to take any chances."

I took her hand. "OK. But please, for the rest of the plan, let's maintain what we agreed upon without any more deviations. We cannot communicate among us. If you decide to make any changes, we won't know about it. It might look to you that the entrance will be easy, but if something goes wrong the exit will be a nightmare. You understand?"

"I do. No more deviations." She got out of the car. Chopin hopped out and assisted her in retrieving her equipment from the trunk. Then he got back in the car as she disappeared into the darkness.

When we arrived at the gate, there was a car in front of us with officers from Cuban naval intelligence. They were thoroughly searched, including the trunk of their vehicle. Once they passed inspection, Chopin drove ahead slowly. Not recognizing the vehicle, they both approached.

As soon as they saw me, they said, "Hello, Commandantico. Back so soon?"

"I'm just back to pick up the car Che told me to take, and then I'm out of here. I might take another drink before I go."

"Yeah, Che told us that you'd be back for a car. You're to take whatever one you want."

He gestured to Chopin to drive through.

Chopin gestured inquiringly about them not searching the trunk with a smile. The sergeant smiled and shook his head. He pointed at me, tapped his shoulders, and gave Chopin a thumbs up.

We drove inside, but by now even the little space I had used for the jeep was taken. I told Chopin, "Wait for me by the door. I'll go in to open the underground garage, and you can park in there."

Chopin smiled happily. "Why would I lie to you guys? I love these privileges! We just got here, not even searched at one of Che's most secure houses. I have butterflies in my stomach at these benefits."

Chandee and I got out and smiled at him. We walked inside and maneuvered through the crowd into the dining room. I went over to the cabinet and took the garage door opener. I picked up a few keys and we went downstairs to the garage. I pressed the button on the opener, and all the doors in the various garages started to open all at once.

I smiled and said, "Open, sesame!"

Chopin drove the Edsel in, smiling like the king of the hill. I pushed the button once more to close the doors. As they closed, I noticed a silhouette slide in under one of the doors and give me a thumbs up. Patricia looked at her watch to check her timing.

She walked up the stair and disappeared. Chandee and I walked through the garage. I turned on the lights and saw Chopin next to the Mercedes roadster.

"What a beautiful machine!" he said.

"It looks better than when I left it last time."

"Who the hell would not be a communist living this way?" Chopin yelled, gesturing at all the expensive cars. "The best of everything," he said sadly, "and it didn't cost even a little drop of sweat to these guys."

I raised a finger to my lips. In a low voice I said, "Be careful. These walls have ears. A guest might be lost looking for a bathroom, and one of them could be Piñeiro, Ramiro Valdes, or even Raul Castro himself!"

Chopin crossed himself and looked at me remorsefully. In a much more moderate voice, he said, "I'm sorry, Commandantico. The display of all these beautiful cars would raise the blood pressure of anyone. I'm just remembering when Fidel criticized the rich people for having more than one car. The people who agreed with them don't even get to see these cars."

I smiled and replied, "Nothing which comes from the mouths of Marxists is ever true. Everything is fabrication and lies—Utopian ideas designed to get the consent of the ignorant useful fools. The worst part is that they repeat the lies to the people so often that they come to believe their own lies. Let's leave our emotions behind and continue with our plans."

I walked along the line of cars and stopped by one of them—a 1956 green and white Ford Thunderbird. I gestured with my head. "What do you think? Is it too flashy? Will it catch anyone's attention too much?"

Chandee smiled and shook her head. "If you don't want to attract attention, you're in the wrong place. Any of these cars will attract attention for kilometers away, no matter where you park it. I think you should stop worrying about that. You do it yourself, everywhere you go, even if you don't want to."

I smiled and stroked her cheek with the back of my hand. She took my hand and kissed it tenderly. While Chopin was distracted by the cars, I moved close to her and kissed, tenderly at first, but with increasing passion.

Patricia infiltrated the house. From the description I had given her, she was able to mark her targets. She got into one of the empty bathrooms and changed her clothes, trading her *militiana* outfit for some very fashionable clothes: a red miniskirt with ribbons of gold that looked like chains running down. They shook and jangled as they walked, attracting attention to her beautiful legs. She put on a pullover blouse, very tight to reveal that she was not wearing a bra. The fabric was silky and white, not quite see-through, but one could make out the pink of her areolas. The blouse also had golden lines and chain decorations.

She had a small gold clutch bag full of utensils which she hid in a cleaning closet near the door. Before leaving, she removed her underwear and dropped them in the trash can.

As she walked through the crowd, every man, even quite a few women, turned their heads to watch her walk by. She was now a brunette, and had put in contact lenses to give her eyes a bottle green color. Her first target was Marko, so she walked by him.

Marko was fascinated with her. Without even excusing himself to the girls he was with, he abruptly said, "I'll be back." He got up and left the table without another word, following Patricia in hot pursuit.

She took a glass of champagne from one of the attendants and engaged him in small talk. She noticed Marko's approach out of the corner of her eye. To bait him, she ignored him and walked further inside the mansion, away from the crowd. She opened a couple of doors as if she were looking for something, never entering any of the empty rooms. All the while, she kept an eye on Marko's movements behind her.

She returned to the hallway. As she passed Marko, she bore an expression of discontented frustration. All she said was, "*Hola.*"

Marko used that as an excuse to approach. "*Señorita*, is there anything I can help you with? I live here."

She smiled as she reached inside her cleavage to pull out some lipstick. She ran it slightly over her lips. "I was just looking for a bathroom. I'm very sweaty, and wanted to take a quick shower before I redo my makeup."

Marko came up to her and said, "Nice to meet you. I'm Marko. My room is right at the corner. If you want to use my bathroom, that's OK. There are ten rooms in this house, all with their own bathrooms. Most of them are empty. My comrade and I are staying here tonight. We leave in the morning."

Patricia said, "My friend Ernesto told me that he would be here tonight. But when I got here, the guards told me he had to leave for an emergency and might not be back tonight at all. I drove all the way from Havana. It's a great disappointment. He's never done that to me before. I don't know if that would be appropriate, Marko. It's a pleasure, but I ought to go back to Havana. Another time, OK?" She turned as if to leave.

Marko stopped her after a few steps. "But why are you going to leave so early, *señorita*? Ernesto's not here, but I am, and I can show you around."

She tugged at the corner of her blouse and shook it. "But I'm so hot and uncomfortable! I would give anything to be able to take a long shower. If there's anything I despise, it's that sticky, sweaty feeling on my skin. All I can think of is that I have to drive all the way back to the Havana, half an hour, and it really bothers me. The air conditioner in my car broke down."

Marko said with a big smile, "Why don't you come with me? Shower, and I'll bring you another glass of champagne, and you can leave if you like. You might change your mind and dance with me for a few songs after you've cooled off and refreshed yourself. It's still early. What about it?" His tone was imploring.

Patricia looked at him indecisively, playing hard to get. After a few seconds, she smiled at him and held her hand out to Marko. "*Mucho gusto*, Marko, and thank you. I am Maria Sandoval. I'll take you up on your offer."

"OK," Marko said happily. "Please follow me to my quarters. You can take that heat off of your body, I'll bring you a bottle of chilled champagne from the bar, and you'll feel brand new."

When they got to the room, Marko unlocked the door with his key. He welcomed her into his room. Patricia took a few steps into the room but tripped and fell facedown onto the floor. Marko had tripped her and shoved her from the back. He closed the door with his foot and jumped on top of her, even as she spun onto her back. He pulled a metal wire from his pants, and with catlike speed wrapped the garrote around Patricia's neck.

Patricia quickly placed her left hand under it to stop it, but Marko had the advantage of surprise. The deadly metal wire sliced into the fingers of Patricia's hand, and they started to bleed as the pressure increased. She finally managed to get her right hand out from under the knee he had pinned it with, and punched him full in the face. It didn't have enough mechanical advantage, however, to have the strength to make Marko lessen his grip. Strangulation began to catch up with her, and her face started to turn red as weakness crept through her body.

Marko knelt on her right hand once more and continued to strangle her. She managed to free her knees and shifted suddenly to throw him off balance. His knee came up off of her hand, but instead of punching him once more, she reached into her cleavage. She rocked back and forth, hitting him once more in the back. His head shot forward, almost hitting her head, and he lost his grip on the garrote.

She took this opportunity to stab him in the neck with the lipstick. A small needle protruded from the stick, and Marko immediately released all pressure on her neck. He felt the stab of the needle, and knew what came next. His eyes opened wide, just as Yoska's had in Madrid. He grabbed at his neck to see what had happened.

Patricia jumped clear of him. Like a mountain lion, she pushed him with both hands. He slid across the marble floor, hitting the back of the door. Marko tried to reach for his gun with glassy eyes. No longer having any power, he numbly let go of it. In broken gasps, he said, "Bitch. We've been waiting for you. How did this happen? You...fucked...me...uhh....."

He grew still, his eyes unfocused.

Patricia took his clothes off and put his body in bed. From an internal pocket inside her miniskirt, she pulled out a small plastic bag containing two roses. She opened his mouth and inserted one of the roses. From another pocket she took a staple gun and a piece of paper on which was written the Jose Marti poem. She stapled the poem to his naked chest.

Before she left, she leaned down so that he could see her. "If it's any consolation, this is the first time I was caught by surprise. You pulled a good trick—I didn't expect you to be a gentleman by letting me go first. Have a good trip to Hell."

She went to the bathroom and checked her neck and hand. The cut on her fingers was superficial. She washed her hands in the sink. She pulled a packet of antibiotic ointment from under her wig. She tore it open with her teeth and squeezed the ointment into her wounds. She flushed the packet down the toilet and wrapped a small towel around her hand. She made certain that her disguise was in place. She left the room and locked it behind her.

On the way back to the main room, she found the same attendant she had spoken to before. With a big smile, she said, "Oh, I need that more than ever! Thank you very much!"

The attendant had an aristocratic look with a pencil

thin beard. He asked, "What happened to your hand, *señorita*?"

She took the towel off. "Nothing important. On my way here, I tried to open the window to my car, and it stuck. Looks like the edge of the glass gave me a tiny cut."

He put the tray on the partition of the planter. He looked inside his pants pocket and pulled out some Band-Aids. "I always carry these for emergencies. I think this will look better for your little wound, don't you think so?"

"Thank you very much," she said as she started to bandage her fingers. Her glass and the towel she deposited on the tray. She affectionately laid a hand on the attendant's hand. "You are really a Lladro doll!"

The attendant said, "Thank you very much, *señorita*." He took it as a compliment, even though he knew nothing about Lladro porcelain.

The attendant got ready to leave. He picked up the tray with one hand, while with the other he handed her a glass. Before she took the glass from him, she pulled some money from her purse and offered them to him as a tip.

He backed away. "No, no, no!" he said in a frightened tone. "Please, *señorita* —do you want to get me in trouble? The Revolution prohibits us from taking any gratuity. It diminishes us! That is a capitalist mentality!"

She said at once, "*Claro, claro*—but such a beautiful gesture like you just made, helping me without any self-interest, sometimes we forget the new rules of our government. I'm sorry, please."

The attendant said with a smile, "Don't worry—it happens to me, too. It's the residue we have from the nefarious past. My name, by the way, is Pedro. What is yours? It must be a beautiful name, because you are a beautiful woman."

After she put her wallet away, Patricia tucked her clutch under her arm and took his hand. "Simply Maria Sandoval, nothing fancy. It's a pleasure to meet you, Pedro."

"The pleasure is all mine," he said. His mannerisms had grown increasingly effeminate as his familiarity with her increased. "You must be someone special, like a movie star, with your angelic face...."

She interrupted, rolling her eyes. "Please, Pedro, if you keep on, I'll start to believe it. All that is not important. Remember, that is the capitalist way to focus on a woman's looks."

Pedro still had her glass, waiting for her to take it. She accepted it, and said, "No, I'm not an actress, movie star, or anything like that at all. Just a simple Revolutionary."

At that moment, Patricia could see Marcelino out of the corner of her eye. At the sight of her speaking with the attendant, he had stopped. She used the opportunity to drop the glass on the floor as if by accident. It shattered against the marble floor. Without wasting a second, she snatched the towel off of the tray and bent over, keeping her now-exposed rear to Marcelino's full view. He froze in rapt contemplation of the view she offered him.

Ignoring Pedro's protests, she helped clean up the spill, moving herself around for Marcelino's benefit. He didn't move so much as an eyelash. She asked Pedro if they had any orange juice in the kitchen for her to make a mimosa. Pedro smiled and informed her that they had everything in that house and that he would bring her a glass. She protested and insisted on going with him. Indicating that it would be a pleasure, she straightened up, and they headed to the kitchen, Marcelino hot on their heels.

Patricia used the decorative mirrors lining the halls to keep an eye on Marcelino. She made sure that he continued to follow her to the kitchens. They entered, and Pedro went to the large refrigerator. She walked over and sat down around the island which contained a grill.

Pedro said, "I squeezed these myself this morning." He filled a brandy glass of the juice and set it in front of Patricia. Utensils hung from the ceiling around the grill, and the counter contained a butcher's block with several knives. She took a bottle opener adorned with a Blackbeard figurine. She admired it for a bit with a smile.

"Wow!" she said. "This kitchen is a fantasy dream for anyone who likes to cook. Everything here is so original and unique. I'm very picky, and I think I could spend hours in this kitchen without getting bored."

Pedro picked up the tray to continue his duties. He said, "Nobody's stopping you. You can spend all the time you want here, *Señorita* Maria."

She smiled. "Thank you. If that's the case, I think I'll stay here for a while and enjoy my champagne in quiet."

Pedro brought an ice bucket over to her and put a bottle in it. "This is in case you decide to be here until I come back."

"Oh, thank you, Pedro! You are a wonderful host. I will tell my great friend Ernesto that you are the best attendant he had at this party today."

"Thank you very much *señorita*. That will make me very happy. Commander Guevara is one of my heroes in this Revolution. Even though it's been a great personal pleasure to serve you, and I will do so until the end of my life, a little recognition for what we do never hurts. Especially since you're a personal friend to my boss. I'll see you in a little while. Enjoy."

He left the kitchen, leaving Patricia to enjoy her mimosa with her back to the door. A few minutes passed, and she heard slight squeak of the swinging door open behind her. Patricia turned her head slightly towards the door. She caught a glimpse of Marcelino quietly entering the kitchen. She smiled and turned her back to him once more.

Marcelino smiled as he said loudly, "Oh, I get lost in this huge mansion, and by chance I wind up in the Garden of Eden!"

Patricia continued to keep her back to him. One of the stainless steel pots hanging overhead was polished to mirror brightness, and she used that reflective surface to keep track of Marcelino as he walked towards her.

Without turning, she smiled and said, "Are you absolutely certain of that? The kitchen can be a very hot place, and so it could be considered the opposite of Eden."

Still smiling, Marcelino picked up a knife from one of the butcher blocks and concealed it behind his back. He continued to advance on her. "With such a beautiful and exuberant woman as you, I wouldn't mind burning in the Inferno."

He was now right behind her back as she sat on a stool before the kitchen bar. She saw him pull his arm from behind his back in the reflection. He raised it with the intention of stabbing down at her. As he did this, he said, "We've been waiting for you, bitch!"

As he stabbed, she dodged to the stool on her left, and his forward momentum carried him down and forward, and the knife point embedded deeply onto the chopping block. He screamed in agony as the bottle opener she held stabbed up into his left eye, corkscrew end first. A quick twist of her wrist, and his agony increased. She yanked it free, the eyeball caught on the tine of the corkscrew, the optic nerve trailing bloodily behind.

Marcelino clapped his hand over the empty eye socket and tried desperately to staunch the flow of blood. Patricia wasted not a moment and jabbed him in the neck with her pencil tip, injecting him with the deadly poison. At the same time, Marcelino managed with his free hand to clear his pistol and fire twice. She managed to avoid the first shot, the bullet going wide and hitting the refrigerator. The second shot, however, hit her in the left shoulder a few seconds before she could administer the poison.

As soon as he was injected, he offered no further resistance. She saw him stiffen as he slumped to the floor, clutching one of the bar stools. He looked at her with his remaining eye, and already the stare was glassy and unfocused. Patricia took a couple of steps back.

She said, "You have to thank your friend Marko. He made the small mistake of warning me that you guys were waiting for me. You lost any advantage of surprise. Welcome to your true home in Hell, you miserable assassin."

She checked her shoulder. From under her wig she took another small envelope with first aid supplies. She tore open the antiseptic package and spread it into the wound, which appeared to be a superficial flesh wound.

She used one of the potholders as a pressure bandage to stop the bleeding.

Once she had attended to herself, she dragged Marcelino's body to the freezer. He was by now semi-conscious, though he was growing stiffer by the second. She smiled as she thought how he might, like Yoska, be wondering how someone who seemed such a bimbo could have put down a professional like himself. Clearly, once more, her enemies had underestimated her.

She finally managed to get him inside the freezer. She took out the last rose she had and put it into the empty eye socket. She pried his mouth open and put the page with the poem on it into his mouth. She stepped back to look him over.

"Don't worry about it," she assured him. "You won't be cold for very long. When you reach your destination, you'll defrost pretty quickly." She reached out and patted him on the head. "You don't look too bad with that rose in your eye. It would have been more appropriate, of course, to bring you a red rose, given your ideology."

She smiled and closed the freezer door. She went to work at once to clean up the blood and put everything back in order as it had been before. She checked the grill at the island. She heard a faint whistle and turned to examine the source. A faint wisp of Freon gas was escaping. The bullet had severed a line. She cut off a small strip of dish towel and plugged the hole so that it was somewhat camouflaged. Only a careful inspection would reveal the bullet hole now.

When she was almost ready to leave, she noticed the bottle opener on the counter with the eye still attached. She removed the eyeball, rinsed off the opener, and put it back in its place on the counter. She wrapped the eye in the remnant of the dish towel. The bundle in her hand, she made a last check to ensure everything was in order.

She went over to the freezer, intending to drop the eye inside with the body before leaving. As she put her hand on the handle, she heard the swinging door open behind her. Pedro's voice called out, more effeminate than ever.

"My Queen Maria, are you still here? Have you gotten bored?"

Patricia immediately shut the partially opened freezer door, hoping that he hadn't caught a glimpse of the body inside. The last thing she wanted was for Pedro or anyone else to see that body before she got clear. As she turned, she concealed the towel and its contents into her cleavage. She walked to the island and removed the bottle of champagne from the ice bucket, and held it against her shoulder to conceal the wound.

"I was just leaving," she said. "After drinking so much champagne and orange juice, I have to go to the bathroom badly. But we'll see each other in a little while, OK? Ciao!"

Pedro directed her to the bathrooms and said, "Ciao, bambina. We'll see you in a little while, *señorita*."

Patricia rushed down the corridor, checking her wristwatch as she went. She grimaced as she saw she had taken more time than anticipated in finishing the job. As she passed by one of the tables in the main room, she put the bottle of champagne down on the edge of a nearby table.

She then went to the bathroom where she had left behind her travel bag and proceeded at once to remove the towel from her cleavage and flush it down the toilet.

She removed her wig and contact lenses. She made sure nothing was left as she packed up her bag. She unwrapped the Band-Aids from around her fingers. Using them, she improvised a larger bandage to apply to her still-bleeding shoulder wound.

    She looked herself over from every angle in the large vanity mirror. Dressed once more as a *militiana*, she left the bathroom with her travel bag. As she passed between the kitchen and dining rooms, she walked by Pedro, who was leaving the kitchen. He did not recognize her, but threw her a distrustful, questioning look. It was clear he was trying to remember her features, so she walked by him rapidly, avoiding his eyes.

    She crossed the dining room and walked down the stairs to the garages below. Once she was downstairs, she saw us waiting for her. She gave us a thumbs up to communicate that everything had gone as planned.

    I had selected a canary yellow 1963 Chevrolet Corvette. I had parked the car behind Chopin's Edsel, which was ready to take off immediately. As we had planned, Chopin opened the trunk of the Edsel, and Patricia jumped inside. I took the travel bag from her and put it in the trunk of the Corvette.

JFK: The Unwrapped Enigma

Corvette

I opened the garage doors, and Chopin drove out of the garage very slowly to avoid catching attention. I left the garage behind Chopin, but I did not drive to the gate. Instead, I stopped by the main door of the house and said hello to the guards.

I walked inside the dining room and replaced the garage door opener. I left the residence at a very slow pace and said goodbye to the door guards. I saw in the distance the gates open to allow Chopin's car to leave, and I breathed a sigh of relief.

I jumped into the Corvette. Even though I didn't want to rush, I sped up slightly so that I could get to the gate before the guards swung them closed. The gates were hand-operated, not electronic, and I wanted to save them the extra effort. I had the top down, so the guards recognized me immediately and I was signaled through without stopping.

As we passed through the gate, I saw a commotion start up in my rearview mirror. Pedro was signaling frantically to the gate guards to close the gate, and they rushed to close it after us. I kept my eyes glued to the interior mirror.

Dr. Julio Antonio del Marmol

The door guards charged towards the gate to provide the guards reinforcement. My eyes still on the mirror, I said to Chandee, "Don't turn your head for any reason at all. Behave very naturally. It looks like something odd happened inside the residence. Something we might not know about has taken place."

Chandee looked at me in concern. "Evidently, not everything went as we expected, eh? I saw—I was watching from the mirror, too. I think if we had taken a few seconds longer, they wouldn't have let us leave that place."

I smiled and took a deep breath. "Don't worry about it. Thank God we're out. Let's hope Patricia didn't leave behind us any loose ends that would incriminate anyone."

Chandee crossed herself. "God protect us. We will know in a very little while when we meet with them."

I nodded and checked my watch. "It will be in exactly twenty minutes. We'll know all the details then." I pointed to the radio. "Why don't you put on a little music to relax our nerves?"

Chandee took a deep breath to control herself. She leaned forward and switched the radio on. As it happened, the song playing at that moment was Perez Prado's "Patricia." We looked at each other and laughed.

I came to know later what had happened at Che's house. Pedro had noticed a small drop of blood on the white marble floor. It was fresh. This, combined with the blonde, blue-eyed militia woman he hadn't seen the entire night at the party, aroused his suspicion. He looked around and saw another drop of blood.

As he started to follow the trail of blood, he saw the

bottle he had opened for Maria sitting on a table. He ran over to it and saw it was almost full. He had been in charge of the party. That was the last bottle of Brut they had in stock, as he had discovered when he specifically searched it out for his guest. Pedro picked up the bottle and continued to follow the drops of blood with the bottle in his hand.

Driven by curiosity more than anything else, he followed the trail to the last empty room, where the trail disappeared in the bathroom. The counters were clean, and no other sign could be seen. He turned to switch off the light. As he did so, he glanced down and saw lying there on the corner of the vanity what he thought was a wrapper with gum. But when he bent down and picked up, he realized that it was one of the bandages he had given to Maria—Che's supposed friend.

He turned the lights off. The bottle of champagne in one hand and the Band-Aid in the other, he decided to return to the kitchen. Everything appeared very strange to him. Before he returned, he looked everywhere for some sign of Maria. Finding no sign of her, his suspicions grew, and he went back to the kitchen.

When he arrived, he went over to the stool where Maria had been sitting. He checked the counters but found nothing, save for one of the footrests, which had something on it. He took a white towel and wiped the footrest and saw that it was blood.

He looked towards the refrigerator and saw that there was some liquid accumulated beneath the appliance. He walked over to the refrigerator and noticed that it was not running. He opened the door, but the light did not switch on. He looked at the interior door and saw that the bottles in the shelf were broken. One of the bottles had a hole in it, and some of the liquor was still in the bottom part of the container. Strangest of all, the bottle was still sealed. As he examined further, he saw a piece of towel. When he pulled on it, it came free, and saw a hole running clear through the door.

He put his hand to his mouth in thought. He was growing worried due to his responsibilities, and clearly the refrigerator had been tampered with. Any damage to the property would earn Che's ire, and he scratched the back of his neck in concern. He could not understand what had happened in his absence.

He remembered that as he had walked into the kitchen, Maria had been in front of the freezer on the other side of the room. He couldn't think of what she might have been trying to find in there, and he walked over there. It was possible that she had damaged the freezer as well as the refrigerator.

He looked at the doors and saw nothing wrong. He massaged his forehead with his right hand in distress. He couldn't imagine what Maria had been doing there. He nearly turned around to leave, but then turned back and opened the freezer door. The sight made him scream.

"Guards! Guards!" He ran out of the kitchen.

The guards ran towards him upon hearing his cry. He showed them what he had found, and they began to remove Marcelino's body. The sergeant in charge of security immediately ordered the sealing of all entrances and detailed a squad of soldiers to do a room-by-room search. Then he called Che. As he spoke with Che, one of the guards approached him.

"Marko is dead. We found him in his room, lying in

bed, with a white rose and another note."

Che's voice was heard clearly over the phone. "God dammit!" He proceeded to rapidly shoot out orders to the sergeant to barricade every road and entrance surrounding the entire perimeter. "You have to find those two women that Pedro described to you. We're looking for a beautiful blond in militia clothing, and the other a sculptured green-eyed brunette with clothing in the latest European fashion."

Che canceled his trip to Algeria and informed the sergeant that he would return to personally lead the hunt for those two women. There was no way they could let them slip between their fingers after this.

All of this resulted in us having our music interrupted on the radio, as an emergency broadcast broke in to describe the two women who were wanted for two murders at Che's house in Boca Siega. We exchanged concerned glances, as it had only been twenty minutes since leaving the house.

We pulled over at the rendezvous point. We made sure to park far enough off the highway to avoid notice and met with Chopin and Patricia, who were waiting anxiously for us under a tree. Chopin raised his arm when he saw me.

"Thank God you're OK," he said. "We just heard the radio broadcast. Did you?"

"Yes," I said, "we did."

"Oh, man! How in hell did that happen so quickly?" Chopin was really stressed. "Oh, man—wait until you hear Patricia's story. Everything that could go wrong went wrong, and then some!"

Patricia had finished cleaning her shoulder wound. She

smiled, and replied, "I think you will be telling him the story. We don't have a minute to waste. We have to be optimistic. I'm accustomed to these improvisations and bullets in my skin from time to time, but thanks be to God we're all OK and no major problems so far. We're all where we're supposed to be, far away from there. The most important thing is for you guys to get away from me immediately—that's your next step. We cannot allow them under any circumstance to find us all together. The worst scenario is that they would accuse Chandee of being the brunette and me the blonde. It would be a disaster that would cost all of us our lives."

Chopin replied, "But we can't leave you here, wounded like you are. You've already lost a lot of blood. Here in the middle of the jungle for two or three days, maybe longer, until our people can get you out of the country...."

I raised my arm and interrupted. "Hey, don't panic." I took a couple of steps towards him and looked at him seriously. "Calm down. First of all, it won't be for more than forty-eight hours, possibly within twenty-four. Our people are never late, especially when I make an emergency call to them. They will be precisely on time. Besides, what Patricia has said is exactly what we're supposed to do. In the first place, we shouldn't have been involved as deeply as we were. We were only supposed to provide her information, and we've gone far, far beyond that. She is absolutely right—if we're all caught together, we'll be the losers in this game, especially Patricia, who will be shot on sight."

Chandee asked Patricia, "Do you have food or water? All the things necessary to stay here for the next couple of days?"

Patricia smiled. "Only if you don't forget to get the bag from the Corvette. I have in there everything necessary to survive for a week, if need be, including an inflatable sleeping bag and a hand air pump. I'll be able to sleep better under these mangle trees than you'll sleep in your own beds."

We smiled. I turned and at once went to the Corvette and opened the trunk. A few seconds later I returned and put the travel bag at Patricia's feet. She looked at her wristwatch. "It's exactly three forty-five a.m. In a few hours, all the news we've heard on the radio will also be on television. Everyone will be up in their houses. Since that is controlled by the government, they will mobilize everyone against me. You have to be far away from me as soon as possible."

I nodded in agreement. I opened my arms and gave her a hug. She whispered in my ear, "Thank you for everything you did. You've made my work a hundred times easier than I expected. These two assassins were extremely well-trained. They almost caught me with my guard down. Take care of yourself, and I pray to God that one day I'll have the opportunity to return the favor to you."

I smiled as we parted and replied. "It's nothing. I did it with extremely good pleasure, *Señorita* Patricia." I kissed her hand. "Let's hope, however, that it will never be necessary."

She smiled and stepped back. She held out her hand once more, which caught me by surprise. "My real name is not Patricia. It is Natacha Sausa."

I smiled at that gesture of trust. I took her hand. "Mine

is Julio Antonio del Marmol." I kissed her hand once more and we smiled. She looked at her watch again and I held up my hand. "I'm already out of here, you don't have to kick me out." I turned and said to Chandee and Chopin. "Say your goodbyes. Chandee, I'll wait for you in the Corvette. Chopin, I'll see you in the Hilton in Havana. We have to complete a transaction with the cars. We can't leave any knot untied. I'll see you there after I drop off Chandee."

"OK," Chopin said.

I looked up at the sky in sadness. I thought about my father's great nobility and integrity that he had always displayed to me. I felt a sharp pain in my chest as I thought of the strong bond I had shared with my father before all of this started.

Leonardo and Julio Antonio at age 16

I thought about the shame he would feel if he realized the depth of the treason he had brought on himself as well as his friends. The magnitude of crime perpetrated by the people in charge of this government who had derailed the Revolution and converted it into a Marxist ideology and pillaged our resources to export those ideas, culminated now in the extreme action of perpetrating one of the greatest crimes in history: planning and executing the assassination of the man entrusted with leading the free world, John F. Kennedy.

I looked at my watch as I started to walk to the Corvette a little behind that exuberant blonde heroine. I said to myself, "Natacha Sausa. Hm." I smiled and shook my head. I said in admiration, "Wow—what an extraordinary woman. If we get more like her with us, we'll definitely win this war."

"In 1979, the House Select Committee on Assassinations concluded that Lee Harvey Oswald fired the shots that killed President John F. Kennedy, but different from previous investigations, in concluding that scientific acoustic evidence established that two gunmen fired on the President."--Louis Stokes (emphasis added)

Some truth inside of all the great, elaborate lies. The men who fired the shots did look exactly like Oswald indeed.--Dr. J. Anthony del Marmol

Declassified by Dr. Marmol in October, 1971, when his cover was blown and he was forced to flee for his life and upon his escape to Guantanamo Base. He used it to verify his identity to naval intelligence authorities and was taken from part of the insurance he had accumulated through the years, as his uncle had recommended:

Lee Harvey Oswald's KGB cryptonym is LIKHOI, which means "Valiant" or "Dashing." The contact between Che and Oswald began in January 11, 1960, when Alexander Zeger, a Polish Jew from Argentina, brought them together. This comrade had been in Russia from 1955, when Che went through one of his debriefings during his intensive intelligence trainings in Moscow.

JFK: The Unwrapped Enigma

Photo Credits

p. 31 Guane
Photo Credit by Oscarphoto at
https://commons.wikimedia.org/wiki/File:Guane_-_Barichara_-_Santander.JPG

p. 32 Tobacco Fields
Photo Credit by Henryk Kotowski at
https://commons.wikimedia.org/wiki/File:Tobacco_field_cuba2.jpg

p. 32 Tobacco Storage
Photo Credit by Alexander Klink at
https://commons.wikimedia.org/wiki/File:Tobacco_Air_Curing_Cuba2.jpg

p. 65 Café Labiada
Photo Credit by katielips at
https://commons.wikimedia.org/wiki/File:Alma_de_Cuba.jpg

p. 95 Swiss Embassy Havana
Photo by Male Gringo at
https://commons.wikimedia.org/wiki/File:Swiss_Embassy_in_Havana.jpg

p. 153 Valley Vinales from another angle
Photo Credit by Severin.stalder at
https://commons.wikimedia.org/wiki/File:Viñales_Valley.jpg

Dr. Julio Antonio del Marmol

Other Works

Cuba: Russian Roulette of the World
The Cuban Lightning: The Zipper

Rites of Passage of a Master Spy saga
Cuba: The Truth, the Lies, and the Coverups
The Havana Conspiracies
The Dark Face of Marxism
The Deadly Deals
The Evil Rituals

Forthcoming
ISIS: The Genetic Conception series
Lack of Judgement

www.ingramcontent.com/pod-product-compliance
Lightning Source LLC
Chambersburg PA
CBHW021801220426
43662CB00006B/142